Federal Government and Urban Problems

HUD: Successes, Failures, and the Fate of Our Cities

Federal Government and Urban Problems

HUD: Successes, Failures, and the Fate of Our Cities

M. Carter McFarland

with an Introduction by Paul Ylvisaker

Westview Press/Boulder, Colorado

Copyright © 1978 by Westview Press, Inc.

Published in 1978 in the United States of America by
  Westview Press, Inc.
  5500 Central Avenue
  Boulder, Colorado 80301
  Frederick A. Praeger, Publisher and Editorial Director

McFarland, M. Carter.
  The Federal Government and Urban Problems.
  1. United States. Dept. of Housing and Urban Development. 2. Housing policy—United States. 3. Cities and towns—United States. I. Title.
HT167.2.M33   301.36'3'0973   77-26301
ISBN 0-89158-085-9

Printed and bound in the United States of America

To
Neal J. Hardy and Philip N. Brownstein,
tutors, friends, and exemplary public servants

Contents

Preface xi

Introduction, *Paul Ylvisaker* xiii

1. Trouble in Our Cities 1

   Urban Ills.......................................2
   How Serious Are Our Urban Ills? 11

2. Cabinet Status for Urban Affairs 15

   Why So Late? 16
   What Was Expected 18
   What Was Accomplished 19
   HUD's Missions 23

3. HUD's Performance................................25

   The Requirements of Leadership 26
   The Skills Required..............................36
   How HUD's Leaders Performed 39

4. Shaping the City 51

   The Holy Grail...................................51
   HUD's Tools.....................................52
   HUD's Performance...............................54

The Deeper Causes of Frustrated Planning 58
What More Can Be Done? 65

5. Renewing the Inner City 69

Block Grants for Community Development.........70
The Urban Renewal Program 76
Neighborhood Rehabilitation 79
The Model Cities Program........................84
Other Categorical Programs for
    Community Development 89
Summing Up 90
Block Grants Revised: A Forward
    Step Backward................................92

6. Housing Needs and the Housing Market 97

HUD's Housing Mission 97
The Housing Market.............................98
Housing Needs and Goals 102

7. Financing Housing Construction and Exchange ...107

HUD's Housing Finance Tools 107
The Tools HUD Lacks 108
FHA's Decline..................................110
Is FHA Still Needed?............................114
FHA's Rise and Early Accomplishments 114
An Effective, Revived FHA Is Much Needed 121
Conclusion......................................123

8. Housing the Poor and Near Poor.................125

The Case for Housing Subsidies..................125
HUD's Housing Subsidy Programs 126
The Section 8 Rental Assistance Program 127
Low-Rent Public Housing.......................130
FHA's Housing Subsidy Programs................134
The Mass Production Drive 141
Program Abuses 141

The Debate over Subsidy Methods 143
Moratorium 145
Some Conclusions 147

9. The Housing Roller Coaster 153

The Facts 153
The Causes 155
The Consequences 158
The Remedies 160
Conclusions 164

10. Reducing Housing Costs 167

HUD's Charter 167
The Upward Leap in Housing Costs 168
Damaging Consequences 170
The Favored Remedy 170
Operation Breakthrough 171
Breakthrough's Forgotten Predecessor 175
The Multiple Causes of Housing Costs 177
HUD and Housing Costs 180
What HUD Could Do 181

11. Equal Housing Opportunity 187

HUD's Mission 187
The Importance of HUD's Mission 188
Limitations on HUD's Power 192
What Has Been Accomplished? 194
The Discouraged 196
Conclusions 199

12. Urban Research 203

HUD's Research Mandates 203
HUD's Current Research 204
Limited Funds 205
An Early Aborted Effort 206
The Dry Period 208

A Minor Miracle 208
A More Mature Urban Research 211
Has HUD Research Made a Difference? 213
Toward Better Urban Research 216

13. Policies and People 221

The Innovators 223
Turning the Idea into a Reality 233
Managing the Programs 234
The "Assistants-To" 236
Agents of Change 237
The Administrators and Orchestrators 239

14. The Underlying Impediments to
     Urban Improvement 241

The Limits of Government 242
There Is Much We Do Not Understand 244
Our Permissive Society 245
The Other Side 246
The Leaders and the Led 246
In Conclusion 247

Appendix 249
Notes 251
Index 267

Preface

This book is about the programs and performance of the Department of Housing and Urban Development (HUD). It deals principally with the present and future of that department and the cities it was designed to serve. History, of which there is much, is considered only to the extent it seemed necessary to illuminate the current issues.

This work evaluates all of HUD's many major programs and suggests ways in which their performance might be improved. This is a vast, perhaps presumptuous undertaking, for it takes us into economics and housing finance, political science, urban planning, the myriad pathologies of slum life, racial discrimination, research, and other subjects—each of which is a specialized field in itself. This broad treatment also makes necessary relatively brief coverage of many subjects which might easily be, and have been, the subject of an entire book. The purpose is to show the broad sweep of HUD's activities and their interrelations.

The performance of numerous past and present HUD officials is evaluated. This is not for purposes of gossip, but rather because it is this writer's conviction that the policies and performance of a government department cannot be understood fully without consideration of the skills and attitudes of the personalities whose influence was crucial. The discussion of personalities is not ad hominem praise or criticism, it is as objective as this writer can make it. Nearly all of those discussed are good friends of the writer.

This book can also be read as a case study of federal government and the people it represents, and its efforts to deal with the increasingly complex problems into which government has been thrust during the past decade or more. This recurring theme appears in nearly every chapter, like the overtones which give color and character to a note of music. The last chapter is devoted entirely to this second, but by no means unimportant, theme. A reader interested primarily in only one or more of HUD's programs, not the entire symphony, can use the table of contents to find those with which he is particularly concerned.

In a direct sense, the substance of this book comes from the writer's many years as a career public servant intimately involved with the programs of HUD and its predecessor agencies (under six presidents), mostly in the role of policy developer, implementor, and evaluator.

In another sense, this book reflects the experiences of an entire generation of urban and housing specialists, for many scores of them, in and out of government, have shared their wisdom with me. Whatever merit this book has, I owe to the generosity of these many friends and professional associates. Its limitations, however, are mine, not theirs.

The people who have given generously of their time and knowledge are too numerous to mention here. But I must make four exceptions. My most sincere thanks go to former HUD Secretary Robert C. Weaver for initially encouraging me to undertake such a book and for the great help he has provided in his penetrating comments on most of the chapters. I am also much indebted to Hilbert Fefferman, who has generously edited the entire manuscript and improved it greatly, and to John Del Vecchio for his careful reading of the page proofs. Lastly, I am grateful to Dean Paul Ylvisaker of Harvard University for the introduction he has written and for encouraging me to pursue the book in terms of the tones as well as the overtones implicit in what I believe to be a subject of great importance to the nation.

I also acknowledge with gratitude the generous support of the Ford Foundation, the National Association of Realtors, and the National Development Corporation of Pittsburgh.

M. Carter McFarland

Introduction

Paul N. Ylvisaker

The word *cities* (by quick count) appears only twice in the sixty pages of legislation that created the U.S. Department of Housing and Urban Development in 1965 and finally recognized that ours was no longer a nation of farmers. Revealingly, those solitary references come when the law gets round to the subject of demolition and deterioration.

There was melancholy genius in the sparing use of the term. *Cities* is the code word for what most Americans want to forget: an environment they have tried to escape; a gathering point for minorities, the poor, the infirm, and others they do not want on their consciences; a way of life that challenges their conventional values; and increasingly, a frightening reminder that neither life nor the American Dream is all that secure.

Knowing as much, those who drafted the legislation in the Kennedy-Johnson era artfully turned to other and more euphonious language to capture the votes of a loosely allied majority. *Urban* was the most attractive and resilient of these supposed synonyms: it spoke to everyone's condition, no matter how disparate those conditions actually were. And the mayors of the big cities did not complain. Quite the contrary: U.S. presidents and the Congress were finally ready to recite something other than a rural creed, and if they felt better saying *urban* rather than *cities*, so be it.

The strategy was politically astute. It did achieve cabinet status for the one federal agency that spoke the vernacular of cities. It has given sustenance to cities, if only to provide a national forum in which they and their problems are routinely on the public's agenda.

But the law and its coalition-building terminology left both HUD and U.S. cities (i.e., the larger, older, and more industrial cities) with the almost impossible task of winning and holding majority support for policies and programs substantial enough to make a difference. What might make a difference? A national land policy that allowed less of a devil-take-the-hindmost exodus from built-up areas and a less anarchic exploitation of open land—with appropriate tax policies to accompany it. A national housing policy that at least reversed the 4-1 edge in subsidies given the wealthier over the poorer. An economic development policy that encouraged industrial cities to move ahead more rapidly into the service economy. Welfare, health, and investment policies that made cities something other than traps for the needy and unemployed.

But to ask for policies of that kind, and programs of that magnitude, would be to ask a majority of Americans to reverse the economic and social directions in which they are racing, and to rewrite the ground rules by which they are "moving ahead."

HUD is a political animal; its secretary serves at the pleasure of the nation's first politician, and its budgets are voted by legislators whose livelihoods depend on accurately assessing where majorities are going. And majorities are not moving toward the older cities, not if they can help it.

Understandably, therefore, HUD—and its predecessor agencies—has become a Janus-figure on the American urban scene: in one aspect, it has facilitated majoritarian tastes and settlement patterns (FHA before the Weaver turnaround showed this face most clearly); in the other, it has looked sympathetically to the central cities and their minority constituents. At one and the same time, it has been a partner in America's growth and the nation's conscience respecting the people and places left behind.

It is precisely that ambivalence that characterizes and bedevils the quest for a national urban policy: is it to facilitate the majority's preference in settlement patterns, or—on behalf of the older cities and the newer minorities—to constrain those preferences?

HUD (like its predecessors) has vacillated in response, moving almost rhythmically from minority to majority and back to minority concerns. Certainly, as Carter McFarland abundantly illustrates, that has been the cycle in the years since HUD's establishment over a decade ago. Weaver's appointment as HUD's first secretary was a signal in itself; the message of his selection and the social unrest of the sixties was powerful enough to bring even FHA to an interest in the cities' poor. Romney, too, had an instinct for the underdog; but his love affair with mass production of housing, and the demagoguery of Richard Nixon, moved HUD again toward the magnet of majoritarian America.

The evidence now is strong that HUD is speaking and acting once more on behalf of America's older cities and their less favored inhabitants. The designation of a black woman as secretary, the shift in block grant formulas to sluice more money toward the older cities, and the emphasis in the president's biennial statement of national development policy ("Cities and People in Distress")—all point in the same direction.

It is not difficult to see what—besides idealism—has prompted the return to city and minority concerns. Rampant unemployment among minority youth in the older cities is frightening everyone, including the black leaders who helped elect Carter and more recently have chided the president about promises unfulfilled. New York City's "bankruptcy"—an omen of many another municipal Black Friday still to come—rivals in its impact the civil uprising of the sixties. The president and HUD have no choice but to respond.

The question is, will HUD and the repertoire of remedies it has managed with much blood, sweat, and tears to accumulate be able to do more than temporize with the city problem the nation faces—or at least fears?

There are a lot of reasons for thinking not. Carter McFarland—with an evenness and openness remarkable for one so caringly involved with HUD's procreation and growth—cites evidence that any reader could convert into disbelief: inconsistent, often incompatible, policies; scattering of responsibilities and powers among agencies not under HUD's control; dismantling of capacities already at HUD's disposal; the inconstancy of leadership and national resolve; the impotence of government in a loosening society in tightening times.

Nor does optimism increase with awareness of the massive forces at work—forces that HUD is somehow expected to redirect by a heroic display of social jujitsu. What seemed a miraculous undertaking in the fifties—Mayor Joe Clark's successful assault on municipal corruption and the "Chinese Wall" of the Pennsylvania Railroad, in his memorable rebuilding of Philadelphia's downtown—now seems minuscule in the perspective of an industrial obsolescence that ashens our cities whole regions at a time.

Skepticism grows as one measures the swiftening flow of immigration (nearing 1.5 million annually, mostly illegal, mostly poor) and then glimpses the prospect that it may be but a starting trickle from the scores upon scores of millions waiting to flood from an impoverished Third World toward our "underused" cities over the next generation. (This process promises to make Hispanics the nation's largest minority, and Spanish our second language.)

During this same generation, those who mind our cities and our society will have to cope with spreading confrontation between two cultures: affluence and attempted stability within the system; rip-off and anarchy at the system's fraying edge. Chronic unemployment and neglect are producing that second culture—a state of nature Thomas Hobbes once described as "solitary, nasty, brutish and short," a condition ripe for Robin Hood at best, marauding bands and syndicated mafiosi at their worst.

Set against those massive forces and their more ominous implications, HUD's chances of making a difference are slender indeed. Increasingly, one gets the sense that urbanites and urbanists alike are discounting any possibility that HUD, or any combination of public and private agencies, will reverse or even halt the downward spiral of the older cities. Business and citizenry continue to leave; segregation by race—and more seriously, by economic class—grows more pronounced; and analysts who once wrote confidently of solutions are now advising the nation that the wholesale abandonment of "uneconomic" cities may be a fact of life Americans will have to get used to.

Realism is one thing; quitting the struggle is quite another. HUD's mission at its core is to keep the struggle for civility alive, to keep this nation at the job of revitalizing rather than discarding its human communities. Battling for the public's attention and ultimately its soul, in my book, is far more important than winning its favor. Currying public favor through fear and promise of practiced neglect, which became the political art of the later sixties and early seventies, cost this nation dearly—infinitely more than the turmoil of hope boiling up in the days of HUD's creation.

Not only in my book, but in Carter McFarland's as well. He writes as a teacher, not a preacher. But through his patient and masterful explication of all HUD's mysterious warrens and weaponries, there is the impatient beat of the drummer calling for the battle to begin again.

But not with the same strategies. HUD and the nation have tended toward the "quick fix"—staccato bursts of new programs featuring in more confident times the virtuosity of federal technicians, and in times less secure (or more manipulative) the delegation of the job to localities whose powers were somehow to be energized through block grants.

If the promise of decent cities is to be wrestled from the darker spirits we now encounter, the struggle will have to persist through a much longer night. The fits and starts of programming, in which innovation has become an end in itself for both politicians and professionals, will have to be evened out into a continuing set of commitments, even if tied to minimal rather than heroic objectives. There is an instinct for a better and fairer life in every "obsolescent" city and in every migrant who comes to it. There is also a latent supply of human power that goes with that instinct. But neither the urge nor the power will show if there is not a continuous and tangible commitment that can be relied upon, whether it be a minimal level of ensured housing, or employment, or income—or, one hopes, a combination of all of them.

HUD is the national symbol of that commitment. Carter McFarland has written of it with the understanding, hope, and affection that are now so urgently called for.

Federal Government and Urban Problems

HUD: Successes, Failures, and the Fate of Our Cities

1
Trouble in Our Cities

Because the purpose of this book is to describe and evaluate the efforts of the federal government to cope with urban problems, it is necessary that we begin by identifying as clearly as possible the complex and closely interrelated litany of urban ills. This chapter will discuss the major problems our urban areas face today. Those that are well known will be mentioned only briefly. The less obvious urban problems will be discussed at greater length. The purpose is to provide background for the chapters that follow.

Concern with these matters is by no means new. For a hundred years, discerning people have been expressing alarm about the trouble in America's cities and forecasting even more dire problems to come. In the 1880s, Jacob Riis wrote *How the Other Half Lives,* a vivid and disturbing account of life in New York's slums. President Theodore Roosevelt established a commission to study possible federal action to improve the sordid human conditions he had seen. The commission's report was published in 1908. Like the reports of many presidential study groups before and since, it produced no action. Later, pioneering urban planners began to sound the alarm that American cities were headed toward deep crisis and impending breakdown. Among these were Ebenezer Howard, Raymond Unwin, Lewis Mumford, Henry Churchill, and J. L. Sert. Sert's book on the subject was titled *Can Our Cities Survive?*[1]

Many of the planners writing in the first half of this century not only saw the physical imperfections of the urban scene—high densities, confused land use, clogged traffic, declining economic function, housing obsolescence, and the deterioration of urban services—but also the deep social problems that would erupt in the conflicts and riots of the 1960s.

In 1960, Catherine Bauer, one of America's most discerning students of urban affairs, wrote of "the purgatory of the immigrants, racial conflict, juvenile delinquency, the dreary lives of the aged, traffic congestion, the lengthening journey to work, the services that never catch up with needs, slums and the chronic shortage of decent moderate-priced housing, smog, crowded schools, ugliness and noise in the center, monotony and inconvenience in the suburbs, the loss of amenity and the lack of recreational opportunity."[2] The following paragraphs will identify the major problems our urban areas face today.

Urban Ills

Slums and Ghettos

Slums are a familiar condition: they exist and have existed in cities throughout the world for a very long time. A century ago, Dickens wrote poignantly of life in the slums of England. A slum is a concentration of poor people living in dilapidated housing in neighborhoods with inadequate facilities and services. It means filth, debris, malnutrition, disease, and despair. It means a breakdown in family discipline and broken families. It means vandalism, violence, and excessive use of alcohol and dope. It means a feeling of alienation from and hostility to society as a whole.

It cannot be said that the slums of America are worse than, or even as bad as, those in some other parts of the world. From the standpoint of sheer poverty and physical squalor, the slums of India and Latin America are much worse.

However, slums in America have two characteristics that do not exist to the same degree in most other countries. The first is that they are intimately related to racial discrimination and segregation. The second is that they exist in a land of unprecedented material abundance enjoyed by nearly everyone but the slum dweller. Yet the expectations and hopes of the slum dweller are systematically raised by the massive impact of television, radio, newspapers, and magazines—both through the advertising they carry and the picture of life their programs and articles promulgate. In recent years, the hopes of slum dwellers have also been raised by a variety of government programs and their expansive promises. Thus, although the *actual* physical deprivation in the slums of America is not as great as that in some other parts of the world, the *relative* feeling of deprivation and the consequent tension and hostility it generates is at least as great. Households with the lowest income and the least competence are trapped in the poorest housing in the poorest neighborhoods, yet they are fully aware and constantly reminded of how the other members of American society live. This revolution of rising expectations is an important factor in producing what urban scholar Anthony Downs calls "crisis ghettos."[3]

Another characteristic intensifies the ghetto-slum condition. When large numbers of the poor and deprived are concentrated in a neighborhood, or even in a single large building, mysterious forces develop that greatly intensify the social and behavioral pathologies. This has come to be called the "critical mass" effect—a term first suggested by Charles L. Schultze, one of our most influential economists, now chairman of the President's Council of Economic Advisers. *Critical mass* is taken from the vocabulary of atomic physics and suggests that when a certain concentration of matter (or persons) is reached, something happens to change greatly the intensity of the interactions, causing a violent explosion. The analogy is an apt one, for we have often seen the explosive results of a critical mass of the poor and deprived.

The slum condition has been further intensified by the relatively new phenomenon of housing abandonment. Fifteen years ago, it was widely accepted that urban slums were overcrowded with too many people occupying too little dwelling space. This situation has changed drastically in the last fifteen years. The cause is housing abandonment. This development has been studied most intensively by George Sternlieb of Rutgers University.[4] But it is still not well understood. In addition to thinning out the population of declining central cities, it seems to reflect purely economic factors related to the low-income tenant's inability to pay rent sufficient to cover the landlord's financing and maintenance costs (both of which tend to be higher in low-income areas); it also seems to be related to tensions between landlord and tenant, particularly if they are of different races; it is certainly related to the tenant's antisocial behavior and his tendency to be destructive of the property in which he lives; it also reflects the landlord's neglect of maintenance and services.

According to Sternlieb's 1973 estimates, New York City has lost approximately 2 percent of its structures by abandonment. In the worst parts of St. Louis, about 16 percent of the structures have been abandoned, and in the Woodlawn and Lawndale sections of Chicago, as high as 20 percent have been abandoned.[5] The acres of boarded-up, empty buildings in many of our cities vividly reflect the growing magnitude of residential abandonment. They show, also, that the thinning out of our urban slums has intensified rather than ameliorated the squalor, hopelessness, crime, and other characteristics of slum life.

The social tensions that all this generates were demonstrated in the urban riots of the 1960s. The riots have now subsided, but the tension and violence in the ghetto slums have not. The rising rate of mindless crime—murder, rape, mugging—in nearly every large city in the country shouts this ominous fact. In February 1976, the magazine *New York* published excerpts from a book about street violence in New York's South Bronx and the inability of the police to keep up with it, much less control it. The book was written by a policeman stationed for several years in a precinct serving a South Bronx neighborhood. It draws a chilling picture, appropriately titled *The Siege of Fort Apache*. The story grimly concludes that this New York neighborhood "may be the closest that men have yet come to creating hell on earth." Unfortunately, Fort Apache is by no means unique among the ghetto-slums of this country.

Racial Apartheid

No less alarming than the explosive ghetto-slum, and closely connected with it, is the fact that the urban blacks and whites live apart from one another. Most blacks (as well as Chicanos and Puerto Ricans) are clustered in inner-city neighborhoods; most whites live largely in the suburbs. Despite twenty years of court decisions, laws, and executive orders aimed at eliminating racial discrimination, and despite some real progress toward this goal, we have made startlingly little progress in achieving an integrated society. The apartheid pattern of settlement was as severe in 1970 as it was in 1960. The percentage of blacks in the suburban population was only slightly greater in 1970 than it was ten years before.[6] It seems clear that less progress toward equal opportunity has been made in housing than in education, jobs, and access to public places.

Urban Sprawl

As everyone knows, our urban areas have grown at a staggering rate since World War I. When large numbers of new residents must be accommodated, cities can either grow up or out. Practically all have grown by spreading. The pressure of a rapidly mounting urban population has created the suburbs and exurbs that stretch for miles and miles around every American city of any size. The growth was inevitable. The character of that growth was not.

The shape, or lack of shape, of suburbia and its sheer size have produced some unpleasant and some ominous results. One of these is "strip development," consisting of streets with a mélange of automobile dealers, used car lots, various quick food establishments, gasoline stations, and other assorted commercial enterprises. Most are embellished with glaring lights, gaudy signs, and billboards, which many tolerate but few admire. Commerce is important to any human settlement. It provides jobs and essential services. But the form it too often takes unnecessarily demeans the environment.

Another aspect of unplanned urban growth results from the private holding of vacant land for speculative profit and the search of developers for the cheapest land on which to build, usually further out from the central city. This leaves hundreds of acres of intervening land unused and vacant, thus stretching suburban development much farther out than required. The result is wasted land and a great increase in the length of such essential municipal services as water and sewer lines, storm drainage, gas pipes, electrical lines, streets, and roads. As Doris B. Holleb has put it, "Urban sprawl is a very costly form of settlement."[7]

This is not to suggest that the expansive and expanding suburbs are always very unpleasant places in which to live. Suburbia has provided millions of Americans who can afford it with what they regard as very pleasant living. Moreover, by any reasonably objective standard, they are right. Their houses are relatively spacious and well equipped. The bathrooms are clean and functional. The kitchens and laundry rooms are marvelously equipped with labor-saving gadgets of many kinds. They often have a plot of ground with grass, shrubs, trees, and flowers. Shopping and recreation are usually easily accessible. Jobs are often nearby, too. So are libraries, schools, restaurants, and even good music and theater. Never, indeed, have so many lived so well, in purely material terms. Even the much-maligned monotony of the speculatively built subdivision with its row upon row of essentially similar houses seems to bother the architects and city planners more than it does the residents, as a study of New Jersey's Levittown revealed some years ago.

Local Government Balkanization

One serious result of urban growth is that our urban agglomerations have long since reached beyond the jurisdiction and responsibility of the central city's governmental mechanism. As our cities have grown, very few, if any, have been able to annex the great stretches of suburbia and exurbia that have grown up around them. Instead, many small suburban governmental jurisdictions have developed, along with various special districts with responsibility for water, sewers, roads, schools, bridges, and other essential sources. This bewildering multiplicity of urban government jurisdictions possesses a wide variation of fiscal and managerial capacity. It creates extreme difficulties in coordination of public services; it diffuses responsibilities to the point of unaccountability.

To say that there is no local government in America that corresponds with, or has effective control over, the intimately intertwined physical, social, and economic unity of our urban areas is to state the obvious, but telling, truth. The consequences of local governmental balkanization are far-reaching and severe. They weaken the capacity of our urban areas to operate effectively, to provide and coordinate services, to plan, and to balance the fiscal books.

The present threat of bankruptcy of New York City, a plight that many other large cities have nearly reached, reflects bad and sometimes reckless management. But it goes deeper than that. It is a sad symptom of the multiplicity of local government jurisdictions plus the large concentration of the poor and deprived in the central city and the dispersal of middle-class families and many business firms to the suburbs. Many large cities have lost much of their industrial and commercial base to the suburbs. This produces high central-city expenditures for welfare, police, fire protection, and other services in the face of sharply declining income from taxes. The central city has to serve not only its poor but also thousands of commuters from the suburbs who pay little or no taxes for the central city services they use.

The Automobile

The present shape of our urban areas was made possible by the flexible mobility provided by the automobile with a big assist from our huge public investment in urban highways and freeways. The cities are also, in many ways, the victims of those powerful and ornate products of Detroit. The way our urban areas are deployed—their wide dispersal of housing, jobs, shopping, recreation, and just friends—makes the automobile virtually essential to most Americans. The poor, who cannot afford one, and the very young and old, who cannot drive one, are correspondingly penalized. But the automobile is to many of us much more than a necessary convenience. It is a status symbol, at least as important to our self-esteem as the clothes we wear, the important friends we know, the jobs we hold, or the clubs to which we belong. Beyond that, the automobile has, in some psychological way, become a means by which we release our deepest drives. America's attachment, some call it marriage, to the automobile has been frequently noted and often decried. But it appears to be one of the most intractable and basic urges of our society. Use of the automobile is pervasive and increasing. Total travel time increased substantially between 1960 and 1971.

Some of the consequences of America's love affair with the automobile have received much attention. An obvious consequence of increased use of the car for travel to work, for shopping, and for recreation (about 85 percent of the time with only the driver and no passengers) is congestion. In most central cities, many streets and freeways are clogged nearly to the point of immobility much of the day. In both central city and suburbs, the morning and evening rush hours' congestion slows traffic movement to the speed of a walk, and lengthy stoppages are common. The commonest untoward event, such as heavy rain or snow, or a large public gathering, can immobilize an entire city for hours. The building of more urban freeways designed to relieve congestion simply generates more of the same.

The automobile is also responsible for much of the pollution and smog that hang heavy over many of our urban areas. (Other villains are industrial pollution, the generation of electricity, and the airplane.) At the beginning of this decade, pollutants in the air equaled about 281 million tons a year, according to Barbara Ward.[8] This is more than one ton for each citizen. It is not surprising that more people are dying of respiratory disease each year.

Another consequence of an auto-dependent urban civilization generally goes unremarked or accepted with equanimity. This is the incredible loss of life and limb produced each year by street and highway accidents. If as many persons were killed and maimed from any other cause—say, a new form of virus—it would be considered a crisis, and the citizens, press, and politicians would demand that something be done. Yet, we have such an affinity for the automobile and such a tolerance of its consequences that the highway carnage hardly stirs public reaction, even when the annual fatality toll is reported in the press, as it frequently is.

Our use of automobiles, both in driving and perhaps even more in idling while we wait for the traffic to move, consumes about 25 percent of our domestic petroleum supply (trucks, air travel, and the generation of electricity take an additional large share). Having begun to recognize that the world's total supply of fossil fuel is finite, many foresee the day when there will simply be no more petroleum (or coal) from which to make gasoline or when the cost of its extraction will be prohibitive. Yet we continue to use gasoline as though it were infinitely abundant. Government studies on the use of automobiles and alternate modes of urban transportation provide little hope that car use can be significantly changed. They find that automobile users are markedly unaffected by steep rises in the cost of gasoline.[9]

Many other urban activities also pollute the air, the water, and the land. Solid wastes pollute the urban landscape; untreated human waste and industrial chemicals pollute our streams, rivers, lakes, and oceans; various home-used sprays and other chemicals pollute the air and the land as well. The ways in which our urban society manages to despoil the environment are numerous, irresponsible, and often lethal to both man and nature.

Impediments to Housing Production

The production of enough decent housing for a growing urban population, particularly for the poor and near poor, is vital to meeting basic human needs and to improving slum conditions. During this decade, at least two million new housing units a year will be needed. Of course, housing will not solve all our urban problems. Factors far deeper than housing alone are at the root of slums—poverty, human behavior, social pathologies—factors that are difficult to untangle and harder to cure.

There are several barriers to the production of a sufficient and steady volume of housing in the United States. The first is the frequent shortages of mortgage credit to finance the purchase of housing. In our urban areas, another problem is a shortage of land upon which to build. There is no absolute shortage of land. The problem has to do with the difficulty builders are experiencing in finding land zoned to permit residential construction and serviced by water and sewer lines and other essential public services. In many jurisdictions this reflects "no growth policies" or other policies that sharply limit the volume of residential building permitted. The most crucial barrier to housing production is the rapid escalation in housing prices. About two-thirds of our people are now unable to afford a medium-priced new house, as compared with about one-third in 1950.

The National Economy and the City

The national economy affects the city, especially the central city, in many important ways. Unemployment reduces tax revenues and increases welfare and unemployment benefit payments. It is invariably higher among the poor minorities and youth, which compounds and makes more explosive the many-sided problems of the slums. Many believe that unemployment, especially among the young, accelerates the alarming rise in crimes against persons and property. Another problem of the general economy—price inflation—affects nearly all urban dwellers. Its effect on the poor is devastating. It also magnifies the central city's fiscal problem by driving up the costs of city services of all kinds and by increasing the cost of the city's borrowing through bonds. Unemployment and inflation thus hit the city on both sides of its fiscal ledger—costs and income.

The Unintended City

There are many city planners and many city plans. But there are few truly planned cities and fewer beautiful ones. A great city should lift the spirit of man as well as serve his more mundane needs. The inefficient and hardly inspiring character of our cities is mostly the result of the interplay of thousands of individual economic and political decisions. They are rarely, if ever, the result of collective, deliberate, sustained acts of public purpose. We pay a high price for relying so heavily on the demonstrated incapacity of the private market and private self-interest to shape our urban living environment. Those aspects of our cities that are shaped by political decisions are equally haphazard. Our cities are a conspicuous example of the nation's difficulty in achieving a reasonable restraint of individual self-interest for the good of all.

Who Cares?

Only once during the past seventy-six years have the troubles of our cities penetrated the national consciousness to the point where there may have been a general recognition that something needed to be done. This was during the mid-1960s, when riots, vandalism, violence, and burning struck in the streets of scores of American cities. Despite the dire warnings of the President's Commission on Civil Disorders, this concern faded quickly. Now, whatever public concern there is has shifted to energy conservation and the state of the economy in general. The public apathy about the city's predicament is probably the most alarming dimension of the problem. If the public does not care or cannot be made to care, very little is likely to be done. In the presidential election campaign of 1976, the cities were scarcely mentioned by either candidate. If the candidates were reading the mood of the electorate accurately, the public, indeed, does not care about city problems and does not want to hear about them.

How Serious Are Our Urban Ills?

Nearly all responsible students agree that many of America's urban ills are quite serious and that the people, through their government, should summon the will to do something about them. Harvey S. Perloff, a widely respected planner, has put his views this way: "The urban problems are basic, pervasive, and complex." They are a "drag on our social and political progress; they drain us of our national self assurance; they poison much of our lives."[10] The National Commission on Urban Problems put the matter thus:

> If there is a sense of urgency and even alarm in our report and our recommendations, it is because the Commission saw the cities of our country first hand and listened to the voices of the people. The Commission members certainly were not less concerned or knowledgeable than the average citizen, but after our inspections, hearings, and research studies, we found problems much worse, more widespread, and more explosive than any of us had thought.[11]

Internationally known author Barbara Ward said, "At no time in human history has the man made environment been in such a state of convulsed and complete crisis."[12] Arnold A. Rogow, a political scientist and psychologist, asserted his opinion in these gloomy tones: "the argument can be made that the American city itself is entering a Dark Age . . . because the city is becoming a fragmented pseudocity of decay, fear, violence, and breakdown." In another place he identifies "racism, poverty, crime, and heroin [as] the four horsemen of the urban apocalypse."[13]

There are a few observers of the city scene who take our urban problems less seriously. The best known is Edward C. Banfield, who writes: "Most of the 'problems' that are generally supposed to constitute 'the urban crisis' could not conceivably lead to disaster. There are some of them important, in the sense that a bad cold is important, but they are not critical in the sense that a cancer is critical."[14] Some others claim the urban crisis is manufactured.

It is true that some urban problems are less critical than others. Some of them have more to do with convenience, amenity, and civility than with the survival of the republic. But many urban problems are quite as grave as the great majority of serious students believe. Among these are slums and the human deprivation they cause, violence and casual crime without remorse, racial discrimination and segregation, the lethal pollution of our air and water, the profligate waste of precious and limited energy, and other perishable natural resources. It is, also, much more than a casual inconvenience that a country as wealthy as ours seems unable to give all its citizens that most basic of benefits, a decent home in a decent neighborhood with the services and facilities we know how to provide. This disparity between our material abundance and our failure to provide shelter and decent living conditions is particularly striking with respect to the poor, the discriminated against, the aging, and the handicapped.

Despite its admitted failures, despite the widespread present disenchantment with government, there is much that government, and only government, can do to deal with the multiple problems of urban America. How the government, particularly the Department of Housing and Urban Development (HUD) has attempted to deal with our complex urban problems and how it might improve its performance are discussed in the chapters that follow. It will become evident, however, that the government can do only as much as the people as a whole permit and support. Thus, our capacity to cope with the grave problems of urban America (where 70 percent of our citizens live) becomes ultimately a test of our collective will and wisdom. It is also a test of our willingness to sacrifice individual interest for the common interest, to forego immediate indulgence for the longer-term benefit of all, and to accept a humane redistribution of the country's wealth from those who have too much to those who, by no fault of their own, have too little.

2

Cabinet Status for Urban Affairs

On a bright fall morning in early September 1965, 150 guests assembled in the White House Rose Garden. Soon, President Lyndon B. Johnson strode out. After a short, solemn statement on the significance of what he was about to do, he sat down and slowly inscribed his name on a bill just passed by the Congress. Following custom, he used a number of dark blue, felt-tipped pens, each bearing the presidential seal and his own signature. That morning the president had established the Department of Housing and Urban Development.

Section 2 of the law described the new department's charter in these words:

> The Congress hereby declares that the general welfare and security of the Nation and the health and living standards of our people require, as a matter of national purpose, sound development of the Nation's communities and metropolitan areas in which the vast majority of its people live and work.
>
> To carry out such purpose, and in recognition of the increasing importance of housing and urban development in our national life, the Congress finds that establishment of an executive department is desirable to achieve the best administration of the principal programs of the Federal Government which provide assistance for housing and for the development of the Nation's communities; to assist the President in achieving maximum coordination of the various Federal activities which have a major effect upon urban community, suburban, or

metropolitan development; to encourage the solution of problems of housing, urban development, and mass transportation through State, county, town, village, or other local and private action, including promotion of interstate, regional, and metropolitan cooperation; to encourage the maximum contributions that may be made by vigorous private homebuilding and mortgage lending industries to housing, urban development and the national economy; and to provide for full and appropriate consideration, at the national level, of the needs and interests of the Nation's communities and of the people who live and work in them.[1]

In his remarks at the signing ceremony, the president said, "In less than a lifetime America has become a highly urbanized nation." We must, he said, "face the many meanings of the new America." We must face this challenge of "our cities and our new urban age [if they are not to become] symbols of a sordid, nightmare society."[2] The legislative charter and the president's sweeping rhetoric gave the new cabinet department a broad assignment.

Why So Late?

The ceremony in the Rose Garden took place in 1965. But the nation had been predominantly urban for fifty years. In 1970, more than 70 percent of the population lived in urban surroundings, and the problems of urban areas had been evident and growing more acute for decades. By any realistic standard, the establishment of a cabinet department to represent urban interests was late in coming. It is not only ironic but also a sad reflection on the nation's priorities that as late as 1960, the rapidly dwindling farm population was represented by a cabinet department employing well over 100,000 people, but that the far more numerous urban dwellers were championed by the Housing and Home Finance Agency (HHFA), a relatively obscure, noncabinet conglomerate of agencies employing about 14,000 persons. Senator Joseph Clark, of Pennsylvania, said in 1959, "A visitor from outer space, looking at the structure of our Federal Government, would surely conclude that America is still a rural Nation, with rural problems the dominant concern."[3]

There are several reasons for this slow federal awakening to urban affairs. Perhaps the most important lies deep in American ideology and cultural values. The country has had a nostalgic attachment to rural and small-town images. As Mark I. Gelfand has put it, "Americans remained tied to the farm and small town. Indeed, the more the United States became urbanized, the more appealing was its rural creed."[4] A more concrete factor was that until quite recently, representatives from rural areas tended to dominate—far out of proportion to the number of people who elected them—in Congress and in State legislatures.

Another factor in the failure to recognize the urbanization of our society is the fact that until the election of John Kennedy, our presidents had reflected the rural bias of the people as a whole. Franklin Roosevelt was a country squire whose tastes and instincts made him aloof to big cities. It is probably no accident that one of the New Deal's first tentative ventures into urban improvement was the construction of several greenbelt towns, reflecting Rexford Tugwell's conviction that the way to solve the concentration of people in cities was to get them out into garden communities or small towns. President Eisenhower was not a country squire, but he was a small-town boy from Abilene, Kansas. During his presidency, Eisenhower displayed no great interest in, or grasp of, urbanization as a significant social phenomenon.

John Kennedy took a different view. While campaigning for the presidency, he bore down hard on the neglect of the cities and the need for an urban department. John Kennedy's contributions to an awareness of the need for national action on urban problems and for an urban department were very great. Shortly after his death, a political scientist observed accurately, "Kennedy will be remembered for many things but in the long run, it may well be that he will be best remembered as the first President to understand the importance of the metropolitan revolution in the United States and as the first to try to do something about it."[5] Kennedy fought hard for creation of an urban department. In 1962, he had a bill introduced in the Congress to accomplish his purpose. When it was defeated, he immediately tried again with a reorganization plan. This approach was defeated even more decisively. The time was not yet ripe. Also, his tactics were bad, his liaison with Congress poor. Another unfortunately damaging element was Kennedy's announcement that the able but black Robert Weaver would be appointed secretary of the new department. Kennedy apparently expected this to help his cause by forcing possible opponents to appear to be voting on purely racial grounds. In fact, by this move, he lost Southern votes he might otherwise have won, including that of Senator John Sparkman, a long-time leader in housing and urban legislation. Kennedy, himself, admitted, "I played it too cute. It was so obvious it made them mad."[6]

What Was Expected

In Washington, a chair at the president's cabinet table is a coveted prerogative. It is also hard to come by. George Washington governed with a cabinet of only three. Since then, the growth in the cabinet has been a faithful record of the nation's priorities. But the birth of each new cabinet post has been a long, tortuous process. The Department of the Interior was established after thirty-three years of discussion; for Agriculture, the debate lasted thirty-seven years; for Commerce, thirty-nine years; and for Labor, over forty years.[7] For HUD, the discussion period was shorter but no less contentious.

Once achieved, cabinet status is expected to bestow many benefits on its holder and on the department he heads. A cabinet member certainly possesses enhanced prestige. He is also presumed to have more clout with the Congress, with other departments, and with the public. Cabinet status is supposed to provide valued access to the president, not only at cabinet meetings but also when personal appointments are sought. A cabinet member normally possesses greater authority than many lesser agency heads to direct and coordinate the usually inert, sometimes intransigent bureaus under him. A cabinet department is also expected to be more effective because it contains all, or most, of the authorities necessary to do its job.

These were the hopes of the many people, in and out of government, who struggled long and hard to achieve the establishment of a cabinet department responsible for dealing with the problems of the nation's urban concentrations.[8] The staff director of Eisenhower's Committee on Government Organization, chaired by Nelson Rockefeller, wrote, "The greater prestige, as well as the more effective access to the President, which cabinet status would afford, would undoubtedly facilitate the effective accomplishment of the programs [HHFA] administers; also it would probably attract better men."[9] William L. C. Wheaton, an early advocate of a cabinet department for urban affairs, expressed his expectations in these words:

> The primary reason for a Department of Urban Development is to secure a seat at the bargaining table in the White House where the Federal pie is cut up and divided. In Washington, unfortunately, the flaming sword of truth is a poor substitute for the broad axe of influence. In Washington, influence is largely measured by prestige, payrolls, budgets, and only a cabinet officer commanding ample amounts of these can represent urban people.[10]

Earlier versions of the departmental legislation had reflected the need for wider powers to cope with urban problems. But it had to be compromised to satisfy vested interests and gain passage of the law.[11]

What Was Accomplished

As a response to the massive problems affecting America's urban areas, the creation of HUD proved a limited triumph, at best. The new department fell short of the high hopes of its proponents in a number of ways.

The new urban department contained by no means all the federal programs affecting the physical shape of the city, not to speak of the many programs directed at human aspects of the urban condition. In fact, the existing Housing and Home Finance Agency (HHFA) had simply been elevated to cabinet level with the secretary's authority clearly established over all of the operating elements. The long awaited new department consisted of these elements.

1. *The Federal Housing Administration.* FHA, created

as a virtually independent agency in 1934 and made part of HHFA in 1947, administered a number of loan insurance programs designed to stimulate the flow of private capital into installment loans for home repair and mortgage loans for the purchase of homes and apartments. In 1961, a relatively small program had been added under which FHA insured loans at below-market-interest rates, thus putting the housing within the reach of families of lower income. More such subsidy programs were soon to come.

2. *The Public Housing Administration.* The United States Housing Authority, created as an independent agency in 1937 and later made part of HHFA, where it became PHA, administered a program of federal subsidies to help local public housing authorities build and manage housing for the poor. This program was known as Public Housing.

3. *The Urban Renewal Administration.* URA, created in 1949 as HHFA's Division of Slum Clearance, administered programs of federal subsidies to localities to redevelop and rehabilitate inner-city slums, to stimulate urban planning, to acquire open space for urban beautification, to build neighborhood centers, to create open space in built-up areas, and to preserve historic structures.

4. *The Federal National Mortgage Association.* FNMA, transferred from the Reconstruction Finance Corporation to HHFA in 1950, managed and sold government-acquired mortgages, provided a secondary market for sound FHA and VA mortgages, and carried out special assistance functions, such as the purchase of higher-risk FHA and VA mortgages and the purchase of FHA mortgages made at below-market-interest rates.

5. *The Community Facilities Administration.* CFA, a division of HHFA, administered programs of federal advances for local public works planning, loans for the construction of local public works, loans for construction of college housing, and low-interest loans for the construction of specially designed and managed housing for the elderly.

6. *The Office of the Secretary* contained staff units inherited from HHFA that were engaged in supervising and coordinating the various operating elements; in formulating

policy; in dealing with the Congress, the White House, and other departments and agencies; and in conceiving and developing new legislation.

HUD also inherited HHFA's authority to finance local planning and construction of mass transportation facilities. However, most of these authorities, except some for planning, were soon to be transferred to the new Department of Transportation, created in 1966.

As important as the urban-related authorities HUD was given were those it was not given. The missing ones were significant and numerous. In housing, the Federal Home Loan Bank Board (FHLBB), an agency supporting and supervising savings and loan associations (which today make more home loans than all other lending institutions combined), and the Veterans Administration home loan guaranty program (VA) were both outside HUD's ken. In addition, the huge program financing the construction of urban and suburban highways, a potent force in shaping urban development, were run by the Bureau of Public Roads, soon to become part of the Department of Transportation. The War on Poverty, aimed at improving the incomes and life of the urban poor, was being waged by the independent Office of Economic Opportunity. Beyond that, federal aids for education, public welfare, social security, unemployment insurance, medical assistance, water pollution control—to name only a few—were lodged in other departments.

If HUD is viewed as a department concerned primarily with the physical improvement of urban places—as it probably was by most in Congress and in the executive branch—then it contained many tools but also lacked some very significant ones. If HUD is viewed as the federal department with primary responsibility for the physical, economic, and social aspects of the urban condition (and in two years, it was to be thrust into all these urban dimensions), then the incompleteness of its equipment becomes even more striking. Thus, HUD's capacity to deal comprehensively with the plentiful and diverse problems of urban America was far more limited than its earlier proponents had hoped.

Another disappointment, which was soon to become

evident, was the secretary's limited influence over the actions of other departments whose programs related to urban matters. This fact of Washington life made it nearly impossible for the HUD secretary to carry out that part of his legislative charter relating to achievement of "maximum coordination of the various Federal activities which have a major effect upon community, suburban, or metropolitan development."

Another gain from departmental status—easy access to the president—proved to be less automatic than those who promoted the idea of an urban department had hoped. They should have known that the influence of a cabinet member varies greatly with the executive style of a president and with the pressure of events, which frequently preempt his time and attention. Not every HUD secretary has enjoyed the easy access to the president that cabinet status was sometimes assumed to confer. Some secretaries lacked access and the president's confidence as well.

However, other benefits of cabinet status proved more real and permanent. The secretary's authority over his department is strong. His power to control the operating elements under him is much greater than that of the previous HHFA administrators. This gives him much-needed capacity to control policy and to achieve organizational coherence. Moreover, a cabinet officer possesses prestige in a government where such things mean much. This has improved the secretary's ability to gain attention from the public, the press, and the Washington establishment in general. This can be a valuable asset if skillfully used.

If the establishment of a cabinet department responsible for urban affairs did not fulfill all the expectations of its proponents, the signficance of this event should not be underestimated. It was an official recognition, at long last, of the importance to the nation of the improvement of urban conditions. In fact, the symbolism of this act was probably more important than the limited authorities HUD was initially given. Once established, the authorities of a cabinet department tend to grow—as, indeed, HUD's were soon to increase. Beyond that, in the scheme of American government, a seat at the cabinet table does give increased importance and momentum to the public objectives for which the department was created. Change is possible in American government, and it is often accomplished through a cabinet department.

To recognize this, one need only reflect on the accomplishments of the Department of Agriculture. With all its bureaucratic inertia, and there is much; with all its unintended side effects, and there are many; with all its elaborate, inequitable, and perhaps too long-lived subsidies, and they are still with us; the fact is that the sustained work of the Department of Agriculture helped revolutionize the art of agriculture, helped make the productivity of American agriculture the envy of the world, and contributed greatly to increased living standards for farmers and the country as a whole. If HUD can do half as well for the cities, it will not have been created in vain.

HUD's Missions

Let us now attempt to identify HUD's major missions, those public purposes explicit in the programs for which it is responsible and in the law that created it. As used here, a *mission* is broader than a particular program authority. Indeed, many individual programs are often directed toward the accomplishment of a single mission. This is necessary to judge its performance. It is also desirable because the chapters that follow will focus on HUD's major missions, how successfully they have been accomplished, and what might be done to improve performance. Briefly, HUD's major missions are:

1. to improve the coordination of HUD's many individual programs toward a coherent and effective assault on urban ills; to increase the efficiency of its performance through the selection and training of its personnel to a high degree of professional competence
2. to assist the president in coordinating all federal urban efforts and to guide and support state, local, and private actions
3. to support the planning of the total urban environment so that it is humanly fulfilling, economically efficient,

and frugal in its use of precious resources
4. to improve conditions in slum areas and revive the central city generally
5. to administer effectively and equitably federal subsidy programs to make decent housing in decent surroundings available to the urban poor and near poor who could not otherwise afford it
6. to support, through mortgage financing and otherwise, the stable production of needed homes in a good neighborhood for all urban Americans
7. through various means, to reduce the cost of housing to the benefit of all housing consumers and so that more will be able to afford it without subsidy
8. to break the age-old barriers of racial discrimination so that every urban American has full, free, and equal access to housing and other urban services and amenities
9. through research, demonstrations, and program evaluation to increase understanding of urban problems, to improve program performance, and to develop better solutions.

To accomplish these missions is, of course, a large order. However, the Congress and the president did not create HUD because its job was easy, but rather because it was believed to be a very difficult one deeply affecting the national interest. If the problems are difficult and sometimes intractable, if the tools available are limited and imperfect, if our understanding is less than complete, HUD would do well to remember the dictum of former Secretary of State Dean Acheson: "The proper role of a statesman is to search for limited ends armed only with limited means."[12] Acheson's view accurately reflects the challenge faced by a HUD secretary.

3
HUD's Performance

This chapter will concentrate on HUD's administrative performance as a cabinet department. Did the secretary's increased prestige, easier access to the president, improved leverage with other departments, and stronger authority over his operating elements—all hoped for advantages—produce more effective performance, improve program coordination, and produce better results? This chapter will avoid evaluation of the various programs HUD inherited and the others added after its creation. That will come later.

This discussion will be carried out in three stages: first, the elements of the secretary's job and the bureaucratic barriers he must overcome; second, the skills the secretary and his top assistants must possess to perform effectively; third, an evaluation of the performance of HUD's six secretaries.

It will be argued that from 1965 to 1970 (under Secretary Weaver and during the first two years of Secretary George Romney's tenure) HUD performed with considerable effectiveness and realized to a substantial degree the potentials of its departmental status; that following several unwise decisions by Secretary Romney, HUD's organizational efficiency declined badly and that this disarray continued under Secretaries James Lynn and Carla Hills; and, finally, that during her first year in office, Secretary Patricia Harris—though recognizing HUD's organizational disorder and announcing plans for major changes—has so far achieved little actual improvement in

HUD's organizational vitality. It is, of course, too early to make a complete assessment.

The Requirements of Leadership

To be successful, a secretary and the top staff must perform many functions requiring varied skills and must overcome numerous obstacles—some predictable, some not.

In the Eye of the Hurricane

In our form of government, the most basic challenge to successful secretarial leadership comes from the fact that he or she will inevitably be under constant pressure from conflicting interests—some well organized and powerful, others less so. These pressures reflect the interests of each group—the home builders, the mortgage lenders, the realtors, the labor unions, the building materials manufacturers, the planners, the cities, those representing minority groups, the housing consumers, and many others. Pressures also come from individual congressmen and senators. Although not all of the demands of these groups are inimical to the public purpose, some are. And it is certain that they will vary widely and often be contradictory.

The challenge to a secretary is to weigh all these demands and seek to turn them into the public interest, as he or she sees it. This is the essence of the art of government. Most of the secretary's decisions will necessarily reflect a compromise of the many pressures surrounding him or her. In democratic government, leadership is the art of the possible as well as the search for the ideal. The job is to combine and blend the various pressures so as to produce public policy that is as near as possible to the ideal and is not so diluted by compromise as to be meaningless nor so internally contradictory as to be unworkable. If the possible falls too short of the public interest, then the secretary, as well as the system, has failed.

Creating an Effective Organization

No organization made up of thousands of fallible human beings scattered throughout the country and relying on the responses of many others, both public and private, can be perfect. To achieve and maintain the optimum organizational effectiveness, the secretary must take wise actions on at least five fronts.

First, the secretary must appoint experienced, talented, loyal leaders to the top positions in the department—the under secretary, the assistant secretaries, the general counsel, the program managers, the "assistants-to." The secretary must be careful to select people suited to the demands of the particular job to which they are appointed. For an able person may perform brilliantly in one type of assignment, such as a program manager, and poorly in another, such as an assistant-to. The secretary must also strive to assemble top executives who will cooperate harmoniously. This is perhaps the most difficult of all the aspects of leadership selection.

Second, the secretary must establish control over the organization. This will depend importantly on the loyalty of the top staff selected. But the secretary must also assert authority in the numerous ways available.

Third, the secretary must establish a workable organizational arrangement. The duties of the various components and subcomponents must be specific, clear, and well understood. People with the necessary skills must be placed in each unit. The lines of authority must run down from the secretary through the operating heads to the remotest outpost in the field. Responsibility must be clearly fixed, and those with responsibility must have the authority to carry out their responsibility. Appropriate means for cross communication must be established so that each operating unit knows how its actions fit into total missions of the department. The various operating elements must communicate with and support one another. The secretary must be ever aware of those potent qualities of morale and esprit de corps, for these are the energizers that turn groups of people into effective and purposeful organizations. The secretary and the major assistants, particularly the program managers, must be constantly alert to the need to place people of skill into positions that challenge and utilize these skills. For a frustrated, underutilized public servant is an inefficient one.

But the secretary and the program managers must see beyond

this idealized and abstract arrangement of people, functions, and lines of authority. This is the phantom organization. Far more important is what the political scientists call the "informal organization"—the way things actually get done, reflecting the special skills, drives, personalities, and relations that spontaneously develop. The informal organization is always different from the formal organization and often much better. The secretary must recognize this fact of organizational life, understand it, and even encourage it. The static boxes of the organizational chart can never accurately reflect the realities and dynamism of the human organizational structure.

Fourth, the secretary must establish programs for the recruitment and training of quality personnel at all levels, from clerks to the more advanced professionals. Programs are needed for the professional development of those in mid-career. This type of training is especially needed in HUD at the present time, for two reasons. During the last ten years, HUD has lost some of its best talent from resignation and retirement. Furthermore, employment in the federal government is not as attractive as it was when FHA and the Public Housing Authority were staffed with unusually high-quality people in the 1930s, or when the National Housing Agency was staffed during World War II. The opportunities elsewhere for truly talented people are much greater and comparatively more remunerative. Beyond that, the public esteem for government is low, and careers in the public service hold less attraction.

Fifth, the secretary should impart to all HUD personnel a sense of purpose, dignity, and the significance of their work. Without these qualities, an otherwise able organization will lose its vitality and harmony. The vital work of HUD will become routine, without imagination and personal commitment.

Positive Polarity

In any department there is always a natural tension between the secretary, who is concerned with broad policy and effective coordination, and the program managers, who tend to focus on their special functions. Indeed, the program managers frequently resist the secretary's efforts at program coordination. "There is no single organizational formula yet discovered which automatically reconciles the centrifugal forces which prompt the coordinators and central administrators and the centripetal forces which work on an operating organization."[1] It was these conflicting forces that caused Robert Weaver to describe HHFA's operating elements as "fiefdoms." Numerous observers have noted that cabinet members are the natural enemies of the president. The program managers, in a sense, are also the natural enemies of the secretary. They always want more than he can give them. They are also surrounded and frequently influenced by the groups whose interests their programs serve. This inevitable tension is one of the greatest challenges a secretary faces. We shall see later in this chapter how two HUD secretaries dealt with these tensions with markedly different results.

Relating to the Career Bureaucrats

It is of the utmost importance that the secretary quickly establish a working relationship with the career bureaucrats in the department, particularly those at high levels. This takes some real effort because the incoming secretary and his political appointees are likely to be both suspicious of their loyalty and dubious of their ability. On the other hand, many career people are certain to be insecure and fearful for their status if not their jobs. The secretary should bridge this gap as soon as possible. HUD's first secretary, Robert Weaver, recently said that "winning over your bureaucrats is one of the most important jobs of a Secretary."[2] There are several reasons why this is essential and in the secretary's own interest. The first is the simple fact that career public servants constitute the essential resource that makes government run. No handful of new political appointees can hope to make HUD run without the wholehearted support of the career people. As Marvin H. Bernstein of the Brookings Institution has observed, "The best thing for the political executive to do is to work closely with his career executives [and others], appreciate them fully, and thank God every night for having them around."[3] The second is that career public servants, with few exceptions, are essentially nonpartisan (most have served under both parties) and eager to support and follow the policies of any secretary. The third reason a secretary would be wise to establish rapport and mutual trust with the career public servants is that they are, on the whole, able, technically skilled, knowledgeable about the ways of government, and committed to their programs and the public service in general. Within the much-abused bureaucracy is a wealth of skills waiting to be tapped. As political scientist Wallace Sayre has written, "the public service requires high competence in administration, integrity, and reliability of performance; and most significantly, the capacity for innovation and creativity . . . to envision and obtain national goals."[4] John Corson, in an exhaustive study made for the Committee for Economic Development, found that the top ranks of the civil service are filled with just such people. In the same book he stated that a secretary must know "how to use his top career staff without being [suspicious], easily offended or unduly sensitive."[5]

Dealing with Bureaucracy's Chronic Maladies

Any bureaucracy—a large group of people working together under conditions in which labor is divided in the interest of efficiency—displays several symptoms that can produce illness unless arrested with the necessary remedies. This is true whether the bureaucracy is public or private. It is probable, however, that the public bureaucracy is more susceptible than a private one to these maladies, because it operates in a far more complex environment with more diversity of purpose and more dilution of authority.

The first malady to which government agencies are prone is premature hardening of the arteries. Any government agency, no matter how sprightly, vibrant, and flexible it may have been at the start, almost always develops aging symptoms. The tentative formulas and requirements of its youth harden into immutable verities, graven in stone. It becomes incapable of change and bristles at the very suggestion. The number of rules and requirements increases exponentially. The paper work multiplies. In its immersion in form and ritual, it may lose touch with the problems it was established to influence, or it may fail to notice that other, more important problems require attention. This process limits an agency's productivity, reduces its creativity, and deadens its adaptability. This condition develops too frequently, but it is not inevitable. It can be prevented, or even reversed, by the skilled leadership of an expert program manager. This is one of the many reasons why a secretary's appointments to key positions are so important.

A second malady to which federal agencies are highly susceptible is a complexity of laws and regulations that greatly reduce its capacity to deliver its services. This grows partly out of the aging process but equally out of the tendency of the executive branch and of the Congress to proliferate laws, one after the other, with little thought of how the new authorities complicate or contradict those that already exist. In our system, laws grow like Topsy; they are rarely considered as a whole, and little attempt is made to consolidate the old with the new in a systematic and simple fashion. Within the past decade alone, government processes and responsibilities have become incredibly more complex, as Joseph Califano, President Carter's secretary of health, education and welfare, has recently observed.[6] HUD's delivery capacity suffers greatly from this bureaucratic malady, as a look at FHA's forty or more specific but differing authorities makes plain. To use FHA, the average applicant needs a highly skilled lawyer to help him decide which of the many laws suits his needs, let alone to complete the complex applications that each law requires. These symptoms, too, can be remedied by alert and forceful leadership.

The third bureaucratic malady might be called persistent obsolescence. Many laws are passed; few are ever repealed. Many federal agencies are created; only rarely is one terminated. Once started, federal agencies and federal programs tend to perpetuate themselves, no matter whether their functions are still needed or even relevant. This tenacity of federal agencies results from more than the simple bureaucratic impulse to survive. It is also related to the power of pressure groups, to the Congress, and to simple inertia. But no federal program or agency should be allowed to continue if its programs are irrelevant or have accomplished their purpose. Either they should be made relevant, with their useless barnacles cleaned off, or they should be terminated.[7] HUD undoubtedly has functions that are no longer needed. It is the secretary's job to weed these out, just as it is the secretary's job to fight for new or expanded programs that are vital to the improvement of urban America.

The fourth, and most destructive, malady to which federal bureaucracies are prone has been called "the unholy trinity."[8] This is the tendency of a government agency or bureau to become the servant, partner, and spokesman for the private interests with which it deals or is presumed to regulate. This incestuous relationship is often compounded by the fact that the congressional committee or subcommittee responsible for overseeing the agency's actions becomes part of the "power cell." If a private power group captures a federal agency and its related congressional committee, the result is a conflict of interest, prone to bring a victory to greed rather than to the public interest. The system is not at fault; rather, the danger lies in its abuse by selfish or misguided people. Indeed, communication on matters of public policy among executive departments, congressional committees, and responsible private groups is both desirable and beneficial to the public interest. But it cannot be denied that abuses of this three-sided relationship do occur, sometimes blatantly, sometimes subtly, and sometimes even unconsciously. HUD's programs have not entirely escaped this disease. FHA has sometimes been unduly susceptible to the interests of its "clients"; public housing is not always as independent as it should be of the interests of local housing authorities; the urban renewal program was sometimes too much influenced by private redevelopers and local redevelopment agency grantsmen. On the whole, the violation of the necessary distance between government and the users of its bounty has not been as serious in HUD as it has been and still is in some other areas.[9] But this bureaucratic malady is one to which the HUD secretary must be constantly alert.

The Scylla-Charybdis Syndrome

A government operating program must steer a delicate course between two dangerous extremes:

The well-adjusted bureaucrat is one who has worked out a tolerable balance between two strong and conflicting pressures. The first pressure is to follow the rules and regulations meticulously, carefully, and to the letter, and to reject applications for federal aid which do not meet the most conservative interpretation of the rules. The second contradictory pressure, which comes both from applicants and often from superiors, is to produce results—to get the cases out, to be liberal and imaginative and to produce in volume. This is a cruel and difficult dilemma, and it is made more so by the knowledge that there are always private groups shrewd and rapacious enough to exploit to their own advantage any relaxation of the rules, any sign of processing weakness.[10]

It is the secretary's job to help his bureaus and their operating employees on the firing line to achieve a fine tuning between these conflicting pressures. Ideally, these opposing forces can be reconciled to produce both volume and quality. But if the balance veers too much one way, the organization can be stuffy, conservative, bureaucratic, and unresponsive. If the balance point goes too far in the direction of speedy production at any cost, sloppy processing results and scandals often follow because the rapacious are quick to see the opportunities for profit and take advantage of them. Although this fine tuning is the final responsibility of the secretary, it should be delegated to the program managers. But the secretary must appoint them, be sure they have the required managerial skills, and avoid putting excessive pressures on them in either direction. HUD and its predecessors have seen numerous instances in which this delicate administrative balance went too far in one or the other direction. Each time, the public purposes were seriously damaged.

What Is Past Is Prologue

In the life span of an organization, numerous things are attempted. Some succeed and many fail. Ignorance or neglect of experience often leads to the futile repetition of past mistakes. Many executives, including some HUD secretaries, have displayed "an uncommon tolerance of repetitive error."[11]

The article from which this quotation is taken described four such repetitive errors from HUD's history. Many more could be cited. This tendency is perhaps particularly characteristic of government departments where political leadership changes frequently and is too often unable or unwilling to benefit from the advice of the career public servants who often know better. George Santayana was profoundly right when he observed that "those who do not read history are destined to relive it."

Dropped Pebbles Send Off Endless Ripples

Many of the fundamental policies of HUD came from legislation carefully conceived and deliberately debated by the Congress. Others came from court decisions, arrived at with equal deliberation. But the shape of HUD's programs has, with surprising frequency, resulted from administrative decisions made routinely, on the assumption that they were matters of no great import. In many cases, these almost casual decisions produced consequences of unanticipated magnitude, like a small sound amplified a thousand times. Examples of this are numerous. Two examples will suffice the purpose of illustration.

There can be little question that the creation by President Roosevelt of the National Housing Agency (NHA), a temporary step for very limited war-inspired objectives, was a crucial, perhaps indispensable, step toward the creation of an urban department twenty-three years later.

In 1934, John Fahey, head of the Federal Home Loan Bank Board, was a member of the committee established by President Roosevelt to design the FHA. He rejected the committee's proposal that the new agency be placed under his jurisdiction.[12] This very personal decision has had untold influence on the government's role in housing finance, an influence still very evident today.

Relating to the President

Much of the power and influence of a cabinet secretary depends on good relations with the president. If the secretary has the president's ear, there is much more chance of achieving the department's goals. Also, the word quickly gets around in Washington. A secretary who has access to the president can exert greater influence over subordinates, with other departments, and with the White House staff. This precious relationship is not, of course, completely under the secretary's control. Many factors—the president's style, the press of events, personal chemistry—all influence cabinet members' relations with the president. Thus, the value of a seat at the cabinet table varies with each president. Those who fought so hard for a cabinet department for urban affairs were pursuing, at best, a movable feast. Yet it is important that the secretary use all his or her ingenuity to make this relationship as close as possible.

Relating to the Congress

The secretary and the chief assistants spend a great deal of their time testifying before various congressional committees and responding to the requests of individual congressmen and senators. The secretary can, of course, never satisfy them all. But the respect in which the secretary is held by Congress, the trust and cooperation achieved, are vital to HUD's success.

Relating to Other Departments

Since the policies of many departments and agencies affect urban matters as much as, or more than, HUD's own programs, harmonious relations with other departments are necessary, even indispensable, to the achievement of many HUD missions. Numerous HUD laws require close program cooperation with other departments. If this program cooperation fails, HUD's programs fail. Moreover, an administration's general economic policies and the state of the economy affect HUD's programs in many important ways. Indeed, they affect urban conditions, for better or worse, more than all of HUD's programs combined. The HUD secretary cannot control these policies. But an understanding of these realities and a capacity to articulate the issues and persuade others are among the most important and difficult aspects of the secretary's job.

Influencing Public Opinion

Public understanding of urban problems and support for the remedies HUD is seeking to apply often mean the difference between their success and failure. Public policy simply cannot go very far without the consent of the people. HUD's cabinet status can often be made a pulpit from which public understanding and consent are generated for actions necessary to the common good. This requires more than routine press releases. It requires the ability to communicate highly technical matters in language that the people can grasp. It means transcending the technical language that too often obscures HUD's programs and purposes to all but the insider and making them reach the mind and the heart of the layman. The secretary's responsibilities for public leadership are secondary only to those of the president.

The Skills Required

What experience and knowledge, what qualities of mind and personality does a HUD secretary need to discharge successfully the awesome and varied responsibilities of this job? When we speak of the secretary, we should include the top political appointees and even some members of the career public service; their skills should complement and reinforce those of the secretary. Top public leadership is rarely exercised by a single person. More often, it is a team performance.

Knowledge of the Problem and the Programs

The HUD secretary must understand the manifold urban problems it is HUD's job to alleviate, if not remedy. The secretary must also understand the often very technical programs for which HUD is responsible as well as the nature and impact of other government programs not under HUD's jurisdiction. These are many, and they require expertise in a variety of subjects ranging from the sociology of slums to the impact of broad economic policy on housing finance (to pick two at random). If the secretary does not possess all this knowledge, he or she must have trusted expert advisers who can supply the broad knowledge required.

Administrative Skill

To be successful, the HUD secretary obviously must be a skilled administrator. This requires an understanding of government organization and how to make it perform efficiently. Also required is an understanding of the maladies to which bureaucracies are prone and the steps needed to avoid bureaucratic decay, or if it has occurred, to eliminate it. The secretary must know how to inspire as well as direct people, how to deal with internecine personal and organizational vendettas. He or she must possess insight into the ways of bureaucracy and study history to avoid repetitive error.

Skill in Selecting People

The HUD secretary must choose wisely the top political appointees and place each in the job he or she can do best. This requires personal knowledge of the best people in the field or the advice of people who possess that knowledge. It means resisting the inevitable political pressures from the White House, from the Congress, from special interest groups, and from politically well-connected job-seekers—except, of course, when politically sponsored candidates are those best equipped for the job.

Skill in Dealing with People

The HUD secretary must be gifted in dealing with many different types of people with widely differing interests, personalities, and positions. The secretary must communicate effectively with subordinates, with Congress, with other departments, with the president and the White House staff, with the many pressure groups, and with the public.

The Power To Persuade

The HUD secretary must possess the power to articulate ideas persuasively—to the HUD staff, to the White House, to the Congress, and to the public.

Public Prestige

The HUD secretary must be, or become, widely respected by the public, by the press, by other departmental heads, and by that elusive but potent reality—the Washington establishment. Without public prestige, the secretary will accomplish far less than the power of the office makes possible.

Access to Independent Information

The secretary's political appointees are likely to be hard-working and able (if the choices are wise), so will be most of the career public servants. But they will rarely be bold enough to tell the secretary the full facts. They are more likely to feel it necessary to tell the secretary only what they think he or she wants to hear. As political scientist Richard Neustadt has written, the HUD secretary (like the president) "needs access to independent information on what is happening and thus freedom from sole reliance on information and advice from staff."[13] The secretary will not get the objective advice needed from the interest groups that will be pounding on the door. Formal advisory committees are generally not a very good method either. As most people know, Franklin Roosevelt used his wife very successfully for this purpose. Truman used for this purpose a small group of disinterested people in a very informal way. If the HUD secretary does not seek and get independent information regularly, he or she may well be the last, rather than the first, to discover what is really going on.

Understanding of the Political Process

The HUD secretary must understand politics. This requires a firm grasp of politics, not in the pejorative sense of ward heelers and power brokers, though that side is real enough, but in the larger sense of politics as a system through which many divergent interests are compromised and (one hopes) transformed into the public interest. To think of a secretary as above politics is to miss an important point of government. Politics is, in fact, the essence of government. A secretary who does not understand it, or feels above it, is ignorant of the requirements of the office and likely to be impotent as well.

Leadership

Finally, the HUD secretary should possess the elusive but vital gift for leadership. This quality combines all the attributes discussed above plus something more. It is not as easy to define as it is to recognize. But when it is there, people instinctively recognize it, and its effects are enormous.

These, then, are the multiple skills a HUD secretary needs.

The position is not a place for amateurs, to borrow Richard Neustadt's phrase.[14] Since this amounts to a portrait of a perfect secretary, few human beings can be expected to measure up to it completely. But they should come as close as human limitations will permit.

How HUD's Leaders Performed

Since 1965, HUD has been headed by six secretaries. A brief look at the accomplishments of these secretaries will provide some insight into HUD's performance, the rise of this important new department, its subsequent decay, and its hoped-for revival. An examination of the history of other federal departments suggests that such cycles are not uncommon.

Robert C. Weaver: 1965-1968

Weaver was an historic figure, if only because he was the first black cabinet secretary in the country's history. He was also uncommonly well equipped for the job by training and experience. He had the benefit of many years of experience in government, at the federal, state, and local levels. A Harvard-trained economist, he understood thoroughly the substance and purposes of HUD's programs. He was also a respected student of housing and urban affairs, having written numerous thoughtful books and articles on the subject. Weaver was especially well known for his studies of racial discrimination and its effects on urban life. He had another pertinent preparation for the job, having been administrator of HHFA (HUD's immediate predecessor) for nearly five years.

When he became administrator of HHFA in 1961, Weaver displayed wisdom in his appointments to key positions. Without exception, the people he appointed in HHFA were talented professionals with long experience in their fields. Considering the political pressures always at work when a new president has been elected, it would not be easy to find a parallel to the uniform professionalism of these appointments. When Weaver became secretary of the newly created HUD, his appointments were equally good. Weaver had good relations with President Johnson, although as a Kennedy holdover, he could not have had intimate relations with Johnson. HUD received strong presidential support, at least until the Vietnam war preempted Johnson's full attention. Though not a charismatic leader, Weaver was respected by his subordinates and by others with whom he dealt. His rapport with the career professionals may have been marred by some suspicion at the outset, but it ripened into a deep, if not warm, mutual respect. Weaver said recently he thought he had the best legal staff in government. He was referring to his very able career professionals. This respect was mutual. In the field of organization, Weaver made several important decisions that displayed a realistic understanding of the ways a bureaucracy works. Here his performance was quite good.

Weaver was less successful in dealing with the inevitable infighting that developed between some of his appointees. This damaged the effective operation of some programs and cast a shadow of intrigue and mutual suspicion on some top-level relations. Some of this is inevitable in any organization. Weaver's relations with the Congress were not always either cordial or successful. This was more typical of his years as administrator of HHFA. Some of this was due to the fact that he was black; some to his reserve and lack of natural salesmanship; some of it resulted from his delegation of most congressional liaison to the general counsel of the agency. By 1967, however, he had authorized the formation of a formidable lobbying group for housing and urban development, and after that he became effective on the Hill. He was, however, victimized by the personalities and ambitions of the congressmen and senators with whom he had to deal. One of his worst experiences with the Congress came in a hearing that Senator Robert Kennedy turned into a quite unfair inquisition, presumably for his own political purposes. Weaver was not notably successful in using his cabinet position as a pulpit to influence public opinion. Though urged by his staff to do so, he remained the analytical, even modest, public servant— which reflected his personality as well as his convictions. He did, however, repeatedly discuss housing and urban affairs issues on college and university campuses as a lecturer and commencement speaker. He also continued to publish books and articles on the subject.

On balance, as HUD's first secretary, Robert Weaver

accomplished a great deal. During his tenure, several significant new programs were added to HUD's arsenal—notably the Model Cities Program, new communities legislation, a significant research program, and several programs to house families of low and moderate income. Other programs were modified in significant ways. The fundamental thrust of urban renewal was shifted from bulldozing slum neighborhoods to their rehabilitation and revival. In addition, the processing of urban renewal applications was speeded up, and the volume of activity significantly increased. If the production of public housing was not significantly expanded until 1968, changes in policy vastly improved its political acceptability, and a move away from high-rise monoliths toward small, scattered site projects represented a positive achievement.

The FHA, long a proud and reluctant member of HUD and its predecessor agencies, became a loyal and energetic component of HUD, fully sympathetic with the secretary's larger goals. The turnaround of FHA, a thing many would have called impossible and some still deplore, was a textbook case in skillful leadership. The key element of this administrative magic was the choice of just the right man to head FHA. Most important of all, Weaver went far toward achieving a coherent department, with department-wide approaches and department-wide thinking.

With the loyal support of the professionals he had appointed, Weaver made remarkable progress in turning HUD into a working entity, in broadening its reach and its vision—all things its creators hoped for.

All was not perfect; of course, there were some dissonant notes in the otherwise harmonious orchestration. One disappointment was the fact that a seat at the cabinet table gave the secretary far less influence on the actions of other departments than had been hoped. This was no fault of Weaver's. It reflected what all seasoned observers already knew—a cabinet secretary cannot coordinate his peers, particularly when he represents the youngest department at the cabinet table.

Robert C. Wood

Robert C. Wood, Weaver's under secretary, served briefly

as secretary between the time Weaver resigned and the newly elected Richard Nixon was inaugurated. He pursued energetically the programs and policies he had helped Weaver establish. He also spent much time preparing for a smooth transition from the Johnson to the Nixon administrations, an act both necessary and responsible.

George Romney: 1969-1972

George Romney—former governor of Michigan, former automobile manufacturer, and short-time candidate for the Republican presidential nomination—was named HUD secretary shortly after Richard Nixon's inauguration. He was a member of a cabinet notable for its similarity in appearance and background. They were all white, all middle-aged, all business-oriented, all self-made. Most were wealthy; at least seven, including Romney, were millionaires. There was much talk, as there always is, about the president's intention to rely heavily on his "working cabinet" and to avoid an administration dominated by the White House staff. But a grim, trim, young former advertising executive named H. R. Haldeman was already beginning the manipulations that would soon bring to the White House the greatest concentration of executive power America had ever experienced. Romney, like many others, would suffer the frustrations of this fateful tide.

George Romney was a likable man, with just a trace of temper occasionally rising to the pleasant, warm surface. He was deeply religious, a practicing Mormon. He tended to think and talk in moralistic terms. Unlike Weaver, he had no college degree.

Romney cared deeply about the cities. He had been governor of Michigan when Detroit was rocked by racial riots. He believed the cities were the chief domestic problem facing the nation. He could be persuasive, eloquent, and evangelical in propounding these beliefs. He had a strong sense of personal mission.

Romney tried hard to persuade Nixon to share his concern for the cities. He argued for a larger volume of subsidized housing for the poor, defended Johnson's Model Cities Program with some modifications, and proposed policies to disperse poor blacks from the ghetto and house them in the suburbs. For a time he made progress, though he never really convinced the president. The Model Cities Program was saved for a time, with the unlikely support of a task force headed by Edward Banfield, one of the country's most outspoken critics of federal social programs. Large subsidies for housing were approved, and the largest volume in history was built.

But Romney's manner and the obvious inconsistency between his racial policies and the White House's Southern strategy irritated the president and eventually produced hostility. It became harder and harder for Romney to break the barriers of the palace guard and to get the president's ear.

Romney's appointments to key positions were, on the whole, good. He brought in the able Richard Van Dusen as under secretary and some bright, energetic special assistants, many of whom had been with him in Michigan. Most of his assistant secretaries were able and experienced. He had trouble securing a man to head the FHA, and the man finally chosen, after months of waiting, left something to be desired.

Aside from his failure to establish rapport with the president (in the light of the tragic events to come, this may have been an impossible dream), Romney's greatest weakness was that he was a bit naive, particularly in matters concerning administration. He made a number of blunders, all prompted by the highest motives. Two were catastrophic. Each reinforced the other so strongly as to start a slide toward administrative chaos from which HUD has yet to recover.

The first of Romney's innocent and high-minded mistakes was to exert excessive pressure for a high volume of housing production, particularly under FHA's subsidized programs. Naturally production-minded from his automobile experience, he made it emphatically clear that the word in HUD was production and more production. It is not surprising that under this fierce pressure for volume, the FHA processing system faltered and then collapsed. Much volume was produced but at the cost of inexcusable program abuses, scandals, and even numerous acts of a criminal collusion between FHA officials and smart but dishonest private promoters. Unfortunately, history could have taught this lesson. For FHA had experienced just such a breakdown in the early postwar period, when President Truman's pressure for production led to a similar but less serious breakdown.

Romney made his second big mistake in a sincere effort to gain control of his department as well as to make it more efficient. He ordered a major reorganization of HUD and its field offices. The details of this wrenching reorganization are too involved to detail here.[15] But the results were disastrous. The essence of good organization is to give a program manager responsibility for a clearly delineated job, give him the people and the power to get the job done, then to hold him responsible for the results. The Romney reorganization of HUD violated this cardinal rule by depriving the program managers of the authority and resources to get their job done. In one case, essential elements of a single operating program were divided up and put under two assistant secretaries, just to compound the confusion. The important distinction between line and staff functions was blurred to the point that officials responsible for essentially service or advisory functions had as much influence over operating decisions as the program managers themselves. Beyond that, the field offices were reorganized in such a way as to be virtually independent of the assistant secretaries theoretically responsible for the programs. Further, following a curious "glob" theory of organization, field personnel with long training and skill in particular program operations were mixed together in such a way that they became responsible for work of which many were totally ignorant. Some resigned; among them were two assistant secretaries. Others shrugged in frustration. HUD, a vast complicated machine, had lost its steering wheel.

It is of significance that the reorganization plan Romney acted on had been proposed to Weaver several years before. Weaver wisely rejected it.[16] His reasons were as simple as they were sound. He thought he could control an operating organization, like FHA, better by keeping it intact and choosing a man to run it who was an able administrator and who shared his objectives. As a result of Weaver's tactics, FHA was efficient, had high morale, and worked hard to achieve Weaver's objectives. But Romney's tactics nearly destroyed FHA. (FHA is used here as an illustration. The same could be said of other HUD operating elements.)

Romney never understood the chaos his actions created. Neither did his two immediate successors. Yet, a *Washington Post* article described the situation in an editorial entitled "HUD Among the Ruins."[17] HUD's sad decline was general knowledge in Washington and elsewhere. One experienced observer said, "We'd be better off without it." This shows how isolated a secretary can become and why he needs independent sources of intelligence.

With respect to public prestige and the power to persuade, George Romney must be given a high rating. He was a well-known public figure when he became secretary. His persuasiveness worked well on many—but not on the president.

James Lynn: 1972-1975

Upon George Romney's resignation, President Nixon appointed James Lynn to be HUD's secretary. Lynn was a personable man whose experience for the job was that of a successful Ohio lawyer. He had also served as general counsel and under secretary of commerce. He was articulate and persuasive. His relationship with his colleagues and the career civil servants was cordial. Whether he trusted them is not clear. Certainly, many of HUD's career people, though finding him likable, were skeptical of his objectives. After all, he came into HUD at a time when many of the programs to which the career staff were dedicated had been put in limbo. His professional reputation in the urban and housing field was certainly not high. He clearly lacked professional expertise for the job. His ability to select able people for key jobs was obscured by the fact that, except for Romney's group of personal assistants, he retained most of Romney's top appointees.

Lynn's relations with the president appear to have been good. The problem was that he worked for a president who had taken a sharp turn against federal social programs. Nixon was also becoming increasingly preoccupied with the looming disaster of Watergate. There is no evidence that Lynn made any serious attempt to revive HUD's suspended programs or to put HUD's chaotic house in order. Indeed, there is every reason

to believe that he went to HUD with orders to maintain its
dormancy and, beyond that, to reduce further whatever else
could be reduced. He saw no merit in HUD's programs. Beyond
that, the administration was anxious to reduce federal
expenditures. In all of this, he succeeded very well. In an
entirely negative sense, then, it could be argued that James
Lynn was a quite successful HUD secretary. Toward the end of
Lynn's tenure at HUD, President Nixon resigned his high
office with an emotional and hardly coherent farewell speech,
as the country watched, stunned. Ironically, just twelve days
later, President Ford signed into law the Housing and
Community Development Act of 1974, the first major positive
executive initiative in the urban field since 1970. This law
contained many provisions of real merit. The value of some of
its provisions is less clear.

Carla Hills: 1974-1977

Not long after Gerald Ford succeeded to the presidency, Mrs.
Carla Hills was named HUD's fifth secretary. She had been a
lawyer with the Department of Justice. Mrs. Hills was bright
and hard-working; like Lynn, she possessed no experience or
expertise in the urban and housing field. Her qualifications for
the job must be considered minimal by any standards. Her
slight knowledge of the political process and her lack of trust in
the career professionals were revealed when, not long after her
appointment, she appeared before a congressional committee
surrounded by a galaxy of her equally new appointees. Neither
she nor her associates could answer even the most elementary
questions about HUD's programs. Nearly all were questions
that at least a hundred of the top career people could have
responded to with ease.

However, as the months went by, she showed a determination to learn. She did her homework. She also displayed a
growing interest in the department's programs and even an
inclination to use her powers of persuasion on the president to
gain positive support for HUD's programs. She tried hard,
despite the pitiful confusion at HUD, its low morale, and the
voluntary retirement of many of its best career people. Her first
major task was the difficult technical one of producing the

necessary regulations and procedures to activate the many new provisions of the 1974 legislation. The job was done with much fumbling, frequent revisions, and long delay. Her launching of the 1974 legislation reflected the unsure touch of an amateur, however sincere and committed she may have been. Beyond that, she did not grasp, much less remedy, the organizational confusion into which HUD had been plunged by George Romney's well-intentioned actions.

On the surface, there were many signs of action and aggressive management. There were well-publicized lists of goals and deadlines, speeches of exhortation and encouragement, and other symbols of the managerial art. But words are not enough. The fact is that Carla Hills failed to remedy HUD's organizational disarray or to make its operations more efficient.

The position of Lynn and Hills on the need for many of HUD's programs reflected the conservatism of a Republican administration. If this reflects the will of the majority of the people, one can disagree with it, but not disdain it. It is hard, however, not to long for the zeal of an Albert Cole, HHFA administrator under Eisenhowever, or the constructive, objective conservatism of the late Senator Robert Taft, who disliked public housing but backed it because he could find no better way to assist poor families whose needs he recognized.

Patricia Harris: 1977

President Carter named Patricia Harris HUD's sixth secretary. It is too early to assess her performance. But some things are known.

Secretary Harris is widely regarded as bright—some say brilliant—as well as persuasive. She has been a successful lawyer, U.S. ambassador to Luxembourg, a delegate to the United Nations, and dean of Howard University's Law School. She has also been a director of several large corporations and active in the civil rights movement. However, she comes to the post with no expert knowledge of urban affairs and housing.

At her confirmation hearings before the Senate, she quickly demonstrated her quick mind as well as her lack of deep knowledge of her new job. She responded with spirit and eloquence to Senator Proxmire's questions about her qualifications. At the same time, she pledged to support a level of subsidized housing production that is probably quite impossible to achieve and that is certainly impossible to achieve if the president honors his pledge to balance the federal budget during his first term—an objective that will mean severe restraints on federal spending. But she is certain to learn more about these matters as time goes on.

Her appointments to HUD's top jobs have been uniformly people of experience and high caliber. Since she has had no experience in the field and, therefore, could hardly be expected to know many of these people, her appointments show that she has had the wisdom to seek the advice of those who do. This is a good sign. So is her commitment to push HUD's programs, even if she somewhat overpromised at her Senate hearings.

As a personality, Secretary Harris has already received much attention from the press. If she uses her celebrity status skillfully, she can increase her influence in Washington and with the public, both valuable assets to a secretary.

After approximately ten months in office, HUD Secretary Patricia Harris must be given rather high marks for her understanding of the substantive problems with which HUD must deal and for the policy directions she has taken. As an administrator, however, her performance so far leaves something to be desired.

During the brief stewardship of Secretary Harris, a number of constructive actions have been taken, and others are under consideration. The Housing and Community Development Act of 1977, proposed by the administration and passed by the Congress without crippling compromises, made several of HUD's programs more realistic and, one hopes, more workable. Needed changes were achieved particularly in the Block Grant Program (for details, see chapter 5).

Secretary Harris has also announced a reorganization of HUD. Its purpose was clearly to eliminate the confusion and disarray produced by George Romney's well-intentioned organizational decisions. Secretary Harris's reorganization plan restores direct authority to the assistant secretaries over the programs for which they are responsible. This move is a return to simple common sense. The Harris reorganization plan also eliminates unnecessary layers in the HUD field structure. One could quibble about details of the plan and wonder why the functions of the FHA still remain fragmented, at least in the field offices. One could also wonder whether a gradual move toward organizational order might not have caused less disruption than the announcement of yet another massive reorganization. But the essentials of the Harris reorganizational plan are sound and much needed. Only time will tell whether the plan becomes a smoothly working reality.

Secretary Harris has also given serious consideration to the future role of the FHA. The role of FHA, both as a support for private mortgage lending and as a housing subsidy tool, has long needed attention (see chapters 7 and 8).

Another sign of Secretary Harris's constructive approach to substantive policy issues is the establishment by President Carter of an Urban and Regional Policy Task Force charged with developing a comprehensive urban policy for the Carter administration. In addition to HUD, the Task Force is made up of representatives of the White House Domestic Council and of the Departments of the Treasury, Commerce, Labor, and Health, Education and Welfare. This is a welcome recognition that urban problems are influenced as much, if not more, by the actions of other departments of the Government than by HUD's programs themselves. It is also significant that Secretary Harris chairs this task force. The final recommendations of the task force have not yet been made public, much less approved by the president. Therefore, it is premature to evaluate either the substance or the effect of such proposals as the task force may produce. But the fact that it exists is a step in the right direction.

For all these actions and initiatives, Secretary Harris and her able staff deserve credit; as one observer has put it, "There is a fresh breeze blowing at HUD."

As an administrator, however, Secretary Harris has shown her lack of experience. She has displayed limited grasp of the difficult art of making a government organization perform efficiently. Personal vendettas between and among her assistant secretaries have already marred organizational harmony—these are a malady to which all bureaucracies are prone. Secretary Harris has had only limited success in establishing a working relationship with HUD's career public servants—the most valuable single resource a secretary possesses. Many of HUD's experienced and committed career public servants are still isolated from the decision-making process by newly appointed and less experienced special assistants. Too often, these hard-working special assistants have blocked rather than facilitated the indispensable process of vertical communication.

Secretary Harris's lack of experience in government is also reflected in her failure to establish a system for making decisions that combine speed with due deliberation. Far too much of the time of her talented top staff is spent attending endless and unnecessary meetings; far too little of it in calm and deliberate consideration of the great and difficult issues with which HUD must deal. To be busy is not necessarily to be productive. Secretary Harris's admirable policy initiatives can remain mere rhetoric unless an effective organization translates the words into action.

It is much too early to reach a reliable evaluation of Mrs. Harris's performance, but the early signs give reason to hope that the sixth HUD secretary may become a good one—just what HUD very much needs. However, if this hope is to be fulfilled, HUD's house must be put in order and its organizational efficiency greatly improved.

4
Shaping the City

This chapter deals with HUD's efforts to improve the planning of our urban areas, a mission on which much emphasis is placed by HUD's legislative mandates. We will proceed by discussing the objective of good urban planning and the methods HUD uses to encourage it. Then we will evaluate HUD's performance and the barriers, many of them lying deep in our institutions and values, that have made HUD's efforts fall far short of success. Finally, some ways of improving HUD's performance will be suggested, and we will discuss some of the characteristics of modern industrial society that are likely to limit even HUD's best efforts. It will be argued that any major improvement in urban planning and the shape of our cities will require fundamental changes in American habits, institutions, and values.

The Holy Grail

The need for improved urban planning has been emphasized in nearly all the laws passed under HUD and its predecessor agencies.[1] Its virtues have been extolled in numerous presidential messages. Over the past twenty-five years, the federal commitment to urban planning has been progressively broadened as various kinds of federal aids have proliferated. Aside from improved housing, there is no remedy for our urban ills to which more official obeisance has been paid than to the enlargement and improvement of urban planning. Paul Ylvisaker, whose introduction graces this book, has recently observed, "Planning has become the holy grail in the federal government's continued search for methods to support the creation of an orderly, efficient, livable urban environment."[2] Urban planning, as a profession and a purpose, goes back to the beginnings of our country, and long before that in Western civilization. Its purpose is to create, through deliberate design, cities suitable for human habitation; cities that serve man's physical needs, encourage humanizing social intercourse, provide opportunities for civilizing artistic expression, facilitate intellectual discourse, and elevate man's spirit with their beauty. The law creating HUD expressed these lofty aspirations in quite pragmatic words. It called for "sound development of the Nation's communities."

HUD's Tools

HUD's tools to encourage and support local planning take three forms: (1) direct financial assistance for the development of state, regional, county, metropolitan, and city plans; (2) financial assistance for various projects capable of carrying out part of a general plan; and (3) incentives that make local planning a condition to receipt of various program aids.

HUD's programs providing direct financial assistance to urban planning include direct grants to finance comprehensive local, metropolitan, and regional planning (the 701 program); funds for mass transportation planning projects; and funds to help coordinate metropolitan development planning and all activities necessary to develop a comprehensive plan. HUD also has authority to provide technical assistance to local planning efforts. HUD funds used to support various types of community development activities can also finance the planning of these projects.

HUD programs capable of supporting planning by turning the idea into reality include a wide variety of community development activities that can be financed under its Block Grant Program (clearance and redevelopment, rehabilitation, urban beautification, conservation of urban open space, code enforcement, provision of public services, and activities designed to guide future urban development). HUD's program to assist the construction of new communities is also an important support to planning. Equally important are HUD's programs to finance housing construction.

Several HUD programs provide incentives, and potentially strong leverage, for local planning; that is, they require planning as a condition for federal financial assistance. As a condition for financial assistance for the various community development activities identified above, local jurisdictions are required to submit a three-year development plan along with the specific ways in which it will be carried out, including cost estimates. To receive HUD Block Grants for community development, localities must submit an acceptable housing assistance plan, one that outlines in considerable detail a plan for meeting their housing needs, particularly those of the poor and the elderly.

When HUD's programs that directly assist planning are added to those capable of carrying out plans, the funds appropriated by the Congress over the years amount to nearly $30 billion. Beyond that, HUD's support for housing construction has amounted to about $194 billion. With regard to HUD's planning incentives, between 1954 and 1974 about 4,000 workable programs and local plans for inner city revitalization were prepared and submitted to HUD. Many three-year community development plans and housing assistance plans have been submitted to HUD since 1974.

Other federal departments also assist and stimulate local urban planning. About three dozen federal programs provide direct assistance to local, regional, or state planning— involving an annual expenditure of $450 million. Planning is a condition for federal aid for mass transit, highways, actions to improve air and water quality, manpower development, health facilities, and many other forms of federal assistance.

There is no question that at least formally, the holy grail of planning is widely supported by HUD and many other elements of the federal government. Many private groups support the virtues of planning. To name only one example, the American Institute of Architects developed and widely promulgated *A Plan for Urban Growth* (1972).[3] This document sets forth in eloquent language a blueprint of how urban areas should be shaped and their growth accommodated. Since then, the architects have held regular discussions with a wide range of private groups in an effort to achieve a consensus on their version of the good city.

HUD's Performance

From a purely legalistic standpoint, HUD has discharged its many responsibilities related to the support and encouragement of urban planning. Its actual performance, however, has been halting and marked by many self-defeating contradictions, lack of clearly defined purpose, and reluctance to enforce its sanctions.

HUD's principal program for assisting the financing of urban planning (Section 701) has, by HUD's own admission, lacked a clearly defined purpose. It has certainly financed the development of many local plans and kept many planners busy.[4] But there is little evidence that HUD has evaluated the quality of these plans or given consideration to their enforceability. Furthermore, too many of the funds have been used for various studies that are only remotely related to any accepted definition of urban planning. In recent years, HUD's planning assistance programs have been deliberately aimed at improving state and local management capacity. This is much needed, but it is hardly urban planning. Much the same thing could be said of HUD's authority to assist transportation planning and the very broad power HUD received in 1974 to support all activities necessary to develop comprehensive local plans. Beyond that, there is little evidence that HUD has carried out with any consistency or meaning its mandate to provide technical assistance to localities in the development of their plans.

HUD administers a number of financial aid programs that, if properly used, could do much to help localities carry out their urban plans. In this regard, HUD's record and that of the communities has been spotty at best.

HUD's urban renewal efforts, aimed at revitalizing the central city and improving its form, have been reasonably successful. But its impact has been relatively small in relation to the job to be done. In some places, such as Detroit, it has failed. Where the creation of inner-city residential neighborhoods was the objective, many cities have found that new structures do not always create pleasant, livable neighborhoods. Washington's Southwest Project is a case in point. The project contains a mixture of residences, office buildings, commercial establishments, a waterfront, and some spacious and well-designed open spaces. But even after many years, it has not yet become a neighborhood. Most of its office workers would rather be somewhere else. The homes and apartments are like fortresses, designed to keep neighbors out. (The social cost of clearing and redeveloping slums will be discussed in the next chapter.)

HUD's new communities program has great potential for shaping urban growth and improving urban amenities. But, so far, its administration has been half-hearted. Only a handful of new communities have been created under this program. Most of these are in deep financial trouble or have been foreclosed by HUD while still incomplete. One of the reasons for this unhappy experience is that HUD has been reluctant to use its authority to make capital grants for the construction of water and sewer lines and other community infrastructure. But the reasons for the failure of HUD-supported new communities go beyond this. Unfavorable economic conditions have been equally decisive. HUD's new communities have suffered from high interest rates on their borrowing as well as a sluggish demand for housing. It is ironic, however, that the most applauded new communities in this country—Reston and Columbia—did not use HUD's support. It is perhaps unfair to point out that no new community yet created in this country is self-contained and independent of nearby metropolitan centers, as the British new towns were intended to be. But even viewed in the narrower sense of an improved form of suburban, satellite development, HUD's ventures into new communities can so far only be called a failure.

HUD's programs financing the construction of public works (specifically water and sewer lines) have rarely been used purposefully to shape urban development in the patterns planners conceive. The construction of these spines of urban shape has for the most part gone its own way without much consideration of its important effect on urban development. The same is true of HUD-supported housing construction. Both of these programs have acquiesced in, if not deliberately supported, urban sprawl. This is an inefficient type of urban development and hardly one consistent with most planners' visions of the pleasant city. As noted in chapter 1, urban sprawl is a reckless use of scarce land, facilities, and energy.

HUD's authorities for stimulating local urban planning by requiring it as a condition for other federal aid—notably the workable program required since 1954 and the housing assistance plans required under the 1974 law—have had little effect because of weak enforcement. It has long been known that a city seeking urban renewal funds was rarely, if ever, turned down because its workable program submission was unsatisfactory, however vague and rhetorical its commitments were. There is ample evidence that HUD has so far proved no firmer in enforcing the planning conditions of 1974 legislation. For this latter, HUD can be excused to some extent, because the housing assistance plan has been inherently unrealistic. A locality can hardly be expected to develop a workable plan for housing its poor and aged when the federal and local subsidy funds are inadequate to meet the needs such a plan will inevitably require.

Some HUD programs have worked not to support good planning, but against it. Some have been unused, others have made modest contributions to good planning. On balance, it must be concluded that HUD has not yet succeeded in harnessing all the horses in a vigorous and consistent support of local urban planning. The same is true of local governments.

To compound the problem, the numerous other departments administering programs that are capable of stimulating and supporting sensible urban planning are often lukewarm and nearly always uncoordinated. Some are affirmatively anti-planning in their impact on the city. The most potent of these is the interstate highway program. Few would disagree that the construction of freeways in and around urban areas has had more influence on the shape and character of America's metropolitan areas than any other single force. Too often, this force has been negative—urban highways have destroyed neighborhoods and shaped urban growth with little regard for reasonable planning and less regard for the people displaced. The Bureau of Public Roads, which ran the program before its transfer to the Department of Transportation in 1966, was dominated by engineers skilled principally in plotting the shortest route from here to there and with little grasp of the larger and far more important consequences of their decisions. Beyond that, they were too often the captives of the highway materials manufacturers and the automobile manufacturers. Their efforts were applauded, too, by the automobile-loving public. The Department of Transportation undoubtedly tried to gain control of this formidable force. How well it succeeded is open to question. Besides, much of the harm had been done by 1966, when the Transportation Department was founded.

Despite massive federal expenditures on urban planning, any casual observer knows that, with a rare exception, HUD has not succeeded in making the city beautiful, orderly, or pleasant. The experts agree that professional urban planners in America have not achieved their lofty goals. The planners themselves are fully aware of this.[5] Barbara Ward, that passionate and eloquent observer of so many of the world's ills, has written of the "unintended city."[6] Elliot Richardson, who must have set a record for the cabinet posts occupied by one man, has suggested that the first step toward better cities "should be to restrain the planners."[7] William Gorham and Nathan Glazer, who fifteen years ago had stars in their eyes about the prospects for urban improvement, have recently expressed their disenchantment: "While planning is now a fixed part of the urban government process, it would be the rare specialist who would place much weight on it."[8] Some years ago, an observer called planning a caricature of Utopia. The obvious question is why all this disillusionment? Why has urban planning failed to achieve its high purposes? The basic reasons are the great complexity of the city-shaping forces that planning must influence, the too frequent abuses of planning tools such as zoning, speculation in privately owned urban land, and the fractionalization and corresponding impotence of local government jurisdictions.

The Deeper Causes of Frustrated Planning

Despite HUD's sometimes uninspired performance in stimulating local and urban planning, it would be unfair to lay all, or even most, of the blame at HUD's door. As we have noted, HUD does not control all federal programs influencing city form. But, far more important, there are deep-seated inhibitions to systematic and comprehensive urban planning, inhibitions against which even the most determined efforts of HUD could prove ineffective.

Complexity

Americans are natural planners, as Harvey Perloff has observed.[9] Business firms plan their production and sales efforts with great care and skill. Most families plan for the future by budgeting, by regular savings, and by purchasing health and life insurance. Expenditures on education of children are a form of planning for the next generation. The federal government plans in innumerable ways. America's landing on the moon was planned for at least ten years. The annual federal budget constitutes a plan and a set of national priorities. The frequent unexpected outcome of the plan embodied in the federal budget suggests that the results of planning become more difficult to achieve as the number of variables multiply. More important, planning becomes especially challenging not only when the variables are many, but also when the desired results depend on the behavior of people with emotions, free will, and self-interest. The city is a human organism, not a machine. The shape and quality of a city are the product of a multitude of interrelated public and private decisions. They are shaped by public, political decisions to build or not to build highways, streets, schools, post offices, parks, water and sewer lines, and many other things. They are also shaped by public decisions on the zoning of land uses and less directly but just as importantly by tax policies. Cities are shaped perhaps more decisively by private decisions to buy or build a house; to maintain it or not to maintain it; to erect a shopping center, a motel, or a drive-in restaurant; to erect a neon sign or a billboard.

This makes it much harder to plan and to produce the

desired results. Planning our trip to the moon was much simpler than controlling the future character of our infinitely complex and unpredictable human settlements.

The Zoning Game

Zoning, the designation of permitted land uses by local government jurisdictions, should and could be a constructive method for achieving planning objectives by arranging, in a sensible way, single-family residential, high-rise apartment, commercial, industrial, and other land uses. Too often, the practical effects of zoning are disorder rather than order, inequity rather than equity, private profit rather than public amenity. Aside from honest misjudgments, the reason is that in the zoning game, the public purpose often clashes head on with the individual interests of landowners and developers. The latter too often win. The decision of a local zoning board can greatly increase the value of a particular parcel of land. Thus, the pressures on the zoning board to make decisions favorable to the economic interests of landowners and developers are intense. Some of these anti-planning decisions are simply the result of pressure skillfully applied. Sometimes they involve bribery. This is a clear case of a failure of local government to perform its most basic function.

There is another dimension to the zoning game. It is called fiscal zoning. Various zoning jurisdictions within a metropolitan area compete to attract property uses that promise to increase tax revenues and add little to the cost of public services; they often bar the less fiscally profitable uses, such as housing for lower-income families. This hardly helps rational and humane urban planning. The dream meets the reality, and the dream loses.

Zoning can and should be a constructive instrument for urban planning. Its abuse makes it fall far short of its potential.

Land Speculation

This country has always held sacred the individual's right to own land. The depth of this sentiment is reflected in the fact that early drafts of the Declaration of Independence identified our inalienable, God-given rights as life, liberty, and the pursuit of *property*. The opportunity to own land, is, of course, fundamental to freedom and the satisfaction of human dignity. Anyone who has observed the landless poor in Latin America can attest to this fact. But all rights, however sacred, can be abused. In our expanding urban areas, individual land ownership, influenced by the opportunities for economic gain, encourages a destructive speculation in land, particularly outlying land. Land speculation is a major obstacle to rational urban planning. This abuse of the valid right to private property is a potent anti-planning force.

Too Many Local Governments

The 1970 census showed slightly fewer than two hundred Standard Metropolitan Statistical Areas (SMSAs) in the continental United States. Because many SMSAs are next to one another (in the Northeast, the Midwest, the Pacific Coast), this figure exaggerates the actual number of urban concentrations in the continental United States. The number is probably 150 or fewer. In 1968, the National Commission on Urban Problems counted over 7,000 local governments in these urban areas. In the Philadelphia area, there are at least 238 cities, boroughs, and townships; in the Chicago area, there are 120; in the New York City area, there are over 500 separate jurisdictions.[10] If the number of special districts and authorities is added, the discrepancy becomes even greater.

Each of these metropolitan areas is an entity—its parts are closely interrelated, physically, socially, economically, and in many other important ways. The disparity between the number of urban entities and the multitude of jurisdictions that govern them is tragic. On this multiplicity of local governments, Daniel Bell observed:

> This is not decentralization, but disarray. The extraordinary fact is that while the United States has the most modern economy in the world, its polity remains Tudor in character, antiquated, and top-heavy with a multiplicity of overlapping jurisdictions—townships, counties, and cities, plus special entities like health districts, park districts, sewage districts, water districts.[11]

This chaos of local governments is a major obstacle to effective planning. These local governmental fragments can, as Harvey Perloff observes, do some planning.[12] However, it is impossible to see how matters that are essentially regional—transportation, air and water pollution, equitable matching of tax revenues and public service costs, efficient deployment of commerce and industry, not to speak of equalizing the burdens of caring for the poor, the sick, the unemployed—can ever be handled without some form of metropolitan government or without at least effective cooperation among existing metropolitan governments.

This problem has been recognized for decades. Efforts to encourage the development of metropolitan governments go back at least twenty years. HUD and other federal departments have attempted to spur community-wide planning through the stick of regulations and the carrot of grants. The results have been notably unsuccessful.

A recent, faintly hopeful, development is the creation in many urban areas of councils of government (COGs). This development was stimulated largely by the Intergovernmental Cooperation Act of 1968 and the subsequent issuance of Circular A-95 by the President's Office of Management and Budget. In essence, the circular requires that local applications for some one hundred types of federal aid with some potential effect on the quality of the physical and social environment be circulated for comment among other governments in the same area. There is no requirement that these comments, if critical, be resolved. Circular A-95 thus does no more than generate a dialogue among local governments on projects of regional impact. The COGs provide a useful vehicle for this interchange. However, the COGs "have shown little capacity to use the A-95 process as a vehicle for implementing their land use plans."[13]

In 1962, the Advisory Commission on Intergovernmental Relations noted that there cannot be equitable and adequate financing of services "unless the basic fact of noncoincidence of service areas and areas of tax jurisdiction for support of such services is clearly recognized and effectively met."[14] The

COGs have not accomplished the crucial task of erasing or even compromising the inherent conflicts of interest between suburban jurisdictions and the central city (in revenue sources, welfare costs, location of housing for the poor), and they have rarely achieved agreement among suburban jurisdictions on issues not nearly so fundamental. At best, the COGs are only a faint first step on the hard road toward metropolitan government, an essential condition to carrying out metropolitan planning.

It is a sad irony that special revenue sharing for community development, passed in 1974 as a substitute for various special-purpose (categorical) programs with the same purpose, has actually discouraged metropolitan-wide planning. Despite the law's glowing language on planning, its distribution of funds to individual urban governments on an automatic formula basis has so far made them more independent of one another. This development has also weakened HUD's leverage to encourage metropolitan-wide planning. However, there are ample authorities in the law to reverse these splintering pressures. There is also evidence the new HUD secretary, Patricia Harris, intends to use these neglected powers.

Some progress has been made toward metropolitan cooperation. Area-wide plans have been developed. Although they are for the most part only advisory in nature, they do exist. They "lack guts,"[15] but their existence is a step in the right direction. Here and there, considerably more positive steps have been taken. In California, Oregon, and Florida, state laws require local governments to adopt land-use plans within a reasonable time; more important, these plans have the force of law.[16] A recent development in Minneapolis–St. Paul may be even more significant. There, certain area-wide functions are planned and financed on a metropolitan scale. Many experts consider this a major breakthrough toward the still distant goal of true metropolitan planning.

Public Consent

At the root of the impediments to effective and humane urban planning lie some of the darker sides of society. The first is public indifference. Too many people are so wrapped up in themselves they take no interest in or responsibility for national and community needs. Indifference is the mortal enemy of public purpose and public achievement. It is also the enemy of the thought and sacrifices needed for realistic urban planning.

Second is the too frequent naked pursuit of gain, regardless of the public consequences. We see this in land speculation. We see it in suburban exclusionary zoning and in many other activities. The laissez-faire doctrine has not served the cities well. Neither has the political doctrine that conflicting interests can be resolved through clash and compromise. As W. W. Rostow has observed, "American politics is shifting away from the classic task of compromising special interests to the task of harmonizing private and public values."[17] In short, if one looks for the villain who frustrates urban planning, he is likely to find that ultimately it is us.

The Planners' Identity Crisis

Faced with the complexity and difficulty of planning the contemporary city, it is not surprising that urban planners are somewhat confused about their goals as well as their roles. The classical urban planners drew schemes for an aesthetic and rational arrangement of land uses, linked by streets and other methods for the movement of people and goods—a picture of urban Utopia. This kind of planning is not now normally attempted. Indeed, it is no longer relevant except in the few cases, such as Brasília, where entire cities are built on vacant land and, to a lesser extent, in new satellite communities. Most of our urban concentrations already exist and are not susceptible to the *de novo* approach. Today's planners necessarily view planning as a process through which the old is improved and new growth guided. Thus, planning becomes an incremental approach to urban improvement.

Planners also differ on the extent of their responsibility. Some believe planning is concerned only with physical shape and function. Others, probably the majority, extend planning to include economic and social improvement. Opinions also differ on the planner's role. Does he simply draw a picture of the shape of the city, leaving it to others to turn it into a reality?

This is what L'Enfant did with the famous plan of Washington. Or does the planner himself enter the decision-making process of local government and become a technically trained advocate? If so, where should he be placed in the local government? Planners can now be found on planning commissions, on zoning boards, and in many other places. If planning is joining in the decision-making process, as most now think it to be, then the planner becomes one of many participants in a complex system. If he chooses this particular role, he is probably wise. But it means he must be prepared to negotiate and compromise in ways that are inevitable and sometimes uncongenial to the artist who lurks in the personality of most planners, especially if they are also architects.

Planners not only disagree but are often quite critical of one another, a characteristic common to most professions. Many planners have become highly sophisticated in the use of computers to predict traffic flows, population growth, demographic characteristics, income levels, and even local economic developments. Lewis Mumford, perhaps America's most respected student of urban matters, sharply criticizes this trend. Planning, he argues, will

> get lost . . . in details of political organization, economic support, population movement, transportation facilities. . . . We neglect the factor that is central to all these things; the dimensions of the human personality. The answer to the problems of human organization and human control will not come from computers; the answers will come from men . . . and not from men . . . indoctrinated with the myth of the machine . . . uncorrected by human wisdom . . . uncontrolled by historic experience.[18]

Mumford clearly finds little to praise and much to fear from the drift of many planners toward abstract, mechanized, impersonal approaches to urban improvement. But he must know that the computer, a useful instrument, cannot be blamed for this trend. Rather, the fault is with those who become so immersed in data for the sake of data that they lose sight of the larger, less quantitative goals of planning. Another voice of dissent comes from Britain. An English planner is critical of the entire approach of much current urban planning on the grounds that planners do not know what kind of environment people want.[19]

This tension within the planning profession undoubtedly accounts, to some extent, for the ambiguities of purpose reflected in HUD's major financial support for planning (the 701 Program).

What More Can Be Done?

Metropolitan planning backed by some form of metropolitan government seems distant and difficult. But it is not impossible. This country has done far more difficult things when the need for them was generally perceived. (The progress we have made toward racial equality is one example.) Several actions can be taken now—all of which HUD can either do or inspire others to do.

1. *More local planning tools.* Zoning, subdivision regulations, and enforcement of building codes have long been the basic tools used to influence land use. They can be made more effective if adequately designed and firmly enforced. Other tools are rarely used. Taxation is one of them. Real estate taxes can be reformed to fall more heavily on land, especially on land that is idle, and less heavily on buildings, especially new buildings. Another neglected tool is the pricing of public services. Schools, sewers, water lines, parks, roads, and other public services are usually financed from general tax revenue. Thus, no user perceives any differential in the charges for these services. This invites urban sprawl and land speculation. User charges, with high rates for those farthest away and thus more costly to serve, would reduce the incentive for urban sprawl.[20]

2. *Needed: a land policy.* The private ownership of land is often exercised in ways that deface the city and defeat sensible planning. Ironically, the increase in land value from which the speculator profits comes not from what he does, but from urban improvements paid for by the public. We have already discussed the ways local taxation might be modified to restrain land speculation and to support more orderly growth. Another approach is through the public ownership of land in the path

of future urban development. The government now owns land for forestry, recreation, and transportation. There is no good reason why public ownership should not be extended to urban development. Land banking, the public purchase of land some years in advance of development, has been used in western Europe for many years. Public ownership of land can facilitate orderly development. The profit that now goes to the speculator would be given to the public. Marion Clawson, one of our most respected students of land use, has said, "it is hard to see how the goals of better cities and better urban land use can be achieved without some extension of public land ownership."[21] The American Institute of Architects has recommended public ownership of land as a method of improving urban development.[22] Donald Canty, a well-known writer on urban problems, has given his views in the following words:

> In the long run, the pressures of the urban emergency will require fundamental reorganization of the patterns of urban development, including tax reform, metropolitan planning, perhaps even metropolitan government. The public interest must assert itself in the disposition and use of land just as earlier social upheaval brought other forms of wealth under meaningful but limited control.[23]

3. *Greater state participation.* With some exceptions, states have ignored the mounting problems of the urban concentrations within their boundaries. Our too numerous urban jurisdictions derive practically all of their powers from the states. What the states have given they can take back. Robert Embry, HUD assistant secretary for community planning and development, before his appointment, told a committee of the U.S. House of Representatives, "If Baltimore City could annex Baltimore County we could handle all of our slum problems."[24] Embry was referring to the more equitable distribution of revenues this would produce and perhaps to the possibility of dispersing the poor. The states have denied central cities the power to annex outlying land as they grew.

This is a major cause of the damaging fractionalization of urban governments. But the states can still simplify local government structure. With the necessary prodding from HUD and other federal departments, the states could play a crucial role in improving urban planning by establishing a more realistic relationship between urban government jurisdictions and the urban organisms they seek to govern.

4. *Toward metropolitan government.* There is clearly a close relationship between truly metropolitan government (or some form of effective interjurisdictional cooperation on area-wide problems) and effective metropolitan planning. The former is virtually a condition for the latter. It is time HUD and the states became serious about this self-evident need.

5. *HUD must exert strong leadership.* If metropolitan planning is ever to be achieved, HUD must do more than pay lip service to it. HUD must become serious. It should let all know that it means business. It must use all the considerable powers at its disposal.

HUD cannot order local governments to take any of the actions we have identified. But there are many ways it can exert leverage toward these ends. The most obvious is to make its financial aid conditional on some of these needed local actions. The project selection criteria are examples of conditions HUD has put on its housing subsidies in the interest of residential racial balance. Conditions attached to other types of funds could be even more powerful because they are more important to most localities than housing subsidies. Former HUD Secretary Robert C. Weaver has expressed the opinion that the incentive approach may be the most promising of HUD's tools for the improvement of local planning.[25] HUD should also seek, with the help of the president, to persuade other departments to use their considerable program leverage toward the same objective.

The HUD secretary should also use the cabinet position to lead and persuade the local governments and the people who live in the cities to take the steps needed, to sacrifice narrow self-interest for the larger self-interest of a well-planned urban environment. If the issue is fundamentally moral, as it is, then moral leadership is required. The ultimate solution to this real, but much ignored, domestic issue calls for an appeal to the consciences of Americans. It will be solved neither by business as usual nor by politics as usual.

5

Renewing the Inner City

This chapter will deal with HUD's efforts to support the wide variety of local actions needed to revive the central city. This means rebuilding or rehabilitating slums, luring back middle-class families who have fled to the suburbs, reestablishing its eroding economic base, and generally making it, if not the core of urban activities, at least an important center of urban life.

We shall examine HUD's current program of block grants for community development (established in 1974), under which the localities are given considerable latitude to select the specific city improvement projects they undertake. We shall also look at the several programs the block grants replaced, especially the Urban Renewal Program (including slum clearance and slum rehabilitation), and the Model Cities Program. The merits of the block grant and the categorical program approaches will be compared. It will be argued that the original block grant approach to urban improvement is a large price to pay for reducing federal red tape, which stifled the various categorical programs, and that with quite possible simplification, the special-purpose categorical approach could better achieve the national purposes. This does not mean a simple reinstatement of the urban renewal or model cities programs—it means careful development and testing of a program that will work.

Needless to say, the revival of our central cities and the

amelioration of slum conditions are of great importance to the cities and to the nation.

Block Grants for Community Development

Title I of the Housing and Community Development Act of 1974 authorized the HUD secretary to make block grants to states and units of local government to finance a variety of urban improvement activities. According to the law, the primary objective of the Block Grant Program was "the development of viable urban communities . . . and a suitable living environment and expanding economic opportunities, principally for persons of low and moderate income."[1]

Objectives and Character

This broad objective encompassed seven major local objectives: (1) the elimination of slums and blight and the prevention of blighting influences; (2) the elimination of conditions detrimental to health, safety, and public welfare through code enforcement, demolition, and rehabilitation; (3) the conservation and expansion of the nation's housing stock; (4) the expansion and improvement of the quantity and quality of community services; (5) a more rational utilization of land and other natural resources and better planned land uses; (6) the reduction of the isolation of income groups within communities and geographic areas; and (7) the restoration and preservation of properties of special value for historic, architectural, or aesthetic reasons.[2]

The law authorizing the 1974 Block Grant Program eliminated, or subsumed into the new program, seven existing special-purpose or categorical programs. Among these were the Urban Renewal Program, the Model Cities Program, loans for public facilities, grants for water and sewer facilities, and several others. Federal subsidies for housing were not included in the new Block Grant Program.

The block grant approach to federal aid in the urban field constituted a substantial change from past practices. Nearly all previous programs sought quite specific objectives and required localities to submit for each proposed project a detailed application in advance showing what the funds would be used for, how and where the project would be built (or carried out), how much it would cost, and so on. Under the Block Grant Program, advance applications were not required for each project undertaken. The locality had considerable freedom to choose how to use the federal funds in a way consistent with the general purposes of the law and was required to report to HUD only after it had made its decisions and obligated the funds.

The fundamental changes involved in the block grant approach to urban aid were three. First, as just described, fewer strings were attached. Second, the amount of funds going to each local governmental jurisdiction that applied was calculated on a formula basis (population, extent of poverty [given double weight], and the extent of housing overcrowding). Thus, the amount of funds going to any local jurisdiction (states, counties, local units of government) was chiefly determined by the formula and bore no relationship to the merits of any specific local project (as had been the case in the past). Third, the government block grant could cover 100 percent of any project chosen (in contrast to the previous programs, which required the locality to cover some percentage of the project cost). Aside from a general application for block grant funds, the only prior submissions required were a three-year community development plan including a detailed assessment of and plan for meeting housing needs, especially those of lower-income families.

Two other aspects of the block grant legislation should also be mentioned. First, the law contained a "hold harmless" provision designed to smooth the transition from the old programs by avoiding a sharp drop in federal funds flowing to a locality and by allowing already planned projects to be completed. Second, a percentage of the block grant funds appropriated were to be used at the HUD secretary's discretion for certain specified purposes.

The Pros and Cons

The reasoning behind block grants for community development—what President Nixon called "the new Federalism"—is plausible enough. The individual categorical programs had proliferated in recent years. They were not only numerous, they were complex and often overlapping. Local officials spent countless hours filling out multitudes of highly detailed application forms, and federal officials spent more hours reviewing them in painstaking detail. The complexities grow year by year, just as the federal income tax form frequently adds new and more bewildering hurdles.

Beyond the elimination of unnecessary red tape, it was believed (with good reason) that Washington does not possess all wisdom. Why shouldn't the decisions on how to spend federal funds for community improvements be made by those closest to the problems—the mayors and their staff? If the decisions were thus made, should they not be more realistically related to the individual needs of each locality? To many, the case for this change in distribution of federal funds went even beyond efficiency and more realistic decisions. It rested on a belief that decentralization of government was a desirable thing in itself, just as centralization of power in Washington was bad in itself.

On the other hand, many questioned the case for block grants on the grounds that the arguments oversimplified the realities. They did not dispute the unnecessary complexity and red tape that had accumulated around the categorical programs, but they questioned whether local governments, because they were so close to their own voters, would be able to resist local political pressures—which are strongest from those who need help least and weakest from those who need help most. The doubters felt that block grants might well defeat the national goals and social priorities reflected in federal legislation.

Informed and public-spirited observers were and are still sharply divided on the merits of block grants for community improvement. Harvey Perloff thinks block grants for community development are desirable. He also believes the development of local capability is a major and desirable objective of block grants. At the same time, he favors categorical programs when a significant national purpose needs to be accomplished.[3] Louis Winnick, of the Ford Foundation, also strongly favors the block grant approach. To the extent mayors prove susceptible to political pressures, he thinks, they must learn to resist them.[4] Carla Hills, HUD secretary in the Ford administration, believed block grants to be a major improvement in federal policy. She was reported to be considering favorably a similar approach to federal subsidies for housing.

Many equally thoughtful observers disagree. Charles L. Schultze, President Johnson's budget director and President Carter's chief economic adviser, has called block grants "a cop out."[5] He has also pointed out how easily the law's objectives could be defeated, yet appear to be carried out, through local bookkeeping devices.[6] Philip Brownstein, former HUD assistant secretary, has expressed the view that block grants will prove "a disaster" because cities are not equipped to resist pressures that will divert funds to purposes other than those intended.[7] Paul Ylvisaker has called block grants "a sly trick" for avoiding federal responsibility for the urgent needs of the urban poor.[8] Former HUD Assistant Secretary Charles Haar has written, "Revenue sharing, as presently enacted, not only virtually eliminates the federal executive role in urban affairs, but ends the Congressional function of setting policy priorities as well." This is much more the case with block grants than with categorical programs. He also predicted that national goals "will be accorded so low a priority on local scales that we can consider them to have been abandoned."[9] Professor Frieden of MIT and Marshall Kaplan said in September 1976, "As a federal aid reform it [block grants] has succeeded in simplifying grant applications and given greater flexibility to local communities, but it has bought these merits at the expense of the poor."[10]

David B. Walker, assistant director of the Advisory Commission on Intergovernmental Relations, an early advocate of block grants, recently made some telling observations about the program. He said the program, like many that preceded it, suffers from too little advance consideration of just how it will affect the urgent problems to which it is directed. Moreover, he noted, the fund distribution formula is already out of date. One of the three criteria—overcrowding—is irrelevant: housing abandonment makes overcrowding no longer an indicator of slum conditions. He observed, further, that the 1974 law is not a pure block grant program. Rather, it is a mixture: that is.

the discretionary funds portion of the program is really categorical in nature.

Walker, a perspicacious observer, maintained that the distinction between categorical programs and block grant programs has been overemphasized. A categorical program does not necessarily inhibit flexibility in local decision making nor necessarily require excessive red tape. On the other hand, the block grant programs could well become burdened with excessive, detailed requirements—precisely because they now lack clear-cut purpose. Finally, he pointed out that although block grants have the explicit objectives of improving slum conditions and helping the poor, they are not effectively targeted to solve these problems.[11]

Others think block grants are not well suited to encourage physical improvements: that is, there are no long-term fund commitments. Another limitation is that too little money is spent among too many local units of government.

Experience So Far

What has actually happened under HUD's Block Grant Program is also the subject of some disagreement. Until the change of administration, at least, HUD found the picture very rosy. It pointed with pride to the elimination of red tape and lengthy processing delays, to the emphasis localities are giving to renewal and rehabilitation and to minority needs, to the coordination of housing and community development, to the innovative approaches many cities have designed, and to the fact that many more jurisdictions are participating than under the categorical programs.[12]

However, others find the results less satisfactory. The National Association of Housing and Redevelopment Officials, who monitored the program under contract with HUD, found a notable shift of activities from lower-income to middle-income parts of the city. It also found that the Block Grant Program was not generating major new investment in our cities.[13] The Southern Regional Council, a nonprofit public interest group, conducted a study of block grant results in twenty-six southern cities. The study led to these conclusions: "Local diversions from the national purpose are not just occasional abuses, but rather form a pattern inherent in the implementation of the act; decisions are made by politicians who often have little regard for the concerns of low and moderate income citizens." Among the specific abuses were: (1) use of $150,000 in block grant funds for a tennis court complex in an affluent section of Little Rock, Arkansas; the city program director was quoted as saying, "You can't divorce politics from that much money . . . we must remember the needs of the people who vote . . . and poor people don't vote"; (2) $50,000 for tennis courts in a well-to-do section of Chattanooga, Tennessee; and (3) use of 7 percent of Nashville's block grants for housing rehabilitation in thirty-six census tracts, only one of which was found to be a low-income neighborhood.[14]

An official in New York City, originally very much in favor of block grants, recently expressed his dismay over petty, politically motivated fighting among departments for a share of the federal block grant funds. He now doubts whether local government can be as objective and as committed to social purpose as is required for a program designed specifically to improve the living conditions of low-income and moderate-income families (a purpose mentioned four times in the law's statement of purpose).[15] As for the capacity of local government to improve the lot of the poor, former HUD Secretary Weaver recalls the many occasions on which mayors thanked him for requiring them, through categorical programs, to do what they knew they should but felt politically unable to do without federal pressure.[16] There is evidence that Secretary Harris has found at least a partial remedy for this deficiency: use of the housing assistance plan required of each community under the Block Grant Program. She has recently announced that several communities will be denied block grants unless their housing plans are modified to provide housing for a diversity of income levels.

In order to put in full perspective HUD's Block Grant Program for community development, we must examine the nature and performance of the major urban-improvement programs it replaced.

The Urban Renewal Program

After more than ten years of discussion in and out of government, authority for the clearance and redevelopment of inner-city slums was given in the Housing Act of 1949. It was initially called "slum clearance." The 1954 law that broadened the program called it "urban renewal."

Mixed Objectives

By 1949, support for such a program came from groups of every political complexion, but for very different motives. The law's language reflected this multiplicity of interests—an outcome common in a government based on the compromise of conflicting interests. Some of its backers saw it as a plan to improve housing and slum conditions. Others viewed it as a way to attract middle-class families and business back to the inner city. Others looked upon it as a means for improving the quality of the inner city. To mayors, it was an opportunity to increase tax revenues. To many private groups, it was simply a profitable real estate opportunity. This led Catherine Bauer to observe, "Seldom has such a variegated crew of would-be angels tried to sit on the same pin at the same time."[17]

How Slum Clearance Worked

The 1949 law authorized loans and grants to localities for the clearance of slums and other deteriorated areas and for the construction of new housing, new commercial establishments, and new public buildings on land that had been cleared. Federal advances were authorized to finance project planning. Loans were available for the acquisition and clearance of land—through use of powers of eminent domain under state law—and for preparing it for reuse. Grants were available to cover two-thirds (in some cases three-fourths) of the ultimate difference between the cost of acquiring, clearing, and reuse preparation and the revenues realized when the land was sold for rebuilding at the "fair market value."[18]

Those who initiated the slum clearance program emphasized improving the central-city tax base by attracting middle-class families and business back from the suburbs. They also emphasized improving the face of the central city through construction of public buildings, commercial centers, centers for arts, and even sports stadia. Another, quite different objective of urban redevelopment—improving slum conditions and providing better housing for the poor—was given less emphasis and sometimes forgotten during the early years of the program's administration.

There appear to be two reasons behind this early thrust of the federal government's first major effort to rescue the central city. First, the federal leaders of the new program felt a need to "sell" the program to mayors, for state enabling legislation had to be passed and local agencies had to be established. Second, Robert Moses, New York City's master builder, and others of like mind quickly saw it for what it could be, a vast, federally supported real estate operation. Many newly appointed local redevelopment directors learned how slum clearance could work—the Moses way.[19] As the slum clearance program gradually gained momentum with federal dollars pouring forth, the bulldozer razed slum neighborhoods in city after city. After a sometimes long wait, expensive apartment houses, stores, public centers, and various other structures began to be built on the cleared slum land. The early administrators of the slum clearance program made another fateful decision. They chose to establish procedures requiring the most detailed review of every aspect of a locality's slum clearance plan. As a result, Washington often second-guessed every detail of the local proposal. This and incompetent local administration also produced a long and agonizing application processing period. From start to completion, the average slum clearance project took seven years or more.

Urban Renewal at the Crossroads

By the early 1960s, the growing urban renewal program began to stagger under a barrage of criticism. It was charged with destroying neighborhoods, callously evicting poor families, and destroying countless small business firms. Beyond that, federal expenditures on urban renewal were said to be wasted. This critical onslaught reached its peak when portions of Martin Anderson's *The Federal Bulldozer* appeared in the April 1965 issue of the *Reader's Digest*.[20] The other side of urban renewal's contradictory purposes—improvement in the lives of the slum dwellers—resurfaced with mounting fury.

Change in Direction

When John Kennedy appointed Robert Weaver HHFA administrator in 1961, Weaver saw the need to humanize the slum clearance program. More help was provided to find decent homes for the displaced and ease their transition to new locations. There was less reliance on the bulldozer, and more slum neighborhoods were scheduled for rehabilitation (authorized by the 1954 act) to improve living conditions for the slum dwellers themselves. Clearance was used more and more on commercial and industrial sites and less and less on residential neighborhoods.

What It Accomplished

When the slum clearance legislation was passed in 1949, it was hailed as a great achievement, one that would change the face of the central cities. Today, almost thirty years later, it is almost universally criticized. The truth is to be found somewhere in between.

1. Slum clearance has made important physical improvements in many central cities—to name only a few, Boston's Civic Center, New York's Lincoln Center, Philadelphia's Society Hill, Baltimore's Charles Center, St. Louis's Gateway Project, Cincinnati's Riverfront, Denver's Mile High Project, San Francisco's Embarcadero Development. In view of the magnitude of the central-city rebuilding job, however, urban renewal has not made a great impact. Between the program's establishment in 1949 and June 30, 1974 (about the time of its suspension), HUD (and HHFA, its predecessor) approved approximately $10 billion in grants to support over 2,000 urban renewal projects. As of 1974, half had been completed, and the rest were still under construction.

2. Unfortunately, the charge that slum clearance has destroyed more homes than it has created is true. In addition, urban renewal did too little to provide housing that was within the means of the urban poor whom it displaces. Thanks to

the efforts of HUD Secretary Robert Weaver, this situation changed in the later years of the program. By 1972, over half the units completed in urban renewal areas were for low-income and moderate-income families—in contrast to only 39 percent five years earlier. The impact of slum clearance on the slum dweller has been, on the whole, more negative than positive, despite surveys that show that most of the displaced have been rehoused in "decent, safe and sanitary housing."[21]

3. There is still a place for slum clearance. It is both needed and accepted in the blighted commercial and industrial sections where few, if any, families must be displaced. Another little explored use for the bulldozer is to remove the growing number of abandoned slum houses, which, if left standing, only make conditions worse.

Neighborhood Rehabilitation

In accord with the general disenchantment with the bulldozer approach to slum improvement, the 1960s saw a marked increase in rehabilitation in an attempt to improve slums and older, declining neighborhoods. The reason for this shift is simple. Clearance displaces poor slum dwellers and thus had become publicly unacceptable; rehabilitation tries to improve neighborhoods for the poor who live in them. Today, it would be hard to find an urban renewal practitioner or student of the subject who does not espouse neighborhood rehabilitation in preference to the once predominant bulldozer. During the 1976 presidential election campaign, the urban platforms of the two parties differed on many subjects, but they agreed on the high priority assigned to the rehabilitation of rundown housing and the need to revive decayed neighborhoods through this approach.

Modifications to the urban renewal program, enacted in 1954, provided various federal financial supports for the planning and execution of neighborhood rehabilitation projects. Later, grants and direct federal loans at a 3 percent interest rate were provided to help poor families finance the rehabilitation of their homes. In 1964, essentially the same aids were made available to support concentrated code enforcement projects aimed at arresting decay in less run-down neighborhoods. In the 1960s, these authorities began to be encouraged by the federal authorities and to be used in earnest by many localities.

But slum rehabilitation proved to be "easier said than done."[22] Rehabilitating slum neighborhoods turned out to be far more difficult than clearance and rebuilding—a complicated process itself. It was also much less glamorous. Translating rehabilitation into a reality took a lot of learning. Many early efforts failed owing to an oversimplified conception of what was required. We now understand more, but we are still learning.

Since residential rehabilitation became a necessary, if not popular, way to treat residential blight, four stages in its development can be identified. The first was in the early 1960s, when the Urban Renewal Administration and the FHA—both in HHFA—joined in several experiments in an attempt to unravel the snarls that had bogged down the few serious efforts at neighborhood rehabilitation. The relatively sophisticated programs in New Haven and Boston, both conceived and directed by Edward Logue and a few others, were the notable exceptions. Up to that time, nearly all urban renewal rehabilitation had closely followed the "Baltimore Plan" of the 1950s, which consisted of systematic code enforcement to induce property owners to improve their houses up to minimum standards, some neighborhood organization and persuasion by the city, the promise of some public improvements (streets, street lighting, small parks, etc.), and financing to help owners improve their properties. But the URA-FHA experiments revealed many deficiencies in this approach. The lessons learned were reflected in greatly modified URA policies on rehabilitation and in changes in FHA rules (particularly in the physical standards required for FHA rehabilitation financing). At that time, the only financing available for rehabilitation was through FHA at full market interest rates. This was changed when direct loans at low interest rates and grants for rehabilitation were authorized in 1964 and 1965.[23] By 1975, about nine hundred urban renewal rehabilitation projects had been started. They contained nearly 500,000 dwelling units. On only about 180,000 of these units, however, was rehabilitation completed. The concentrated code enforcement grant program produced 233 projects, and about 250,000 units were repaired to code standards.

The second stage—in the mid-1960s—grew out of a lesson learned in the first: that the urban renewal approach to rehabilitation often worked very poorly with absentee owners and that 50 percent or more of the buildings in a typical slum are owned by absentee landlords. This prompted FHA to start several rehabilitation experiments, using its own rental subsidy programs. They were designed to learn how to bring about the rehabilitation of absentee-owned, rental properties in decayed neighborhoods. FHA conducted these rehabilitation experiments in over half a dozen cities. Some succeeded; some failed. But they all produced better understandings of urban decay and the remedies needed. They also made clear the formidable obstacles that must be overcome.[24]

The third phase came in 1969, when HUD Secretary George Romney—building on FHA's earlier efforts—mounted a major effort to stimulate massive rehabilitation of absentee-owned properties. The Romney program was called "Project Rehab." Under the leadership of an FHA assistant commissioner, the plan involved the concerted use of all of HUD's various skills and financial resources. By the end of 1972, about 26,000 living units had been rehabilitated in twenty or more cities. Secretary Romney expressed satisfaction with the results, and the Arthur D. Little Company, commissioned to evaluate the effort, concluded Project Rehab had proved that massive rehabilitation is possible. However, both judgments were premature: the success of residential rehabilitation depends not only on the number of units completed but also on the long-term improvement of the housing, the living conditions of the people affected, and conditions in the neighborhood. As a recent review of the long-term results of a sample of these efforts shows, many proved financial failures, but for very different reasons. Some failed because the families did not maintain their homes, others because the wrong properties were selected, others because of a misjudgment of the size of units the market required, others because the subsidy program used was not flexible enough to cover necessary repairs under conditions of rapid cost inflation. The fact that only one of the financial failures reviewed was directly attributable to destructive tenant behavior seems a hopeful sign. It also suggests that we need more thorough and careful examination of the long-term results of rehabilitation. Such a study would provide the basis for more realistic guides for the many cities now undertaking rehabilitation to help them establish where and under what conditions residential rehabilitation will be successful.[25] Clearly, there is still much to learn about the complex process of rehabilitation.

The fourth stage is now taking place in the many cities using the block grant funds for rehabilitation. Many variations in financing and approach are being used. HUD is also promoting urban homesteading, where HUD's foreclosed properties are made available to families at nominal cost if they will rehabilitate them with the help of low-interest rate loans, with their own efforts, or both. HUD has also been promoting another rehabilitation approach, one that stresses organization of the neighborhood residents in self-help efforts. This is by no means new, but it cannot be dismissed solely for this reason. Indeed, neighborhood participation and the training of neighborhood leadership are basic to rehabilitation, especially in neighborhoods where home ownership predominates. From this lengthy experience, some general conclusions can be drawn.

1. Neighborhood decay is a complex, self-reinforcing process involving many physical, economic, social, and political forces. Thus, it is extremely difficult to reverse this many-sided process through neighborhood rehabilitation.

2. Local government has too few people who have the understanding and skills required to carry out successful neighborhood rehabilitation. These skills involve neighborhood organization, property inspection, financing, and related matters.

3. There is, with very minor exceptions, no rehabilitation industry. Therefore, there is little or no entrepreneurial drive to respond to government efforts. It is often difficult to find even a general contractor with the interest and capacity to organize the needed subcontractors and to perform rehabilitation for an

owner who has been persuaded, or coerced, to rehabilitate and who has somehow been provided with the crucial financing needed.

4. The establishment of rehabilitation standards, the physical level of improvement to be achieved, involves a difficult compromise between the desirable and the possible. The local housing code is often of little help. A code violation notice does not cover all aspects of minimally livable housing, and it does not provide a detailed description of work to be done—which is essential for the contractor and for his ability to estimate his costs.

5. Because most residents of blighted, inner-city neighborhoods are poor, long-term financing and some form of subsidy are usually required to bring the needed rehabilitation within the means of the occupants. Not enough such financing is available to support rehabilitation on a large scale. Project Rehab required millions of dollars to support the rehabilitation of 26,000 living units.

6. Neighborhood rehabilitation means more than the physical improvement of living units; it also means improvements in neighborhood facilities and services. Although it is less costly to improve facilities and services in an existing neighborhood than it is to create them from scratch in a new one, it still costs the city money—money it often does not have.

7. Neighborhood rehabilitation must be accepted, affirmatively supported, and even led by the residents. The organization of this essential grass-roots support takes time and great skill. In some neighborhoods, it is impossible.

8. Neighborhood decay does not stem entirely, or even primarily, from physical causes. It results from poverty. It results from human apathy, disinterest, and despair. It frequently comes from the deep-seated social pathologies that produce property destruction, vandalism, crime, roving gangs, fear, and all the other antisocial behavior that the daily newspapers so often report. Under these circumstances, bad housing is more the consequence than the cause of the slum condition. No amount of physical improvement will cure these social pathologies. Any physical improvment will not last long. We still know too little about the causes and cures

of this human side of urban decay.

9. There is still much to learn, but successful rehabilitation is by no means impossible—if the neighborhoods are carefully selected and the needed skills and money are applied.

10. The techniques and authorities used in urban renewal rehabilitation (neighborhood organization, public improvements, code enforcement, etc.) should be merged with those used in Project Rehab (purchase, rehabilitation, subsidized financing of absentee-owned rental properties, and good management).

Neither is complete without the other. In theory, cities can use block grant funds to merge them. In practice, however, it is almost impossible: block grants do not include HUD's major housing subsidy programs. The latter are still categorical and must be applied for project by project.[26]

The Model Cities Program

Also included in the 1974 block grant legislation were the objectives of the Model Cities Program. This was the boldest, most sweeping effort of President Johnson's Great Society to deal with the physical and social problems of the inner city. Unlike urban renewal, which was long in gestation, the model cities idea came quickly from suggestions presented to and developed by a blue-ribbon presidential task force. Its chairman was Robert C. Wood, soon to become the first under secretary of HUD. Its members were distinguished people of broad experience. The Wood task force proposed a full-scale attack on the physical and social ills of slums, an attack that would use the complete arsenal of relevant federal programs, with HUD as the leader and coordinator. The purpose was no less than to rebuild completely, on a scale never before attempted, entire slum neighborhoods.[27] As Charles Haar was later to write, the hallmark of the proposal was "its ambitious comprehensiveness and its vaulting promises."[28]

The Conception

Recognizing the immense difficulty of the job as well as the need to learn more about the roots of the manifold urban pathologies, the task force proposed an experimental effort, limited to a few selected cities. The strategy of the Model Cities Program, as conceived by the task force, had five ingredients: (1) *concentration* of all federal resources on a target area; (2) *coordination* of the complex array of urban aids; (3) *mobilization* of local leadership; (4) *local initiative* in shaping and carrying out its efforts; and (5) *experimentation and innovation.*[29] The proposal was notable for two other reasons. In its emphasis on local initiative, local leadership, and limited federal review, the plan anticipated the Block Grant Program passed nine years later. It also wisely recognized that the slum problem is as much social as physical—a lesson that many toilers in the urban vineyard had learned through bitter experience.

Its Modification

About one year after the Wood task force delivered its recommendations to the president, the Model Cities Program became law. But something happened to it on the way to passage. The number of eligible cities was increased from a few to fifty (and thereafter to well over a hundred). At the same time, the funds were reduced. This was a drastic transformation of the original conception.

The task force's plan for a massive concentration of effort and money in a saturation attack on the troubled neighborhoods of a few cities had vanished. The law provided too little money for too many cities to come even close to the vision of the task force.

Short Life

HUD plunged into the job of administering this highly compromised new law with great zeal and high hopes, and the presidential rhetoric continued to soar. President Lyndon Johnson insisted on referring to what was legally "the demonstration cities" authority as the Model Cities Program, thus giving it the over-hopeful name by which it was to be known and judged. The still new program even survived for a while during Richard Nixon's presidency, chiefly because HUD Secretary Romney embraced it and fought hard to keep it alive.[30]

So did Floyd Hyde, the HUD assistant secretary responsible for its administration. The program even survived the review of a committee Nixon appointed to review it. The committee's chairman was Edward Banfield, an urban scholar whose skepticism of federal action in the urban field was well known. To the surprise of most, the Banfield committee recommended continuation of the Model Cities Program. However, Nixon was never convinced of its merits.[31] Besides that, it was a Lyndon Johnson creation. Slowly, the drive behind the Model Cities Program ebbed. It was probably inevitable that such a bold, if flawed, plan for urban improvement would be abandoned in an administration dominated by the politics of expediency and based on a "Southern Strategy" inimical to the needs of blacks.

The Lessons

The Model Cities Program was in operation for about eight years: from its passage in 1966 until President Nixon terminated it in 1973. Its short life was rocky, filled with confusion, and darkened by the inevitable contradictions between big promises and small results. From it there are many lessons to be learned, both about the program itself and about the operations of federal and local government.[32]

1. *The quick fix.* The Model Cities Program proved once more than a federal program of this magnitude cannot be put together in so short a time by any group, however brilliant they may be. The instant fix does not work in government. Our most successful programs are those that have been carefully and painstakingly conceived, pretested, and then given years to season.

2. *Too much to manage.* The program, certainly heroic in conception, probably was too comprehensive and contained too many elements to be manageable by mere men, however skilled.

3. *The limits of a cabinet secretary.* The Model Cities objective of orchestrating all the federal programs in a grand inner-city rescue operation proved impossible. The effort did not always receive full support, even from the various HUD principalities. It received practically no support from many

of the related programs located in other departments. Although the law gave HUD some authority to call on other departments for support, a cabinet secretary simply cannot issue orders to his peers.[33] But the problem is even deeper than that. The design of categorical programs, not to speak of the pressure groups who use them, makes them resistant to cooperative activities of the Model Cities type. Most categorical programs have specific eligibility formulas. Some are funneled through states, others are not. As Ralph Taylor, the original HUD assistant secretary for Model Cities, has said, "There was no one in HUD who really understood the way HEW's programs worked and what formulas controlled the disbursement of funds."[34] When a secretary was eager to support Model Cities efforts, as HEW Secretary John Gardner was, he was likely to be told by his technicians that there was no free money under the laws governing categorical programs. This was clearly one of the major flaws in the Model Cities Program and a major reason why it did not work as intended. The presidential task force had recommended that a multibillion dollar fund be given HUD for grants to localities for the mix of physical and social betterment to be carried out in selected neighborhoods. HUD's legislative counsel, Hilbert Fefferman, advised the task force that such an invasion of the turf of other departments and other congressional committees, even for selected neighborhoods, could not be passed. Faced with this realistic advice, the task force, the secretary of HUD, and the Bureau of the Budget chose to water down the proposal to give it a reasonable chance of passage. As submitted to the Congress, the proposal converted the multibillion dollar fund into one that HUD would use to supplement funds already available through itself and other agencies under existing law. Even with this major compromise of the original idea, Congress passed the Model Cities legislation by only a small margin and only after further compromise. Thus, faced with the political realities, the task force saw its initial idea transformed into a program with little chance of working effectively.[35]

Jay Janis, formerly a special assistant to HUD Secretary Robert C. Weaver and now HUD under secretary, confirms the necessity for this type of compromise. He has said the only way to overcome this rather basic defect is to plan and legislate three years ahead so that free funds will be available in the various non-HUD categorical programs.[36] This would be a big, perhaps impossible job, requiring action by many different congressional committees, each with its own turf to protect and its own interest groups to satisfy.

4. *The fight for local control.* The Model Cities Program generated struggles between mayors and neighborhood groups over who should make the local decisions. Neighborhood participation was an important element in the program. But when neighborhood leaders compete openly with the mayor for final authority, the result can only be impasse and even chaos. (It is an irony of history that many of the radical leaders of the time, who openly advocated rebellion against all government authority, were financed by the government itself through the Office of Economic Opportunity's War on Poverty and Model Cities programs.) In this regard, the Model Cities Program revealed the fragility of the bonds that hold many local governments together.

5. *Lack of local skill.* If the federal government proved unable to coordinate its efforts, local governments were even worse. Former HUD Secretary Robert Weaver has commented, "The localities displayed a lack of skill and sophistication" in discharging the formidable tasks expected of them.[37]

6. *Between the dream and the reality.*[38] Some have argued that the Wood task force was naive in its expectation that the Congress would accept so large a federal expenditure in a few cities. Given our political style of balancing special interests through compromise, events proved these observers to be correct. But whose plan more nearly reflected the larger public interest in curing slum problems? Is it still realistic to make policy on deep social ills in the fashion of a group of crafty men sitting around a poker table, each seeking to capture the major share of the pot? In this larger sense, Johnson's task force may well have had a more realistic vision of public good than the Congress was able to summon up, organized, as it is, in committees and subcommittees.

As it turned out, we will never know whether the original idea of Wood and his colleagues could have been made to work.

These doubts will remain, not only because the idea was gravely distorted on the road to passage, but also because what was enacted was given too little time to prove itself. George Bernard Shaw's comment about Christianity is perhaps apropos: "It's impossible to know whether it works because nobody has ever tried it."

Other Categorical Programs for Community Development

Other categorical programs replaced by the 1974 block grant legislation included (1) grants for the creation of open space, such as parks in built-up areas, urban beautification, and historic preservation; (2) grants for basic water, sewer, and other neighborhood facilities, such as community centers and facilities for health, recreation, and social services; and (3) loans for public facilities of various kinds. By 1974, nearly $2 billion of federal grants and loans had been made for these purposes in nearly 4,000 projects. Over half of the total consisted of grants for basic neighborhood water and sewer facilities.

These programs will not be discussed in detail here. They all can improve the physical face of the central city and thus reinforce the objectives of urban renewal and model cities. As discussed in chapter 4 the water and sewer programs can also supply important support to urban planning.

Another approach to inner-city revival—not explictly embraced in the 1974 block grant legislation—deserves brief mention. It is the idea of building new towns in-town, towns that are comparable in nearly every way except location to the new communities discussed in chapter 4. This idea was advocated by Harvey Perloff at least fifteen years ago.

Specific efforts to build new towns in-town have been few, and most have failed. They follow two approaches: (1) the use of vacant land in or near the central city, and (2) the development of new towns on inner-city land already developed. An intensive effort at the first approach was ordered by President Johnson in the mid-1960s. He believed that much vacant land suitable for this purpose could be found on abandoned military and other reservations, for example. His imagination was stimulated by the fact that in Washington, D.C., a large area of practically vacant land existed very close

to downtown Washington. HUD assembled an expert team, led
by Richard L. Steiner, head of the Urban Renewal Program
during the Eisenhower administration, and the search began.
After much frustration, eight locations were finally identified.
Despite much effort, none got off the ground—for a variety of
reasons, including a lack of statutory authority, difficulties in
achieving interdepartmental cooperation, and the unwillingness of local military commanders to respond to the wishes of
the Pentagon. This experience is documented in a 1972
publication of the Urban Institute.[39] There is reason to believe,
however, that the District of Columbia project has since been
revived.

The second approach (development of a new town in an
already built-up inner city area) is perhaps best exemplified by
the Cedar-Riverside project in Minneapolis, close to the main
campus of the University of Minnesota. This project was
assisted under HUD's New Communities Program. It, too, is in
trouble. Harvey Perloff has analyzed this and other efforts at
new towns in-town in a recent book, which also gives his views
on how the job can be done and the types of federal assistance
needed.[40]

Both of these approaches to inner-city revitalization have
great promise. But the idea remains a gleam in the eye.

Summing Up

We shall now attempt to reach some broad conclusions from
our discussion of the block grant, urban renewal, and model
cities approaches to central-city revitalization. Each program
was flawed in some way. None of the three proved to be the
hoped-for method for eliminating slums and reviving the
central city. Yet each had its merits as well.

The Urban Renewal Program was aimed at the major
problems of the central city. One of its problems was that the
actions required to achieve its various goals (improving the
conditions of run-down neighborhoods, raising the tax base,
attracting middle class families and business back to the central
city) proved to be mutually contradictory. Yet, urban renewal
clearance is a workable and needed method for accomplishing
several specific limited purposes. It works well for the clearance

and rebuilding of deteriorated central city commercial and industrial areas, as well as for rock-bottom slums. It is needed for spot (limited) clearance in the improvement of residential areas. It is an appropriate tool for ridding slum areas of the further curse of abandoned housing units, especially where many residences are still above the slum level.

The Model Cities Program was also clearly aimed at the most difficult of central-city problems. Its greatest merit was its recognition that slum problems are as much social as physical and that both aspects need to be treated in a coordinated way. As finally passed by the Congress, the Model Cities Program was doomed to fail. As an experiment (the original idea of the Johnson task force), it is unfortunate that it was not carried out. For we must learn how to deal with the complicated and not fully understood physical and social web of urban decay. Experimentation is probably the best and cheapest way to learn. The most expensive and futile is to throw massive, untested programs at the problem. This view is shared by President Carter's top economic adviser, Charles L. Schultze.[41]

The 1974 Block Grant Program has its strengths and its weaknesses. It was not targeted at problems with which it is designed to deal. Too much of the money went to suburban jurisdictions and even to nonurban areas, which have few, if any, of the problems to which the program is directed. According to Stuart Eizenstat, director of the President's Domestic Council, the Carter administration recognizes this limitation and has urged the Congress to target block grants more to the poor and to increase the secretary's discretionary fund.[42] (Incidentally, these changes would make the program more categorical in character.) These Carter proposals are in the right direction. Whether they go far enough to overcome some of the Block Grant Program's fundamental weaknesses is open to question. If the Carter administration insists on **sticking with the block grant approach (one that is bound to** become less block grant and more categorical and restriction-ridden), it should make very basic changes in the distribution formula to eliminate the formula's negative impact on metropolitan government, to prevent local governments from misusing the funds, and to preserve the important national purposes embodied in the law. (The changes in block grants proposed by the Carter administration and passed by the Congress in later 1977 are discussed in the final section of this chapter.)

This writer has become convinced that, on balance, categorical programs, properly simplified and stripped of unnecessarily detailed review and red tape, are the most appropriate methods for achieving specific, high-priority national objectives—such as improving slum conditions and relieving other urgent problems of the inner city. Block grants, along with general revenue sharing, are a more appropriate method for federal relief of the fiscal problems being experienced by many, but not all, local government jurisdictions. This is an important public purpose if the funds are transferred to jurisdictions in real need. This view does not mean that the urban renewal and model cities programs should be reinstated in their original form. It does mean that categorical programs, properly streamlined and without excessive bureaucratic controls, can better serve the national purpose. The deliberate design of such a program or programs is better than having the Block Grant Program with all its inherent weaknesses become, willy-nilly, another categorical program without design. This can easily result from attempts at adjustment (some of which have already occurred) and from the modifications likely to come out of this year's congressional review. We had had enough of that. Devising a realistic program of federal assistance for central-city renewal will require deliberate thought, experimentation, and better understanding of matters we now only dimly perceive. This is not an argument for inaction. It is an argument for carefully conceived, realistic, workable programs, programs that draw on the lessons of the past as well as new understanding. It is an argument for responsible government.

Block Grants Revised: A Forward Step Backward

The Housing and Community Development Act of 1977, signed into law by President Carter on October 17, 1977, is a move in the right direction, though it can hardly be called the basic rethinking of urban revitalization policy referred to in the previous paragraph. The 1977 law made numerous modifications in block grants for community development. Four of these legislative changes are so fundamental as to modify the objectives as well as the character of the Block Grant Program.

First, the 1977 law establishes new formulas for the distribution of block grant funds. The previous distribution formula (based on population, extent of poverty, and housing overcrowding) was retained. But two additional fund allocation formulas were added. The applicant's grant is based on whichever formula produces a greater amount of money. For metropolitan cities and urban counties, the alternate formula is based on: (1) the extent of growth lag in the city or county (counted once); (2) the extent of poverty (counted one and one-half times); and (3) the age of the city's or county's housing (counted two and one-half times). For states and for nonmetropolitan areas, the alternative formula established by the 1977 legislation is based upon: (1) the age of housing (counted two and one-half times); (2) the extent of poverty (counted one and one-half times); and (3) population (counted once). This change in the distribution formula for block grants is intended to provide greater assistance for older central cities that are declining owing to loss of population and business to their own suburbs or to other parts of the country.

Second, the block grant provisions of the 1977 legislation are laced with injunctions that funds should be used primarily to meet the needs of low-income and moderate-income families.

Third, the 1977 law establishes a new Block Grant Program—Urban Development Action Grants. The purpose of this program is to assist—through neighborhood revitalization—severely distressed cities and urban counties experiencing loss of population, physical and economic deterioration, housing abandonment, and declining tax base. The UDAG program, as it is called, authorizes a multiyear commitment of funds directed toward the revitalization of a specific distressed neighborhood.

Fourth, the 1977 revisions to the Community Development

Block Grant Program lay great stress on the rehabilitation of run-down housing and the revitalization of distressed, slum neighborhoods.

These modifications in the Block Grant Program for community development appear to remedy some, but not all, of the program's initial weaknesses. (These weaknesses are discussed earlier in this chapter.) If effectively promulgated and strongly administered, these changes could improve the Block Grant Program considerably. The law's modification in the fund distribution formula as well as its emphatic emphasis on serving low-income and moderate-income persons could go far toward redirecting block grants to the urban problems of highest national priority. The same is true of the law's new multiyear Urban Development Action Grants. Central cities that are severely distressed because of loss of population, jobs, and tax revenues clearly need federal assistance more than those that are growing and prosperous.

On the other hand, the Block Grant Program still tends to direct federal funds to too many suburban jurisdictions that need them least. This diffusion of limited funds to too many local jurisdictions is growing and will be hard to reverse. Once a prosperous suburban community has tasted federal funds, it is naturally reluctant to relinquish them. Beyond that, no provision of the 1977 law addresses the fact that block grants go to many individual urban jurisdictions, thus tending to work against the metropolitan-wide cooperation so essential to the solution of many of our gravest urban problems. Whether the 1977 amendments to the Block Grant Program will make it easier for mayors to resist political pressures to spend funds on low-priority needs remains to be seen.

One thing is clear: the 1977 changes make the Block Grant Program less a revenue-sharing device and bring it closer to the categorical programs it replaced in 1974. The new law's principal step forward—Urban Development Action Grants— will probably become a step backward to something similar to the early urban renewal program. This is not necessarily a bad thing. For the original urban renewal program was aimed at the real problems of the inner city. So was the Model Cities Program. Had the original urban renewal program been administered with more flexibility and less detailed review of local proposals, it could have produced that sensible balance between federal oversight and local freedom that the new approach might achieve. A step backward, seasoned by the wisdom of experience, can become a step forward.

6
Housing Needs
and the Housing Market

This chapter will deal with the importance of HUD's mission to provide an adequate supply of "decent, safe and sanitary housing" for all Americans.[1] It will discuss the way the housing market works and the characteristics that set it apart from other markets for consumer goods. It will also cover the legislative pledge to provide decent housing for all, especially for the poor living in substandard housing; the quantitative national housing goals established in 1968; the difficulties of measuring total housing need; and the difficulty of measuring the amount of substandard housing. This chapter is introductory to the three following chapters, which deal with HUD's programs for supporting general housing construction and for subsidizing housing for the poor and near poor.

HUD's Housing Mission

It is not entirely an accident that the first word in HUD's name is housing and that its immediate predecessors were the Housing and Home Finance Agency and, before that, the National Housing Agency. Before any coordinating agency existed, the 1930s had seen the creation of at least three separate agencies concerned with housing. Improving housing conditions for the population as a whole and particularly for the poor is thus a HUD mission of great importance. This is not surprising. Housing is, along with food and clothing, one of man's most fundamental needs. Government involvement with housing is not unique in this country. Almost every country in the Western world has developed supports for and controls over housing. In Britain about half of all housing is government-subsidized. Scarcely anywhere is housing left to the free play of market forces alone.

The Housing Market

Like most other commodities, housing is constructed, sold, and purchased largely through the interplay of supply and demand. Government controls and supports modify the behavior of the market, but do not substitute for it. The market for housing has special characteristics that make its behavior different from the market for popcorn, pins, and pianos.

Housing as a Commodity

As a commodity that is bought and sold in the market, housing is peculiar in several ways. First, it lasts a very long time—thirty years or more, sometimes over a hundred years. Second, housing is fixed and immobile. Once built, it cannot be moved except at great expense. Thus, an oversupply in one place cannot be shifted to another, where demand is greater. In this regard, it differs from automobiles, works of art, and nearly everything else sold to the consumer. Third, a house is by far the most costly expenditure ever made by the typical family. Fourth, a house is not a self-contained commodity. It is a complicated combination of elements. It is a structure; it is also land. It is dependent on streets, sewer lines, gas, and electricity—all provided by someone else. The value of a house is also much influenced by the value of the houses that surround it, by the character of the neighborhood. All these things make the house a unique consumer commodity.

Reliance on Mortgage Finance

Because a home is a family's largest investment, its purchase depends heavily on the availability of mortgage financing. About 95 percent of all new homes and the overwhelming majority of existing homes are purchased with the aid of credit; obviously, credit allows the cost of the house to be repaid in relatively small amounts over a number of years. If mortgage financing is not available, few houses can be sold. Also, the mortgage terms (down payment and repayment period) and the interest rate charged by the lender greatly influence the number of families who can purchase a home.

Housing Markets Are Local

The interplay of housing supply and housing demand—what any market is about—is primarily a local matter. There are as many housing markets as there are cities and towns where houses are bought and sold. In fact, there are more. A large metropolitan area can have several housing markets, simply because the distance from one part of the city to another is so great. Beyond that, a single metropolitan area can have separate markets for units available for rental and purchase, as well as for units of various sizes and prices. As Ernest Fisher, one of FHA's founding fathers, put it, "the [local] real estate market cannot be analyzed as a single market, but only as a series of localized, fragmented, and particularized markets for a wide variety of rights to assorted services flowing from numerous unique sources, and only roughly comparable one with the other."[2] At the same time, certain national supply and demand forces affect housing costs, such as interest rates and the cost of lumber and other materials.

Market Miscalculations

Because a house cannot be moved, because its purchase is so dependent on the availability of financing, and because local markets are so fragmented, the housing market is harder to predict than most markets. Likewise, the results of a miscalculation take longer to correct themselves. (As this is written, many places in Florida are experiencing a serious housing surplus, particularly in condominiums. As years pass, demand slowly catches up with supply. In the meantime, builders are going broke, and even banks that made the loans are in trouble.) These complicated circumstances make the analysis and prediction of housing markets a highly uncertain task at best.

The instability of local housing markets is intensified by what might be called the "law of mutual miscalculations."

Because the building industry consists of so many small firms, the miscalculations of one are multiplied by those of many competitors in a way that reinforces the collective error exponentially.

The Theory of Filtering

The filtering process is an important element of the local housing market. It works like this. New construction is introduced into the housing market and is purchased by families of relatively high income. To buy a new house, they sell an older house, which has deteriorated somewhat in value, to a family not quite as well off as they are. Over time, the same house, as its price is reduced relative to new homes, becomes available to families of lower and lower income. Thus, families, as their incomes improve, filter up the housing ladder, and a house, as it ages, filters down with successive moves. This chain of moves causes the total supply of housing, new and existing, to serve a wider range of family incomes.

According to Anthony Downs, the "trickle down" process works very well for most households in urban areas. The exception, he says, is the very poor—who are excluded. For them, the process is a social disaster: it forces them "to concentrate together in the worst-quality housing located in older neighborhoods near the urban center," thus helping create slums.[3]

The National Commission on Urban Problems, of which Downs was a member, said of the filtering process:

> Undeniably the trickle-down theory does work for part of the population, but it falls short of supplying enough housing for low-income families principally because: (1) the availability of the lowest cost housing is not always where the poor can get to it, and because (2) so much of the cheapest available housing is substandard . . . virtually all slum housing is filter-down housing—which is proof enough of its inadequacy.[4]

It must also be remembered that the process of filtering works best only when new housing production is high and housing markets are relatively loose, that is, when housing production exceeds household formation by a good margin. When new housing production is relatively slow, the filtering process bogs down, and many families cannot find suitable housing.

The effectiveness of the filtering process has been debated for decades. Many argue, with considerable validity, that the filtering process does not even serve well many families of moderate, much less low, income. This argument is fortified by the current inflation in house prices and the fact that the prices of most existing homes are only slightly below those of new ones.

One other characteristic of the housing market limits the filtering process. When a housing unit has, after passing through the hands of many households, become no longer useful, there is no way to dispose of it. This contrasts markedly with the automobile market. When an automobile has outlived its usefulness, it disappears from the market (it is put in a junkyard or crushed with heavy machinery and its metal recycled). But the useless house often remains standing, whether occupied or abandoned. It is a blight in the neighborhood. This constipation of the housing market is a damaging defect of the market mechanism.

Since any reasonably effective filtering must be triggered by relatively high production of new housing, two further facts are worth mention. First, annual new housing production has lagged behind household formation since about 1973. Second, at an annual production rate of 1.5 million units, we are adding less than 2 percent to the total existing housing stock. Thus, filtering is hardly a major factor in upgrading housing for low-income families, at least in the short run.

Government Intervention

Despite the fact that there is a private housing market—in the sense that individual builders, sellers, and buyers exercise their free will in consummating thousands of transactions each week—the hand of government is heavy on the housing market. Local governments influence the housing market through building regulations, zoning, subdivision regulations, eminent domain, and in other ways. The federal government influences the housing market through its support of housing finance. The federal and local governments also influence the housing market indirectly—among the many ways are the property tax, tax exemptions, and the federal income tax.[5] Miles Colean, also one of the founding fathers of the FHA and an influential writer on housing and urban matters, has said, "Real estate activity and its financing [are] more fully subject to governmental influence, regulation, and control than any part of the economy not distinctly of a public or public utility character."[6] This fact is not reported to imply that all such public influence over the housing market is undesirable. It does suggest, however, the need for wise and consistent use of these public influences.

Housing Needs and Goals

The Goals

In the Housing Act of 1949, Congress pledged the nation to produce enough housing to provide every American with "a decent home and a suitable living environment." In 1968, the Congress required the president to establish a quantitative ten-year goal for the annual production needed to fulfill this pledge. It also required the president to report each year to the Congress on progress made toward reaching the housing goals. The goals it established called for the production within a ten-year period (1969-1978) of 26 million housing units—20 million without subsidy and 6 million with subsidy to meet the housing needs of the poor and near poor who could not afford decent housing without public assistance. Thus, the goal implied an average annual housing production of 2 million unsubsidized units and 600,000 subsidized units. It was expected that the annual rate of production would rise gradually over the decade as the capacity of the industry increased.

The 26-million-unit goal was arrived at by calculations familiar to housing economists. It included over 13 million units to accommodate estimated increases in household formation (families, individuals, or groups of individuals living together in a separate housing unit)—household formation, not population increase, has long been recognized as the foundation on which the demand for additional housing construction rests. It included additional production to increase vacant units substantially. Clearly, a reasonable, but not excessive, vacancy rate is necessary to permit population mobility and to promote filtering. It included production to compensate for units abandoned because of population shifts and the demolition of existing units. Finally, it included the construction of enough new units to replace dilapidated units (not capable of being rehabilitated) and those expected to become dilapidated during the ten-year period.[7]

Thus, the 1968 national housing goals represented a national commitment to eliminate all substandard housing in the country in a ten-year period and to build enough to take care of new households. It was a bold and heroic promise, very much in tune with the other large domestic commitments of the Johnson administration.

Their Weaknesses

The housing goals established by the Congress and the president were not without critics. Charles L. Schultze, then with the Brookings Institution, wrote that no such precise measure of housing need is possible and that the concept itself is a dubious one. He also observed that the goals contemplated an annual rate of housing construction about one million units higher than projected household formation, a greater surplus than had occurred during the previous twenty years, and suggested that the high vacancy ratio this would produce might actually discourage new housing starts.[8] Henry Aaron, also of the Brookings Institution, also questioned the realism of the goals, calling them "more an expression of political commitment than of realistic forecasting."[9]

Housing economist Leo Grebler of UCLA recently said, "the whole idea of quantitative housing goals is phony." Former Secretary Weaver, though not as critical of the concept of goals, thinks that an annual goal each year would be more realistic than a ten-year goal.[10]

As a measure of the basic shelter needs of the American people, there are various weaknesses in the concept of national housing goals. First, the idea of a national goal is, to a considerable degree, fictitious: housing markets are local, not national. Second, much of what the goals reflect is market demand, which is not necessarily the same thing as urgent need. Some household formation does represent real need, for example, when young people marry and seek a house in which to raise their families, when a family is required to move from one city to another, or when an older couple or widow seeks a smaller place in which to live. But much household formation is neither a biological nor a social imperative. A household is formed when a young person with a job decides to leave the parental home and take an apartment to become more independent. A household is formed when two or more single men or women decide to rent an apartment or a home to live together. A household is formed at colleges when one or more students decide to forsake dormitory life and rent an apartment or home near the campus. These household formations are often desirable, but they hardly represent indispensable housing need. The same is true when families move from one good house to a larger, better-located house. These cases reflect economic affluence more than vital shelter requirements. However, it must be recognized that in a free market, the less basic needs can and do compete with the more basic ones. And when supply is limited, the unmarried young singles may prevent the husband-wife families from satisfying their housing needs.

What Is Decent Housing?

Now let us turn to the goal calculations that identified the number of subsidized housing units to be built (6 million over ten years). For decades, decent housing was defined as housing that was not dilapidated or overcrowded and that contained a private bath for each family with hot and cold running water. These characteristics, reported by the Census Bureau every ten years, were the only relevant guides available. The Census Bureau and nearly everyone else knew that this was a poor standard for identifying unsatisfactory housing. The National Commission on Urban Problems characterized it as the definition of a nearly watertight box with plumbing.[11] That is, the census-derived definition tells us what plumbing exists, but not how it works. It tells us whether the structure appears on the surface to be run-down but nothing about its basic structural soundness. It fails to reflect the size of the structure, its interior finish, its fire resistance, the light and ventilation it provides, its storage space, its kitchen and bathroom equipment, and many other things. The census-derived definition provides no hint of the quality of the neighborhood in which the house is located and nothing about the adequacy of public services. No one seriously believes that we now have in this country a satisfactory basis for measuring substandard housing. There is, therefore, no reliable way to estimate how much of it exists.

We know that our urban areas contain much substandard housing, probably more than given in the estimates on which the housing goals were based—simply because of the very crude measures that had to be used. But no one can say just how great the number is. The latest attempt was made by the MIT-Harvard Center for Urban Studies. Their estimate of current "housing deprivation" (including those who must pay too much for decent housing as well as those who live in substandard housing or substandard neighborhoods) is about 16 million.[12] This is far larger than the number of substandard units used in calculating the housing goals.

The Importance of the Goals

As technically difficult as it is to calculate housing goals, the fundamental significance of what the Congress did in 1968 should not be obscured. For the first time in the federal government's nearly forty-year involvement in housing, it had specifically pledged the production of an adequate quantity of housing for the nation. It thereby suggested that improved housing should become a matter of high national priority.

Thus, although there are differences of opinion on the appropriate numbers and even questions about the realism of explicit, quantitative goals, particularly if spread over a long period, there is general agreement that a high volume of housing production is needed in the coming years. In mid-1975, HUD estimated that "from 1.9 million to almost 2.4 million housing units would be needed annually just to respond to net additional household formation, household

mobility, and replacement of net housing inventory losses."[13]
The latest estimate of housing economist Anthony Downs is
2.6 million per year, exactly what the 1968 goals called for.

Although good housing will by no means solve all of our
urban problems, the production of an adequate and steady
volume is vital to urban improvement. The support of housing
production, both subsidized and nonsubsidized, is one of
HUD's major jobs and most difficult challenges. HUD
secretary, Patricia Harris, has publicly committed her department to a high level of housing production. She has also
stressed the need for stability in the volume of housing
production.[14]

7
Financing Housing Construction and Exchange

This chapter is concerned with the mortgage financing necessary to support both an adequate volume of construction and the purchase and sale of the large stock of existing housing. Financing for both is needed to facilitate the efficient performance of the numerous housing markets to be found in our urban areas. Federal subsidies for households unable to afford decent housing because of low income will be discussed in a later chapter.

Here we shall discuss HUD's tools for supporting housing markets through support of private mortgage lending as well as the significant federal aids to housing financing that operate outside of HUD. We shall examine the sharply reduced influence of HUD's Federal Housing Administration (FHA), the reasons for its great decline, and whether FHA is any longer needed. We shall argue that a revitalized FHA is needed to support the housing market. We shall also examine the performance of the now private Federal National Mortgage Association (FNMA) and discuss the government's other mortgage finance supports (the VA Loan Guaranty Program [VA] and the Federal Home Loan Bank Board [FHLBB], both of which are outside of HUD).

HUD's Housing Finance Tools

HUD possesses one primary and one supporting tool to carry out its mission of encouraging the production of an adequate volume of new housing (whatever the exact number may be) and of facilitating the efficient use of the existing housing supply through the purchase and sale of older dwellings. The primary tool is the FHA, which designed a system of federal insurance of privately made mortgage loans to stimulate the flow of mortgage funds. The supporting tool is the FNMA, popularly known as "Fannie Mae," which was originally in the New Deal's Reconstruction Finance Corporation (RFC), then transferred to the Housing and Home Finance Agency (HHFA), and in 1968, made a private corporation under federal charter and operating under the general guidance of the secretary of HUD. As a private corporation, FNMA's function is to buy and sell sound FHA-insured, VA-guaranteed, and conventional mortgages in the so-called secondary market, that is, after the mortgages have been originated by a private lender. The purpose is to encourage lenders to make mortgage loans because the lending institution knows that if it needs to, it can sell the mortgages to FNMA. In banker's parlance, an FHA-insured loan is a "liquid" investment, a highly valued condition. Other of FNMA's original functions (purchase of high-risk mortgages and purchase of FHA-insured mortgages at below-market-interest rates) were transferred to the Government National Mortgage Association (GNMA), which is still a part of HUD. The privatization of FNMA has reduced HUD's control over its activities, thus making it a kind of stepson rather than a blood relative. The law, however, gives to the HUD secretary stronger authority over FNMA operations than any HUD secretary has so far chosen to exercise.

The Tools HUD Lacks

As noted in chapter 2, HUD did not include all the federal activities related to its missions. Mortgage finance is a good example. Several federal programs have a substantial impact on mortgage lending and thus on home building and home purchase, but they are not within HUD's domain.

The program of loan guarantees (along with some direct loans for veterans) is operated by the Veterans Administration. This program is similar to the FHA program, except that it does not follow the insurance principle, with reserves and premiums, but provides a simple federal guarantee against loss. Its loan terms are also somewhat more liberal, equalling 100 percent of a house's value. A substantial volume of mortgage loans has been guaranteed under the VA program since it was created in 1944. A total of 9.3 million VA loans amounting to over $131 billion had been made as of March 1977.

Even more important, the Federal Home Loan Bank Board (FHLBB) still thrives outside HUD's purview. The FHLBB was once in HHFA, but congressional action made it an independent agency. The FHLBB (1) serves as a central bank for savings and loan associations (much like the Federal Reserve Board does for commercial banks) through advances to member savings and loan associations, which provide essential support should one of its members experience a squeeze because its total loans exceed its deposits; (2) stimulates and charters the creation of additional savings and loan associations where housing needs and financial circumstances justify; (3) insures (through its Federal Savings and Loan Insurance Corporation) the deposits, or savings, placed in savings and loan associations by individual families, a function almost identical to the Federal Deposit Insurance Corporation's support of commercial banks; (4) regulates, supervises, and audits the operations of savings and loan associations to assure their financial soundness.

For over four decades, this galaxy of federal supports has generated what is now by far the largest single source of mortgage loans in the nation.

In 1970, the savings and loan associations were given further important support by legislation that authorized FNMA to purchase, hold, and sell mortgages not insured or guaranteed by FHA and VA. Therefore, FNMA support is now available for mortgages originated by savings and loan associations and other lending institutions. The same law also created the Federal Home Loan Mortgage Corporation, which is managed by the FHLBB. This, too, provides a secondary market for savings and loan mortgages as well as for FHA and VA mortgages.

The savings and loan industry, spawned and supported by

the FHLBB, has grown in size and vigor as the country's population and urbanization have increased. It is a highly competitive "growth industry" in every sense of that Wall Street term. In 1976, it could advertise, with accuracy, that savings and loan associations made more home mortgage loans than all other types of lending institutions combined. (In the fall of 1976, 56 percent of all mortgage loans were made by savings and loans.)

The absence of the VA Loan Guaranty Program and of the vastly powerful FHLBB constitutes a significant gap in HUD's capacity to influence and coordinate federal support for private mortgage lending.

FHA's Decline

From 1934 through 1974, FHA insured about $190 billion in mortgage loans, making it the biggest insurance operation in the world. The FHA insured over 11 million home mortgage loans for the purchase of new and existing homes and over 2 million loans for rental housing units. For years, FHA-insured loans financed from a quarter to a third of all new homes constructed each year as well as a substantial volume of existing home sales.

The FHA's position in total mortgage lending began a gradual decline after 1950. Its share of total housing units started was 18 percent in 1950; less than 3 percent by early 1974. As the volume dropped, the percentage of so-called conventional loans (largely by savings and loan associations but also by commercial banks and others) jumped from 62 percent in 1950 to 89.3 percent in the early part of 1974. The once influential FHA, a Samson with shorn locks, has lost its clout.

There are a number of reasons why the FHA's role in private mortgage lending has faded. Some reflect the growth of the savings and loan industry. Others have to do with the deterioration in FHA's own performance.

External Causes

1. *Growth of savings and loan associations.* Full of vigor and intensely competitive, savings and loan associations have greatly grown in number. Their total assets, 90 percent of

which go into mortgage loans, have also grown enormously. In 1935, all savings and loan associations had assets of $6 billion; by 1977 they had more than $300 billion. They have made many mortgage loans that would otherwise have been insured by FHA. Private mortgage loans have not, however, won out over FHA's federally assisted loans. Although the savings and loan industry's publicity often suggests that its loans are "private," this is not true. Their loans receive just as much support from the federal government as do those insured by FHA, though the type of support is different. The FHLBB provides savings and loan associations with federal insurance of deposits, advances from the FHLBB, and federal chartering. For those purposes, the FHLBB can borrow at least $2.5 billion from the Treasury Department.

2. *Liberalization of mortgage terms.* In the late 1930s, the only long-term, low-down-payment loans available were those insured by FHA. But over the years, the savings and loans, mutual savings banks, and commercial banks have progressively liberalized the terms on their mortgages. Changes in FHLBB's policy and changes in state and federal laws have made this possible. Today, a conventional loan can be made for a thirty-year term with a 5 percent down payment. In some places and under some conditions, a non-FHA-insured loan can have even more liberal terms than an FHA-insured loan.

3. *Private mortgage insurance.* FHA's competitive position has suffered from another development: the growth, since the late 1950s, of private mortgage insurance companies. These companies, the largest of which is the Mortgage Guaranty Insurance Corporation (MGIC), insure the top portion of a conventional loan. These companies have multiplied and grown rapidly. They have made it possible, and presumably safe, for the savings and loan associations, mutual savings banks and other lending institutions to offer more liberal loan terms and thus to compete with the FHA. By 1972 private mortgage insurance written had grown to 60 percent of the loan insurance of FHA and VA combined.

4. *Secondary market support.* For many years, the FHA (and VA) were unique government instrumentalities: only their loans could be purchased by FNMA. In 1970 this changed.

The Emergency Home Finance Act made conventional mortgages eligible for purchase by FNMA—an unprecedented shift in federal policy. Previous policy had limited FNMA purchase to FHA and VA loans for several reasons. FHA and VA loans were uniform in character and in underwriting standards. Furthermore, they both were backed by the full faith and credit of the United States. These factors were thought to make them solely suitable for trading in the secondary mortgage market and for purchase by FNMA. This radical change in policy clearly gave the conventional loan—whether made by a savings and loan association, a mutual savings bank, a commercial bank, or a life insurance company—a much greater competitive advantage over an FHA-insured loan. The 1976 law went even further. It created another government-supported secondary market for conventional loans—the Federal Home Loan Mortgage Corporation. Not surprisingly, it was created as an adjunct to the FHLBB, with its board serving as directors of the corporation. The reason for the creation of an additional secondary market facility was that the savings and loan associations were reluctant to use FNMA and wanted their own instrument. Thus, the conventional mortgage suddenly had not one, but two, crucial supports it had never before enjoyed. Both made it easier for them to usurp the very liberal mortgage terms once thought to be appropriate only with FHA or VA backing.

Internal Causes

There are also important internal reasons for FHA's fast fading role in channeling the flow of private funds into housing.

1. *Complexity and delay in FHA processing.* As the homebuilders are fond of reminding us, "time is money." They mean that extensive delays in responding to applications for mortgage loans cost them money in many ways. When construction costs are rising rapidly, long waits cost the builder even more and may make the proposed project infeasible. FHA's often tedious and prolonged review of loan applications makes builders as well as individual home purchasers reluctant to use its loan services, especially since every other type of

mortgage financing can be secured in much less time. Beyond that, use of FHA has become very complicated. Its programs are numerous and complex. Its regulations are equally so. All of this hardly encourages use of FHA's services.

2. *Poor management.* The organizational chaos at HUD (discussed in chapter 3) has had its effect on the FHA. Not only is the processing time longer, but different field offices use different criteria. No applicant can be sure he will receive the same decision—if he can get a decision—from one office as from another. This happens because no single person is steering the FHA ship.

3. *Front-end costs.* Various worthy objectives, especially environmental protection and racial equality, have been added to FHA's application requirements. These objectives become, in effect, conditions that must be met before the application for mortgage insurance can be processed. Among these worthy but added requirements are: (1) project selection criteria, to discourage segregation by race; (2) affirmative marketing, to assure equal access in marketing; (3) environmental impact analysis; and (4) evidence of equal opportunity employment practices in the production of housing. These all take time, however worthy their objectives are. The FHA has added so many worthy objectives to its loan application requirements that there is little wonder builders and others are reluctant to use it. If FHA is to stay alive, much less regain its proper place in financing of housing, something has to give.

4. *The delicate balancing between volume production and caution.* We discussed in chapter 3 the delicate balance that must be achieved between the pressure to produce at any cost and excessive caution and reluctance to make decisions. We did not elaborate on the fact that a liberal cycle is usually followed by a conservative cycle. This happened to FHA as a result of the criticisms and scandals in the early 1970s, which resulted largely from Secretary Romney's excessive pressure for volume. FHA personnel appear to have overreacted to this traumatic experience by putting their heads in the sand of extreme caution—a very human impulse. But this has not improved FHA's role in mortgage lending.

5. *Loss of professionalism.* For many years, FHA was blessed

with technical personnel who were well trained and skilled in the various technical specialties required to perform their jobs. In recent years, retirements and a reorganization often gave inexperienced people major responsibilities. The result is a weakening of FHA's professional competence.

6. *The penalties of success.* FHA's early success in demonstrating the feasibility of the long-term, low-down-payment mortgage and its adoption by all lending institutions, accounts, to some extent, for its own decline. In a sense, it is the victim of its own success. Ironically, the decline in the use of FHA's ironclad protection against losses on mortgage loans came about the time mortgage lending became much riskier owing to the elimination of the postwar housing shortages.

Is FHA Still Needed?

Given the rapid growth and increased federal support for conventional mortgage lending (non-FHA or VA-insured) and the decline of FHA as a major factor in normal mortgage lending, many are now asking whether the FHA is still needed. Some argue that the FHA, having pioneered in popularizing the low down payment, long-term mortgage, has done its job and should close its doors. Others argue that there are needs only a federal mortgage insurance system can meet. This question can be discussed in better perspective after we have examined FHA's early accomplishments.

FHA's Rise and Early Accomplishments

FHA was created in 1934 "to encourage improvement in housing standards and conditions"[1] and to stimulate the national economy by providing jobs for workers in the home construction and related industries. As originally conceived, FHA was a public insurance company designed to insure the risks involved in private mortgage lending. (It was also authorized to insure installment loans for home repairs and modernization, as a temporary measure. After many extensions, this authority was made permanent.) FHA charged premiums for its insurance, premiums based on actuarial calculations and out of which it accumulated reserves to cover losses. It was also expected to pay its operating costs from fees charged for its services. Its most significant original program, the insurance of home mortgages, included the idea of mutuality. Premiums collected in excess of actual losses were returned to home purchasers. Insurance claims were paid to lenders not in cash but in government debentures, a hedge against a run on the FHA insurance reserves.

FHA home mortgage insurance found willing users, but not without intensive efforts to persuade skeptical lenders of its merits and the profitability of such investments. Life insurance companies, mostly the small ones, were the first to dip their toes into the strange, chilly waters of FHA. Large life insurance companies and other types of lending institutions soon followed. In 1935, its first full year of operation, the FHA insured over 23,000 home mortgages, and by 1941 its annual volume topped 200,000 loans. Between 1935 and 1939, its insured loans for new housing units amounted to 24 percent of all homes built. From 1940 through 1944, it insured mortgages on almost half of the country's new home construction—a result of the restraints on mortgage lending imposed during World War II. The FHA's normal share in mortgage lending was closer to 25 percent.

The FHA plan was conceived by Winfield Riefler, a brilliant economist, in a committee ("task forces" had not yet become fashionable) President Franklin Roosevelt established to find a way to stimulate residential construction, a labor-intensive activity and therefore an obvious way to create jobs for the unemployed. Riefler's concept was supported vigorously by Marriner Eccles, then assistant secretary of the treasury and later chairman of the Federal Reserve Board.[2]

Roosevelt's committee originally wished to place the new FHA in the already existing Federal Home Loan Bank Board. John Fahey, a member of the president's committee and head of the FHLBB, not only opposed this proposal but also vigorously resisted the creation of an FHA; he believed it might prove a competitor in mortgage lending with the savings and loan associations, the clients of his FHLBB.[3] According to Miles Colean, Fahey's failure to grasp the implications of meshing the proposed FHA into the Federal Home Bank Board—thus creating an integrated federal mechanism to support mortgage lending—was a mistake of historical significance.[4] One observer put it this way, "We took John Fahey up the mountain top and showed him the kingdoms of the earth and he would have no part of it."[5]

Unlike several New Deal programs (some were declared unconstitutional, some passed quietly into oblivion, others survived but only amid continuous political controversy), the FHA quickly gained public and political acceptance. As housing student Catherine Bauer has so aptly described the birth of successful government agencies such as FHA: such schemes are first declared unconstitutional, then they are declared unsound and socialistic, and soon thereafter, the very same people are claiming, "I thought of it first." Like those who came over in the *Mayflower,* those who "had something to do with starting FHA" are now legion.[6]

Dr. Raymond Saulnier, chairman of the Council of Economic Advisers under President Eisenhower and an authority on housing finance, has said that he considered FHA one of the greatest social inventions of the 1930s.[7]

The early accomplishments of FHA are many.

1. *Organizational competence.* Beyond the simple, but ingenious, concept embodied in the system of mortgage insurance, the FHA was organized by several men of singular skill and vision. The second administrator of FHA was Stewart McDonald, a man of strong, commanding personality with great leadership skills and an unusual capacity to deal with the Congress. Among the others was Miles Colean, an architect turned economist and later the author of several important books on housing and urban problems. Colean soon brought Frederick M. Babcock and Ernest Fisher into the new agency. Babcock was a brilliant and innovative real estate appraiser. Fisher was a noted real estate economist, later a professor at Columbia University. Also on the scene early was William Flanders, a successful and persuasive New York real estate operator.

FHA's guides for real estate appraisal were developed by Babcock, and they were classic in their ingenuity. Even today, they have an impact on the assessment of mortgage risks. Colean developed FHA's property and subdivision standards.

Fisher developed FHA's system of analyzing local housing markets as well as its highly regarded system of operating and actuarial statistics. Flanders, Colean, and Babcock selected and deployed FHA's original staff, including its far-flung field offices. FHA's organizational structure was sound, and the personnel were of rare competence. The quality of the staff assembled reflected not only the good judgment of the men involved but also the Great Depression, which made it possible to attract highly trained architects, land planners, appraisers, credit experts, and administrators at the low salaries then paid by the federal government. To train its technical staff, an effective apprenticeship program was instituted, something that HUD needs today.

In the early years, the FHA trained an entire generation of housing experts, including several who were later to play a leading role in public housing. Moreover, the system of mortgage risk rating, created by these rather special men at FHA, has been copied by nearly all the country's responsible mortgage lenders. Unfortunately, as we shall see later, the performance of these able men was seriously flawed by a blind spot with respect to the just claims of ethnic and racial minorities.

2. *Reform of residential financing.* FHA did not invent the long-term, low-down-payment, fully amortizing mortgage with uniform payments spread over the life of the debt. (This was done by Roosevelt's temporary real estate rescue operation, the Home Owners Loan Corporation.) But FHA did popularize this significant advance in mortgage financing, and it did prove its soundness as well as its benefits for home purchasers. Because this type of mortgage has become virtually universal today, it is difficult to realize what a revolution this was in the 1930s.

Before the Great Depression, and certainly contributing to it, lenders considered a ten-year home mortgage to be long-term. Many mortgages ran only one, two, or three years, with most of the loan amount due in one large payment at the end of the short term. At the end of this short period, the home purchaser faced great uncertainties. Could he persuade the lender to renew his mortgage? At what interest rate? If he failed to get a renewal, he often lost his home. The standard plots in the melodramas of the time were not entirely fiction: this type of financing greatly contributed to the record level of home mortgages foreclosed during the Great Depression. FHA thus revolutionized home mortgage financing. Perhaps the most important measure of the mortgage lending revolution led by FHA is the fact that nearly all present mortgage lending, whether government assisted or not, follows closely the model originally popularized by FHA.

Some have argued that long-term, low-down-payment mortgages add to the inflation in housing prices, that is, they cause families to think not of the price of a house but only of the down payment and monthly charges required. There is some truth to this. Others decry the modern habit of living on credit as a violation of the Protestant ethic of thrift and frugality. But however one views these matters, the FHA revolution was real.

3. *Increased volume of mortgage credit.* FHA's mortgage insurance and the revolution in lending practices it triggered made it possible for many more families to purchase homes. FHA also tapped new sources of funds for mortgages, such as insurance companies and eventually even pension funds. This perhaps explains President Eisenhower's affection for the FHA. He believed widespread home ownership strengthened the social fiber of the country.[8] Whether such homely and nostalgic virtues can indeed be ascribed to home ownership or not, many others felt the same way.

4. *Creation of a mass-production home building industry.* In the 1920s, the building of a home was a single, customized transaction. FHA changed all this. Not only did it provide a long-term, low-down-payment mortgage, it developed a conditional commitment to insure mortgages on homes not yet built, provided only that an acceptable purchaser was later found. This conditional commitment was based on FHA's examination of house plans, subdivision drawings, and its estimate of the house's value. This single step of providing an advance commitment for future financing markedly changed the home-building industry by making it possible for builders to plan and construct large subdivisions without identifying the particular purchasers in advance. This made possible

speculative, relatively large-scale home-building ventures. It introduced the true entrepreneur into the construction of dwellings. All this did not turn the home builder into a General Motors, but it was a revolution of no mean proportions. It was not long before all mortgage lenders, FHA-assisted or not, were making conditional commitments. The significance of this is that home building is the only major industry in this country where the consumer financing (through the conditional commitment) has to be arranged before the production financing can be secured. The typical builder takes his conditional commitments for consumer financing to his bank and uses them as security for a short-term construction loan, thus getting his working capital.

5. *Creation of a mortgage banking industry.* The FHA stimulated the creation of yet another industry. Because life insurance companies and similar capital sources have no local facilities for originating and servicing home mortgage loans, the mortgage banking industry came into being. Mortgage bankers perform several important functions. They originate mortgage loans locally, dealing with the builder and the FHA. They also service such loans by collecting monthly payments, handling delinquencies, foreclosures, and related matters. The mortgage banker has an important role. They make it possible for capital accumulated in New York, Boston, and other centers to be lent to home buyers in states and cities far distant. Thus, they distribute capital from centers that have more than can be used locally to distant places that have too little for their needs.

6. *Consumer protection.* It is often overlooked that an FHA-insured mortgage provides significant protections to the home purchaser. FHA requires that the house be constructed according to its carefully developed standards for structural soundness, fire protection, sewage disposal, lot size, subdivision planning, and many related things. It inspects the house while under construction and upon completion to assure a reasonable degree of conformance. In addition, FHA's credit reviews usually protected a capricious purchaser from getting into an obligation that was financially over his head.

7. *An ingenious form of government intervention.* There are a variety of ways in which government can and does intervene

in private affairs—e.g., through direct construction and through various types of direct control over producers and consumers. Rhetoric to the contrary, the government is involved in one way or another in most aspects of private enterprise, from subsidizing farmers to supporting airlines. Thus, the key issue today is not whether the government is involved, but how. The conception of Winfield Riefler and others who developed the FHA has some important virtues. The FHA did not seek to substitute its decisions for the multitude of complex decisions that can better be made by buyers and sellers in the market. Rather, it sought to influence and condition the range of choices available to individuals in the private market. It did not seek to repeal the strong forces of the market. Rather, it sought to redefine and enlarge the range of options available to those making their private decisions. It did not seek to stifle private and individual initiative. Rather, it sought to enlarge the choices available and the number who can participate in the free decisions relating to home purchase and sale.[9]

Many federal agencies attempt to substitute public for private decisions. Often they become so bogged down in the complexity of this job that they can neither cope with the volume nor be confident that their choices are right.

FHA's Debits

The FHA story is not all sweetness and light. Like any other human enterprise, FHA had its blemishes, one of which was especially serious.

Racial discrimination. As we shall see in chapter 11, the early FHA abetted and even led racial discrimination in the housing it supported. Although this was prevalent in the national society at the time, FHA should nevertheless have displayed far more vision and leadership than it did. The record of public housing, during the same years, was strikingly better.

Excessive red tape. Unfortunately, despite the inherent simplicity of its original design, FHA has gradually become clogged with red tape and inclined to second-guess every applicant's decisions in unnecessary detail. But these are barnacles on the FHA system; they are not inherent and can be removed. To some extent, FHA's present complexity reflects the fact that the Congress has greatly increased the number of FHA programs and has done so in a manner that creates excessive diversity and confusion in its program requirements.

Urban sprawl. FHA, perhaps unknowingly, fostered expensive urban sprawl by assisting home builders to scatter subdivisions far and wide on outlying land. Ironically, its subdivision standards were a good influence. But a well-planned subdivision is not the same as a well-planned total suburban environment. FHA displayed little vision of what good general planning is.

A captive of its clients. As too often happens in government, FHA sometimes became the pawn of its clients—mortgage lenders, homebuilders, and real estate dealers. Their interests did not always coincide with the public interest. For many years, FHA disdained publicly assisted housing for the poor, a sentiment that public housers heatedly reciprocated in their attitude toward FHA and its programs. An incident will illustrate the extent of this early rivalry. Stewart McDonald, the head of FHA, boarded an airplane in New York and found himself sitting beside Nathan Straus, who then headed the U.S. Housing Authority. McDonald attempted to strike up a conversation by asking Straus how things were going. Straus's brusque reply was, "Does Macy's tell Gimbels?"[10] Such animosity between two arms of the federal government, both created to improve housing conditions, is hardly healthy and can be destructive.

An Effective, Revived FHA Is Much Needed

Despite the great growth in conventional mortgage financing (especially that done by savings and loan associations) and the decline of FHA, an FHA with the vigor and efficiency of the past is still needed. There are a number of reasons why this is true.

1. *Conventional financing serves fewer families.* Savings and loan and other conventional financing, even when backed by private mortgage insurance, is a highly selective process. It chooses the best risks, namely, the best-located properties being purchased by families with relatively ample financial re-

sources, families of relatively higher income. This situation is changing somewhat, but without a revived FHA, many Americans would be deprived of mortgage financing. This would be a step backward.

2. *Important sources of mortgage funds would be lost.* The absence of a workable FHA would also permanently reduce the flow of funds into the mortgage market from sources that are not equipped to originate mortgage loans throughout the country. Through the system FHA generated, these institutions can make mortgage loans in reliance on FHA insurance and with the aid of the mortgage banking industry, which originates and services loans on their behalf.

3. *Efficient geographic distribution would be diminished.* One of the key functions of the FHA system is to make it possible to distribute mortgage funds from capital-surplus areas to capital-scarce areas. This is accomplished by the mortgage banking industry, supported by FHA's standardized mortgage instrument, which is readily acceptable in the secondary market. Without an effective FHA, such cross-country mortgage lending would be greatly curtailed.

4. *Rental housing would suffer.* Non-FHA-insured, or conventional, mortgage lending is available predominantly for the financing of one-family to four-family structures. Without an effective FHA, there would be less credit available for large-scale rental projects. This type of housing is likely to be needed in tomorrow's land-short urban areas. Many experts believe that mortgage funds for apartment construction will become very hard to find in the years to come.

5. *Can private mortgage insurance survive a severe depression?* There is another important reason why an effective (revived, simplified, and streamlined) FHA is much needed for normal mortgage financing. The present dominance of conventional mortgage lending, particularly that with liberal terms and low down payments, relies heavily on the insurance provided by several private corporations. This is a welcome and promising development. Nevertheless, this system of private mortgage insurance has not been fully tested. Some studies have concluded that such a private system can survive a severe real estate (and general economic) crisis. But so far it has not

stood the test of an actual depression. The FHA, backed by the full faith and credit of the federal government, is far better designed to do just that.

6. *FHA's sound mortgage lending standards would be lost.* The absence of an effective FHA would also significantly erode the influence that FHA's underwriting, property, and subdivision standards have exerted on all mortgage lending, an important consumer protection. FHA mortgage underwriting standards have long been a yardstick against which all mortgage lending is measured. One expert group has observed:

> It can be said that the elimination of a Federal guarantee of home mortgage debt, surrounded by the various standards and protections which have historically been attached to such a guarantee as a matter of public policy, would in all probability initiate a trend in the very mortgage lending practices which these systems [FHA and VA] were initially instituted to correct; preferential selection of higher income families and higher priced properties; shortening mortgage terms; high downpayment and carrying charges; and growing use of secondary financing and other forms of junior liens to generate supplementary credit.[11]

Conclusion

The conclusion to be drawn from these considerations is clear. An efficient, effective FHA is still much needed as a federal instrument to support, stimulate, and channel private capital into mortgage lending. It is as much needed as the equally important Federal Home Loan Bank Board, another social invention of the early 1930s (created under President Hoover shortly before the wave of New Deal legislation). Only FHA-insured mortgages can attract into the mortgage market funds that would not otherwise be available. For example, HUD's Government National Mortgage Association (GNMA) sells securities, like bonds, backed by FHA and VA mortgages. Not only do GNMA securities cause otherwise unavailable funds to flow into mortgages, but during the recurrent periods of credit shortage these funds become virtually the only source of mortgage credit available. Only the FHA can take marginal risks, so much needed by families of lower income and those living in decaying central-city neighborhoods, which non-government-insured mortgages are unable to take. Only FHA-insured credit can take the risks of innovation (the currently much discussed variable payment mortgage, for example) to demonstrate what can be done by all lenders without unreasonable risk. This last is a role FHA has played many times during its history, and it is an important one.

But to perform its role, the FHA must be simplified, streamlined, and made attractive to use. Its unnecessarily complex laws should be simplified. This will require legislation. (A bill directed at this end has been prepared by the Mortgage Bankers Association of America.) Beyond that, the HUD secretary must rescue FHA's operating effectiveness from the chaos into which unwise organizational decisions have thrown it. The secretary must also relieve FHA of the bewildering array of unnecessary processing hurdles that have made its use an almost insurmountable challenge, rather than an inviting opportunity to home purchasers and home builders alike.

8

Housing the Poor and Near Poor

In this chapter we will discuss HUD's various, often overlapping, programs for subsidizing housing to bring its costs within the means of the poor and near poor. We will describe and evaluate HUD's current housing subsidy programs (the Section 8 Rental Assistance Program, passed in 1974; public housing, dating from 1937; and the various housing subsidy programs tacked onto FHA, some active, some suspended by administrative action). We shall delve into the hectic history of these programs during the past decade as well as into the disputes over the merits of housing production subsidies in contrast to direct subsidy payments to the poor (favored by the Nixon administration). Also considered will be the conspicuous absence of a coherent subsidy policy. We shall draw some conclusions from this tangled affair and offer some recommendations. It will be argued that the development of a coherent housing subsidy policy is a HUD mission of great importance.

The Case for Housing Subsidies

Few in this country or elsewhere seriously believe that the private housing market, left to itself, has ever succeeded in providing minimally decent housing (not to speak of decent neighborhoods) to all. The free housing market has failed conspicuously to meet even the meager needs of the very poor. Many of the less poor—those families below the government-defined poverty line who occupy decent housing (as measured by our very faulty statistical tools)—have done so at the sacrifice of other necessities.

Under the right conditions, the filtering, or hand-me-down process, does provide acceptable shelter to many who cannot afford a new house. But as we saw in the last chapter, the filtering process does not help the very poor or even many better-off families. As Anthony Downs observed, "for the poor it is a disaster."[1]

In a recent book, Barbara Ward said, "If a wealthy nation does leave any of its citizens in poor, unhealthy, substandard housing, the issue is one of choice, not necessity. It means that government and people alike have not given the provision of homes the attention and priority which, in justice, in humanity, in dignity and compassion, they require."[2] Since 1937, the legislation authorizing federal housing subsidies for lower-income families is replete with references to providing minimally decent housing for all citizens. But as will become evident, the performance does not match the noble legislative commitments. Most Western countries have for decades provided housing subsidies to a significant percentage of their people, but in this country subsidies seem to have gone against the national grain. During the past thirty years, we have subsidized only a tiny fraction of those in need. Of all the missions of HUD and its predecessors, subsidized housing has been among the most controversial. Disputes, often bitter, have continued even as the subsidy programs multiplied. The controversy that has hung, like a dark cloud, over HUD's housing subsidy programs accounts, to a considerable degree, for the discrepancy between the ambitious rhetoric ("A decent home and a suitable living environment for all Americans") and the meager results.

HUD's Housing Subsidy Programs

As the Carter administration took office early in 1977, HUD had several authorities for subsidizing housing. The Section 8 Rental Assistance Program was the largest. Others, administered rather reluctantly by the Ford administration, include traditional public housing, FHA's programs of subsidized mortgage interest rates for home purchase and for the construction of rental housing (Sections 235 and 236), and a direct loan program (Section 202) at below-market-interest rates to finance rental housing for the elderly. Also in the law, but not active, is the FHA Rent Supplement Program.

The Section 8 Rental Assistance Program

The Section 8 Rental Assistance Program was established by the Housing and Community Development Act of 1974. It authorizes HUD to make annual assistance payments to owners of rental housing for the purpose of closing the gap between the normal market rent and the amount that a low-income or moderate-income family can afford to pay—generally the family is required to pay 25 percent of its income toward rent. A family is eligible for rental assistance if its income is 80 percent or less of the median income in the locality. Rent subsidy payments can be made, in behalf of eligible families, to private owners—profit or nonprofit—and to public agencies such as local housing authorities and state housing finance agencies. The program does not help owners finance the cost of building, rehabilitating, or purchasing the housing in which the rents are subsidized. Unless the housing is already owned, those who use Section 8 rent subsidies must find some other means, which may include other FHA programs of financing construction, rehabilitation, or purchase. However, Section 8 aims to stimulate all three of these types of housing.

As promulgated by HUD (through its regulations issued during the Ford administration), Section 8 is a somewhat ambivalent form of housing subsidy. It is not a pure cash payment to tenants (a housing allowance), since the rental subsidy goes to the owner rather than the tenant. Nor is it a pure production subsidy program—as nearly all its predecessors were—for in itself it provides no mortgage financing for housing production. In this regard, it is neither fish nor fowl, but something else. As formulated by the Ford administration, it is a rent supplement program messed up by taking away its financing machinery.[3]

The Section 8 Rental Assistance Program was the solution promised, after two years of study, for the supposed structural weaknesses of the previous housing subsidy programs that the Nixon administration had vigorously carried out for four years and then abruptly suspended in January 1973. The Section 8 Program was supposed to replace the previous programs which the Nixon administration found so flawed. The new program did not quite live up to the promise Nixon had made, while the study was under way, of simple, direct payments to low-income families for housing. However, as shaped by HUD's regulations, it leaned in that direction. It did not even solve the high cost of housing subsidies, an issue President Nixon made much of when he suspended the previous programs. On the contrary, the per unit subsidy cost under Section 8 was considerably higher than under the programs it replaced.[4] It is also considerably more complicated to use and to administer than the earlier subsidy programs. As a vehicle for supporting new construction, the HUD interpretation of the Section 8 law may well be the most complicated housing subsidy tool ever concocted. Most private builders gave up on it after a few months. Only state housing finance agencies found it reasonably feasible to use for new construction or substantial rehabilitation—the law gave them more favorable treatment, and they had their own mortgage financing facilities. After a long wait, some private builders found a way to use the program for new construction: they used FHA mortgage insurance plus funds made available by GNMA at below-market-interest rates. It is by no means certain that this will continue when GNMA's cheap money runs out.

After two years, Section 8's accomplishments—aside from the use of existing housing—were unimpressive. In June 1976, Secretary Carla Hills reported to Congress that funds had been reserved for 85,000 new or substantially rehabilitated units, or about 30,000 a year. But as of the same date, HUD's reports showed that only about 3,500 units of Section 8 new and rehabilitated housing had been completed and occupied. Clearly, fund reservation figures are not a reliable estimate of how many units will ultimately be built.[5] This record is puny compared with the 1.6 million subsidized units George Romney got *started* between 1969 and 1973.

To add to the confusion, the Congress has been unwilling

to abandon some of the earlier programs. This is understandable in light of the Section 8 program's slow start. The FHA Section 235 program to finance home purchase was revived in 1976, but only for much higher income families than it its original form. The FHA 236 program to subsidize rental housing was also extended. The public housing program was born again on a limited scale. The Section 202 program of direct loans for rental housing for the elderly, which the Johnson administration wanted to fold into the Section 236 program, was also reestablished by the Congress. None of these programs were administered with any enthusiasm by the Ford administration. The 236, 235, and 202 programs were further extended and liberalized by the Housing and Community Development Act of 1977, as was the Section 8 program.

On a more optimistic note, nearly all observers agree that the Section 8 law itself is potentially quite a good one. With realistic modifications in the administrative rules HUD has promulgated and with one minor legislative amendment, it could be an effective and flexible means for subsidizing new construction, rehabilitation, and the use of existing housing where this is appropriate. However, it lacks a built-in method for financing construction and is not as appropriate for subsidizing new construction as its predecessors were. In addition, it provides no way for assisting homeownership.

The Housing and Community Development Act of 1977 remedies at least one of the flaws in the Section 8 program, flaws that have made it a less than ideal vehicle for subsidizing new construction and major rehabilitation. The law authorizes HUD to make payments to project owners equal to the mortgage payments required on vacant units. This assurance that vacant units will continue to receive financial support under Section 8 should make the program somewhat more appealing to those seeking to build or rehabilitate under it. HUD has recently made some of the administrative changes needed to improve the program. However, Section 8 still lacks a built-in method for providing mortgage financing for new construction, a deficiency that will continue to make it cumbersome and complicated to use.

Low-Rent Public Housing

The Beginning

In 1937, Congress passed the first important program for subsidizing housing. This program for low-rent public housing followed and grew out of a brief sally into the direct construction of low-rent housing by the New Deal's Public Works Administration. David Krooth and others in the Public Works Agency, and New York Senator Robert Wagner and his staff assistant, Leon Keyserling, engineered the public housing law of 1937. Catherine Bauer, a respected student of housing matters,[6] Charles Abrams, a New York lawyer and teacher, and Ernest Bohn, an Ohio Republican who helped to gain the support of Senator Robert Taft, supplied important leadership from outside the government.

The public housing law established a United States Housing Authority with power to assist local public agencies (some directly under the mayor, but most of them relatively independent) to construct and manage new housing for the poor. Federal aid consisted of loans for planning and construction as well as long-term annual contributions contracts to subsidize debt service on local authority bonds. Armed with the annual contributions contract—in effect, a federal guarantee—local housing authorities then issued long-term bonds on the private market to repay the temporary government loans. Public housing projects also benefited from two indirect subsidies—they were exempted from federal taxes on interest earned on the local public housing authority bonds (this reduced their interest rate) and partly exempted from local property taxes. With this array of subsidies, local housing authorities could reduce rents to levels that most poor people could afford.

Public housing bonds soon became a favorite form of investment for well-to-do people, who often opposed the public housing program. Self-interest overcame political conviction. John Mitchell, later the U.S. attorney general and of Watergate fame, became both renowned and wealthy as an expert in the development of public housing bonds.

For nearly twenty years, public housing provided decent

shelter for many poor families. Except in New York City and a few other places, early public housing was mostly two-story and three-story construction, widely scattered in large and small communities. The families it served were largely working-middle-class and upwardly mobile but temporarily short of income. (President Carter and his family occupied public housing for a while after World War II.) Though often monotonous in design, this type of housing with this type of tenant presented no great problems and helped many.

The Trouble Begins

But by 1955, a significant change had occurred. Because of sustained national prosperity and low unemployment, the Jimmy Carters of the country no longer needed public housing as a temporary way station. In addition, the massive migration of poor blacks from the rural South to the larger cities was well under way. Increasingly, public housing became the haven of the rural blacks, the culturally deprived, the broken families, the welfare recipients, the permanent poor. Social prejudice produced bitter local resistance to public housing projects and social turmoil within them. As a result, it was difficult for local housing authorities to find sites on which to build. Where sites could be found, the land was expensive. Expensive land made high-rise construction an economic necessity. Too many public housing projects became concentrations of culturally deprived families packed into large, tall structures—an environment ill suited for normal family life (what mother can supervise the play of her children from the twelfth floor?) and very conducive to the disruptive behavior encouraged by the anonymity and monotony in which the deprived families lived.

The infamous Pruit-Igoe Project was built in the mid-1950s at a cost of $36 million. Its architect was highly esteemed. The American Institute of Architects gave it, with justification, an award for design excellence. But it soon became the apotheosis of all these negative forces. It became a disaster area, in all respects like the worst slums in America. As Arnold Rogow wrote:

> the planners of Pruit-Igoe apparently assumed that a concentration of 12,000 poverty-level blacks in high-rise apartment

buildings would spontaneously produce a city within a city or at any rate establish a basis of a community. If they were aware that 60 percent of the blacks were on welfare, or that two-thirds of the families had no male heads, or that more than 60 percent of the project residents were children, their plan did not show it, and there was even less awareness that the basic high-rise design of Pruit-Igoe was incompatible with the needs of the poor, fragmented and fundamentally demoralized population.[7]

A former public housing commissioner, Marie McGuire, has stated that Pruit-Igoe's problems came principally from the fact that the original plan (including recreation and other facilities) was never completely carried out and that it was badly managed.[8] These deficiencies undoubtedly played a role, but it is hard to believe they were decisive in the Pruit-Igoe disaster. Finally, in desperation, HUD Secretary George Romney ordered the project torn down.

Pruit-Igoe was only the most dramatic of many similar public housing debacles. Neither HUD nor the local housing authorities responded to these unhappy developments with great speed. Slowly, local housing authorities abandoned such projects. Many of them turned to construction of projects for the elderly, simply because the elderly presented few management problems and no community resistance. Finally, in the 1960s some public housing authorities shifted to scattered sites (small projects in several locations) and then to the leasing of a limited number of units in existing buildings. These constructive changes were inspired by HUD Secretary Robert C. Weaver with assistance from Public Housing Commissioner McGuire.

The Unrealized Dream

By 1974, over a million units of public housing had been built by over 1,200 local housing authorities, and another 165,000 units were under way—not a large volume for a program nearly forty years old. When this production volume is judged against the many millions of poor people living in substandard housing, it is clear that public housing has made but a small dent in the problem it was created to solve. There are many reasons for this.

1. *Early hopes.* Public housing started with high hopes. The passage of the law realized the dream of a generation of dedicated people, deeply concerned about urban slums and the plight of the poor. Many first-rate people joined in the effort, both at the national level and in the cities. The United States Housing Authority benefited from good leadership and competent staff. Its first head, Nathan Straus, a businessman who believed in the program, was a strong leader. In its pristine years, public housing had many of the aspects of a missionary movement. It was a cause. Its early leaders moved public housing ahead of its time in its policy on racial equality. And it provided good housing for many blacks and whites who needed it badly. Under Philip Klutznick, another able businessman, the program shifted gears and contributed much to housing for war workers and military personnel shortly before and during World War II. Its principal problem in the early years was a paucity of funds, which reflected the fact that too many in Congress viewed the program with suspicion and even hostility. Public housing never arrived politically. Its very existence was an annual political cliffhanger.

2. *Hammer blows.* After a hopeful beginning, public housing suffered a series of setbacks that would have disheartened Don Quixote himself. Public opinion viewed it as some kind of socialistic conspiracy. During the Eisenhower presidency, public housing considered itself lucky to get appropriations for a mere 25,000 units a year. Some years it got no money at all. Meanwhile, the poor themselves had changed: there were difficult management problems, vandalism, and local resistance. Public housing became a bad word. It is not surprising that the Public Housing Administration lost some of its best people and that those who remained became somewhat paranoid. This was reflected in bureaucratic decay, loss of efficiency, and slow, tedious processing of applications. Many local housing authorities stopped applying for more subsidies and turned to managing the housing they already owned. The once fervent U.S. Housing Authority had become dispirited.

3. *Faint rebirth*. In the late 1950s, newly passed authorities to provide specially designed housing for the elderly gave public housing a new and publicly acceptable raison d'etre. Many quite good projects for older people were built. Among the leaders in this development was Marie McGuire, soon to be appointed public housing commissioner by President John Kennedy in the early 1960s. Public housing took a turn for the better with the Weaver-inspired approach of scattered sites, leasing of existing units, and even attempts to provide ownership for its tenants. But public housing never fully recovered from the Pruit-Igoes it perpetrated and the disasters they produced.

On Balance

Not all public housing projects were Pruit-Igoes. Despite the bad press it has received and the rocky life it has led, public housing has provided decent housing to thousands of families who would not otherwise have been able to afford it. Certainly, it has been a great boon to the elderly. It must be doing something right: otherwise, the vacancy rate in most public housing would not be so low, and there would not be so many long waiting lists for admission. Often overlooked is the great number of small projects built in small towns. Here, the results have been good. At the same time, the public housing experience underlines the deficiencies of high-rise construction for family living, especially for the supervision of children. It also demonstrates that too many culturally deprived families cannot be packed into one large project without disaster. On the whole, public housing does not deserve its bad name. Many of its well-publicized failures reflect deep social forces in our society. No one knows exactly how to cure vandalism, crime, and antisocial behavior in America's slums. Public housing cannot be blamed if it did not solve these same problems in some of its projects.

FHA's Housing Subsidy Programs

The Change in FHA

In the early and middle 1960s, two major developments substantially changed the FHA. The first was the establishment in 1960 of a program in which the normal market interest rate on FHA-insured loans was reduced by a federal subsidy to bring housing within the means of moderate-income families and in 1965 within the means of the very poor. The second was an increasing recognition that FHA's programs should be directed to the growing problems of inner-city neighborhoods. These developments constituted a far-reaching change in the original conception of FHA as a public insurance company taking actuarially sound risks. The significance of this change should not be underestimated. Nor should we forget the challenge to leadership represented by so basic a change in direction of an agency that had long gloried in the "soundness" of its mortgage insurance operation and its basically suburban orientation.

FHA now had to take risks it had always considered unreasonable, to enter slum and blighted areas where any sensible banker would consider mortgage loans to be dubious investments at best. FHA even became involved with the social problems that frequently accompany poverty. This was a strange new world for an agency accustomed to measuring only the economic aspects of a proposed application. During this period, four different subsidy programs were given to the FHA. Each reflected the new social mission expected of it.

FHA's Below-Market Interest-Rate Program

The first of these programs—to subsidize housing for families of moderate income—was authorized in Section 221 (d) (3) of the first housing legislation initiated by President John Kennedy. (It came to be known as the "BMIR" program, or the "d3" program—typical examples of housing's obscure jargon.) Through the FHA loan insurance mechanism, the law provided what amounted to a direct government loan at an interest rate of 3 percent. That is, the newly made FHA-insured loan was quickly converted to government credit when the mortgage was purchased by the then federally owned FNMA. In effect, this scheme reduced rents by about 20 percent below those required in a comparable nonsubsidized apartment. Nonprofit private groups could use the program (profit-motivated groups were added later), and the loan was very liberal (100 percent of FHA's estimate of replacement cost to nonprofit groups and 90 percent for profit-making organizations).

Subsidies for families of moderate income were prompted by the 20 percent gap requirement placed in the public housing law in 1949. It was designed to make certain that public housing would never compete with privately built, unsubsidized housing. The law required that public housing rents should always be kept at least 20 percent below the lowest rents at which a substantial supply of private housing was available. By definition, this provision meant that a substantial number of families, unable to afford decent private housing but ineligible for public housing, would be left out in the cold. During the 1950s, federal and local officials, as well as students of housing, became increasingly concerned about this segment of housing need. There was much discussion of and experience with families who had too much income to be eligible for public housing and who then could not find decent housing in the private market. If the law worked as it was designed to, this was inevitable.

By 1965, about 90,000 rental units had been or were being financed under the BMIR Program. Because of the limited subsidy, the program reached only the top of the moderate-income families, but it was notable because it was the first program to bring private groups into the job of housing lower-income families. It also brought to the fore the difficult dilemma of which type of private sponsorship was best equipped for this job. Nonprofit groups—churches, fraternal societies, and ad hoc civic committees—had the strength of charitable motivation. But they were amateurs. They knew little about home building, mortgage finance, FHA procedures, and economic realities; they knew little about how to manage a rental housing project. On the other hand, the professional home builder knew the complexities of building and financing, but his experience and his commercial motivations were not always compatible with the social purposes of the program. He knew little about managing housing for this type of tenant.

On the whole, the BMIR Program produced good, though

limited, results, largely because the subsidy was not large enough to attract families with extremely low incomes and the social problems they often bring.

The Rent Supplement Program

In 1965, the Johnson administration proposed yet another FHA subsidy program effort—the Rent Supplement Program. It was aimed at an income group similar to that served by the BMIR Program. But it employed a different financing and subsidy formula (an FHA-insured, privately held mortgage with the government making annual subsidy payments to the owner to bring rents down). The change was motivated almost entirely by a desire to reduce the annual impact on the federal budget. Since the annual subsidy was a lesser amount, it was hoped many more housing units could be supported than under the BMIR formula. (Under the BMIR Program, the total amount of each mortgage appeared on the federal budget as an expenditure in the year it was originated. Under the Rent Supplement formula, only the much smaller annual subsidy payment appeared on the budget.)

This rather technical change in the financing formula met unexpected hostility from the Congress. After bitter debates, the Congress changed the program drastically. The changes were not in the financing formula but in the income levels to be served. The Rent Supplement Program emerged from the Congress as a private substitute for public housing, a substitute designed to serve the same low-income levels as public housing did. The president signed the bill, although it was very different from what he had proposed.

FHA was handed the job of administering the new program. There was some logic to this, for the government subsidy to reduce rents was applied to an FHA-insured mortgage. On the other hand, FHA, long accustomed to dealing solely with the private real estate and financial community, had no experience with the manifold problems involved in housing the very poor. The same can be said of the private groups who used FHA programs. FHA's top staff accepted the assignment dutifully and made an heroic attempt to train its field staff of appraisers, architects, and related professions in the difficult task of housing the poor. It was a job that had baffled and frequently defeated the public housing people for twenty years. It was perhaps too much to expect FHA staff to learn how to perform this difficult job virtually overnight. In its training sessions, FHA called upon Abner Silverman, a public housing veteran, from whom it heard for the first time about the special problems of managing projects filled with poor people, about non-upward-mobile families, their behavior, and other such matters—all arcane to FHA. If FHA's solid, business-oriented staff did not look bewildered, it should have been.

The Rent Supplement Program was followed in less than three years by two more subsidy programs.

The Section 236 Program

In 1968, two more subsidy programs were placed in the lap of FHA. The first was yet another plan to subsidize rental housing for low-income and moderate-income families. It, like most other FHA programs, was known in the trade by the number of its paragraph in the FHA law: in this case, Section 236. The financing formula was similar to that used for rent supplements, but the subsidy was not as great. The maximum subsidy was that necessary to reduce rents to what would be required if the mortgage carried an interest rate of one percent. The families to be served were those whose incomes were just above public housing eligibility ceilings in each locality. Section 236 was thus aimed squarely at families in the income gap between those served by public housing and those who could be served by the private market. The Rent Supplement Program was not completely abolished but put in a subsidiary position. Up to 20 percent of the units in a Section 236 project could use rent supplements. In effect, the rent supplement subsidy could ride piggyback on the Section 236 subsidy.

The Section 235 Program

The 1968 act also authorized FHA to subsidize the purchase of new and existing homes by families just above the public housing income level. The financing formula was similar to the Section 236 plan. The home ownership program, however, was not proposed by the Johnson administration. The initiative came primarily from Senators Charles Percy and Robert

Kennedy, who believed strongly that home ownership would produce desirable social benefits for lower-income families. The two senators gained wide support in the Senate and elsewhere. To be sure, HUD Secretary Weaver was skeptical about the wisdom of placing the responsibilities of home ownership on families with such low income. But his was a lonely voice. Most saw it as a way to make slum families stable and responsible. The senators won, though their original home ownership plan was substantially modified. Despite skepticism, Weaver worked with the senators to improve their initial plan.

FHA Loans in Older Neighborhoods

The 1968 law contained another significant provision. FHA was authorized to use any of its programs for the purchase, repair, rehabilitation, or construction of housing located in older, declining urban areas without regard to its normal requirements if it found that the area was reasonably viable, giving consideration to the need for providing adequate housing for families of low and moderate income, and if the property was an acceptable risk in view of this consideration.[9] Thus, FHA's traditional principles of low-risk lending could be ignored, and loans could be made in the inner-city, declining areas—if FHA judged the extra risk justified in view of the social need to improve these neighborhoods. This provision, plus the various FHA housing subsidy programs enacted in the 1960s, constituted a historic change in FHA's role. More precisely, it added an entirely new social dimension to FHA's mission, a dimension that would have astounded some of its earlier patriarchs.[10]

Philip N. Brownstein and FHA's Changed Direction

Philip N. Brownstein, federal housing commissioner and later also HUD assistant secretary, headed the FHA during this momentous time. While pointedly warning the Congress that mortgage loans for the poor and in the decaying inner city would inevitably result in higher rates of foreclosure than FHA's traditional insurance activities, he put all of his substantial administrative skills into the job of educating, leading, and exhorting FHA's staff to throw its best efforts into its new role.

In an often-quoted speech, delivered on October 23, 1967, to all FHA field office directors and to its top Washington staff, Brownstein said:

> it is our job to enlist and encourage private enterprise to play a leading role in providing decent housing for families of low and moderate income, and in improving housing and related human conditions in the inner city. This is the purpose for which the Department was created; it is one of the major objectives the Secretary [Weaver] has announced again and again. It is what the American people, the Congress and the President [Johnson] expect of us. It is the greatest and most urgent responsibility of FHA—its principal reason for existence in the year 1967.

Brownstein concluded his speech with this passage:

> I have given you a number of reasons why I believe FHA must mount a major effort to accelerate and expand use of those of our programs which can serve families of low and moderate income and revive and rebuild the inner city. Let me give you one more reason. You should work at this task as though your job depended on it . . . because it may.[11]

The speech also carefully put limits on the risks FHA was asked to take. It urged, even demanded, innovative, venturesome, but not irresponsible decision. This is admirably straight talk. Such explicitness, such boldness are rarely heard from the lips of bureaucrats. It marked a watershed in the FHA's long history. Senator Mondale of Minnesota, now vice-president of the United States, came down from the Capitol to listen to Brownstein's speech.

Many questioned the wisdom of giving the FHA programs and purposes so clearly social and unbusinesslike. They thought that FHA was not only unprepared to carry out programs of social reform and heavy federal subsidy but also that such a mission was incompatible with and weakened the purposes for which the FHA was created.

Some are now working to divorce the original FHA from the social mission it undertook in the 1960s. It is true that the original FHA must be revitalized, as we have argued in the previous chapter. But it does not follow that the two functions cannot be performed by a single FHA within HUD.[12]

The Mass Production Drive

Not long after the Section 236 and 235 programs were passed, Richard Nixon was elected president and George Romney became secretary of HUD, thereby verifying Anthony Downs's Law of Inescapable Discontinuity: "High federal personnel change so fast that almost no major federal program is ever initially conceived of, drafted into legislation, shepherded through the Congress and then carried out by the same officials."[13] For nearly four years, the production-minded Romney used every resource at his command to achieve the ambitious national housing goals established in the 1968 legislation (600,000 subsidized units and 2 million nonsubsidized units a year).

The immediate results were spectacular. In 1970, over 400,000 subsidized units were started (using Section 236, rent supplements, and public housing). This was not merely an all-time high. It was a spectacular quantum leap. In 1971 and 1972, subsidized housing starts remained high, and with the help of an improved private mortgage market, unassisted starts also rose. Total housing starts (not counting mobile homes) reached 2.1 million in 1971 and 2.4 million in 1972—another all-time production record.

Program Abuses

As Romney's production volume continued to soar, he began to hear reports that administration of the programs was breaking down. The full extent of this development was uncovered by the House Committee on Banking and Currency, which smelled the trouble and made its own investigations. Informed of the committee's finding, Secretary Romney was at first reluctant to believe them. But he became convinced after his own investigators gave him similar reports, which showed that there was indeed something seriously wrong with the way HUD's housing programs were operating.

In fact, many things were wrong. Using FHA Section 235 subsidies (as well as related nonsubsidy programs), callous speculators were purchasing run-down houses in slum areas for a song. Then they applied for FHA-insured loans under Section 235 and other programs. The FHA's mortgages were much higher than the purchase price. The houses were then sold to poor families, too inexperienced in such matters to protect themselves. The speculator's profits were outrageous.

Two examples, out of many, will illustrate. A broker bought a house in southeast Washington, D.C., for $9,600; three months later, he sold it under Section 235 with minimal improvements to a poor family for $17,500. In Spokane, Washington, a house was purchased for $3,375 and sold for $11,250.[14] This could only have been accomplished with FHA mortgages that were inflated beyond any possible justification. Most of these poor families were exploited in another way. They were burdened with mortgage payments that left them little surplus to pay for normal maintenance, much less cover breakdowns of the furnace or similar major expenses that almost always occur, especially in older houses.

In many cases, the houses sold to poor families under Section 235, sometimes with the connivance of the mortgage lender, were in such poor condition that the FHA could hardly have inspected them. Some were in such bad condition that municipal authorities condemned them soon after their purchase. Much newly constructed housing sold under Section 235 (and also under FHA's nonsubsidized programs) was found to be inflated in cost by thousands of dollars. Many suffered from shoddy construction and the cheapest materials.[15]

This was nothing less than a racket, a racket perpetrated by some sellers of existing homes and some builders of new houses. The FHA—long respected for its careful appraisals, examination of the purchaser's capacity to pay off the mortgage, and its inspections of properties against its detailed minimum property standards—tragically failed to apply its own rules to these transactions. Similar, but fewer, problems occurred in apartments financed and subsidized under the

Section 236 program. The abuses were equally bad in some of FHA's nonsubsidized programs.

When they woke up to what had happened, thousands of low-income families walked away from the houses they had been sold with government help. This left FHA the owner of an unprecedented number of old, run-down houses in inner-city neighborhoods. It became, unwillingly, a large slum landlord, with many of its homes vacant. Those who suffered included disappointed homeowners and tenants, the FHA (whose insurance reserves were endangered), and the residents of central-city neighborhoods blighted by the abandoned housing.

The vaunted FHA system, often accused of being unduly conservative, had clearly broken down. In time, it became clear that the problem had another serious face. There were well over a thousand criminal indictments of real estate dealers, mortgage bankers, and a few FHA employees. The great majority were convicted.

The Debate over Subsidy Methods

As Romney strove to break one production record after another and as clouds of program abuse began to gather on the horizon, a debate over subsidy techniques began. People in and out of HUD began to question the cost as well as the effectiveness of the housing subsidy programs being used. Although the facts had been clear from the beginning, it slowly dawned on Romney's staff and others that the total public cost of subsidizing 400,000 or more housing units a year would be huge. The programs had been designed to stretch out the subsidy cost over the life of the mortgage and thus minimize the annual impact on the federal budget. But the ultimate cost of subsidizing a unit over the life of the mortgage could be estimated—by simple arithmetic—with reasonable accuracy. If all 6 million of the subsidized units pledged by the housing goals were built, it could well cost the government $7 billion. This was a frightening thought to administration officials not deeply concerned with any social programs. Such cost estimates became even more alarming in the face of the largest budget deficits in the country's history.

At the same time, HUD's policy analysts began to brood over the equity of the programs. Since even 600,000 subsidized units a year could not possibly serve all those eligible for aid, they raised questions about the social equity of helping some and not others. They forgot that nearly all social programs operate with limited funds and cannot immediately serve all those who are eligible. They also ignored the fact that not all families whose incomes made them eligible actually lived in substandard housing. Another equity question was not theoretical, but came from complaints of nonsubsidized homeowners who discovered that their neighbors were buying a better house than theirs with the help of a subsidy. Many wrote understandably bitter letters to Secretary Romney. The unequal geographical distribution of subsidized housing was also cause for worry.

In the course of this soul-searching, HUD program analysts, the Urban Institute, as well as scholars at the prestigious Brookings Institution became fascinated with a very old and frequently rejected idea—direct subsidy payments to needy families for housing. Once called rent certificates, in their reincarnation they were called "housing allowances." The Brookings Institution published a book by Henry Aaron that seemed to favor the housing allowance over production subsidies such as provided under the 235 and 236 programs.[16] On close reading, Aaron's book is much less dogmatic on this question than many casual, and perhaps wishful, readers concluded. Charles L. Schultze, then with Brookings, made a strong argument for housing allowances and attempted to prove that their long-term costs would be considerably lower than the programs then current.[17] That the calculations on which this brilliant and experienced government student based his conclusions were somewhat dubious escaped notice for a while. So did the fact that both Aaron and Schultze made it plain that any housing allowance program would have to be accompanied by programs to support a considerable volume of new construction.

Soon, HUD's research staff and the Urban Institute were busy designing an expensive experiment to test housing allowances in selected cities. Thus, the government's chronic tendency to reinvent the wheel built momentum. Anthony

Downs has called this the "Law of Compulsive Innovation."[18] It is also a sad commentary on the stubborn unwillingness of high government officials to study history. Whatever the merits of the housing allowance idea, it certainly would have been instructive had the revisionists looked and learned from the careful examinations of this idea made by knowledgeable and responsible people in 1937, 1945, and again in 1953.[19] One who studied the question was the widely respected Senator Robert Taft. There is no evidence that these previous studies were considered or even known about, except by senior HUD civil servants unable to stem the tide of enthusiasm for the reborn old idea.

Moratorium

In early 1973, President Nixon ordered Secretary Romney to declare a cessation of activity under all FHA-subsidized housing programs. Romney sadly announced an indefinite stoppage of the programs at the annual convention of the National Association of Home Builders in January 1973. The shocking decision extended beyond the housing subsidy programs to include urban renewal, model cities, and related HUD authorities for inner-city improvement.

According to Charles Orlebeke, then HUD's deputy under secretary for policy, the primary reason for Nixon's cancellation of so many of HUD's programs was their high cost.[20] It is hard to believe, however, that the administrative abuses and the growing appeal of the housing allowance approach did not also influence this drastic decision. When the moratorium evoked consternation in the Congress and elsewhere, HUD Secretary James Lynn (Romney left shortly after the programs were suspended) promised a thorough and objective review of the entire housing subsidy issue. The study was carried out by more than 100 government personnel recruited from HUD and nine other government departments and agencies. A preliminary draft of the results was circulated to Congress and a few others in September 1973, eight months after the programs had been suspended. Thirteen months later, a final, printed draft was made generally available. The report, called *Housing in the Seventies*, was an abstruse indictment of the suspended housing subsidy programs on the basis of their lack of equity, efficiency, and viability.[21] The report was superficial, its reasoning was fragile, it contained numerous errors of fact and what could only have been deliberate distortions of the language of laws and congressional reports. President Carter's new HUD secretary, Patricia Harris, said at the March 1977 meeting of the National Housing Conference that the money spent on this study would have been better used to build houses.[22]

All these weaknesses and more were exposed in a careful, nonpartisan analysis made by the Congressional Research Service in the Library of Congress.[23] Senator Sparkman called the HUD report "an elaborate study . . . hastily written . . . to support the already announced opposition to the kinds of housing subsidies which the Nixon Administration had inherited and administered for four years."[24] In Sparkman's opinion, the alternative proposed by the HUD study—housing allowances—probably would have quadrupled federal expenditures on housing subsidies.[25] No serious and experienced observer took HUD's report as anything more than an unconvincing argument leading to a conclusion that had already been reached.

The problems HUD experienced in administering the Johnson housing subsidy programs were real enough, and their long-run cost was undoubtedly substantial at the high production volumes Romney achieved. But the problems did not result from deficiencies in program structure, as the HUD report argued. The very real abuses, if not the scandals, were produced by two of Secretary Romney's greatest misjudgments. The first was a major reorganization of HUD and the FHA, which destroyed effective control over field office operations and often put the job of processing FHA applications in inexperienced hands. The second was excessive pressure to produce volume at any cost. As experience has demonstrated many times, any organization will falter under such pressure, particularly one that has been paralyzed by organizational chaos.[26] One more factor also played a part. The once-competent FHA staff had been allowed to decline over the years. Many able people had been lured into private industry by higher salaries or had retired because of age or disenchantment with the organizational chaos. There was no effective recruitment and training program to replace these attritions in skilled personnel. At the top leadership level during the Romney-Lynn-Hills days, at least two knowledgeable FHA commissioners and one FHA assistant commissioner resigned in frustration.

Moreover, the overall performance of FHA's subsidy programs was not as bad as HUD and others painted it. The Section 235 and 236 programs suffered substantial losses, losses made necessarily higher by the inexcusable looseness of administration. But as Anthony Downs has observed and Romney's Charles Orlebeke has agreed, "It seems rather short sighted to accuse policies deliberately designed to operate in high risk situations of encouraging unusually high losses. This essentially ignores the purposes of the programs."[27] When the Section 235 and 236 programs were being considered by the Congress, then HUD Assistant Secretary Philip N. Brownstein made it clear that abnormally high losses were inevitable given the social objectives involved.

Some Conclusions

Subsidized housing in the United States has produced more rhetoric than roofs, more confusion than coherent policy. As we have seen, the subsidy techniques have varied widely over the past forty years. There has been dismal failure and considerable success. There has been much hard work by dedicated people; there has also been ineptness, poor administration, and even scandal. From this spotty, inconclusive forty-year record, there is much to be learned.

1. *Other ways to improve housing for the poor.* Direct subsidy for housing is only one of several ways in which lower-income families can be helped to improve their living conditions.

One is a nonhousing program that puts funds into the hands of the poor, notably social security and welfare payments. Some observers think that federal transfer payments of this kind improve housing conditions more than all the direct housing subsidies combined.[28] However, the welfare payments do not necessarily produce improved housing standards. The welfare system does not require that the housing occupied by the recipients of its payments meet any minimum level of decency. Thus, welfare payments too often subsidize and perpetuate substandard housing conditions.

A general rise in affluence, or effective income, also increases the proportion of people able to afford decent housing. The general increase in incomes has contributed greatly to a progressive reduction in the number of substandard housing units, measured by the crude statistics we possess.

2. *Housing cost reduction.* If HUD, with the help of others in the government, could devise a way or ways to reduce the mounting cost of housing, or even to keep housing cost increases below the increases in effective income, many more people could afford decent housing, and the cost of housing subsidies could be reduced greatly. (This difficult question is discussed in chapter 10.)

3. *Production subsidies versus housing allowances.* The idea of giving poor families cash to pay for their own housing has always been appealing. Cash payments would certainly give the poor greater freedom of choice. They might well eliminate bureaucratic rigidities, unnecessary red tape, and the stigma attached to living in "a project." If existing housing can be used as it should, the cost of subsidy per unit might be lower. Some believe cash allowances would upgrade the existing housing supply.

But for each of these hopes, there are troubling questions. Will housing allowances prove simpler to administer? Will they improve the quality of housing? Can we be sure that they will actually be used to purchase or rent better housing? Will the general use of housing allowances inflate the cost of existing housing, especially whenever or wherever the supply is tight? Would it be politically feasible to install a housing allowance system that did not cover all people in the eligible income bracket, thus driving the total subsidy cost above anything the Congress is likely to tolerate? How would one assure the necessary growth of the total housing supply as population increases, and how much would that cost?

The housing allowance experiments HUD has under way in

twelve cities may answer some of the major questions. They may well support the judgments of those who studied and rejected the housing allowance approach in 1937, 1948, and 1953. Preliminary information from these experiments suggests that the administration of a housing allowance program will be quite complicated and expensive. Furthermore, no limited experiment can answer the key question: how much would a full-scale housing allowance program further inflate the cost of housing for the poor?

4. *Why not use the most economical subsidy technique?* By far the most important influence on the type of housing subsidy used in this country is the federal budget. As the national books are kept for most programs, "no distinction is recognized between out-of-pocket expenses for current operations and outlays which are in the nature of recoverable investments."[29] Because of this budget practice, the political practice is to devise a program that has the least visible impact on the current budget. For example, the FHA Below-Market-Interest-Rate Program had a large, immediate budget impact: the entire amount of the mortgage loan was reflected on the budget the year it was made, despite the fact that it was a repayable loan secured by a piece of real estate. In contrast, under the Section 236 program the federal subsidy took the form of an annual payment throughout the forty-year life of the mortgage. Thus, only the relatively small annual payment appeared on the budget each year. Whether the latter approach is likely to cost the government more in the long run becomes irrelevant to politically motivated policymakers. In fact, the Section 8 Program has been more costly than the programs it was intended to replace.

Among the various housing subsidies, the direct government loan at a low interest rate is probably the least costly in the long run. Yet this method is the least acceptable—in large part because of the way the federal budget is calculated. It is irrational that the budget barrier should have so dominant an influence in shaping housing subsidy programs, often at considerable cost to the taxpayer. There must be a way to deal with this budget impediment, which is based more on tradition than reason.

5. *Home ownership is not necessarily uplift.* American tradition holds that owning a home builds character, responsibility, and the other middle-class values. But although most Americans certainly prefer to own a home, it would be hard to prove that the typical middle-class homeowner behaves very differently from the middle-class renter.[30] For certain of the poor, as the Section 235 program showed, home ownership can be more of a burden than a blessing.

6. *Housing alone is not enough.* The provision of decent housing for all, including those who cannot afford it without help, is a public purpose of high importance. However, we should remember that improved housing alone will not automatically uplift the permanent poor. Neither will it solve such problems as crime, delinquency, and broken homes— problems that extend beyond the poor and hopeless. This fact does not diminish the virtues of improved housing and a more felicitous environment. But it does suggest that people and governments should proceed with reasonable humility, recognizing both the value and the limitations of better housing.

We should have learned by now another, less cosmic, truth. The improvement of the housing structure itself is not enough. The Urban Institute has accurately characterized good housing as a package of services, many of which come not from the structure itself but from the city and the neighborhood.[31] Among these are heat and light, streets and sidewalks, police and fire protection, convenient shopping, medical and many other facilities and services. The quality of the neighborhood and of the city itself is decisive in determining the kind of living conditions a single structure can provide. The pledge of the 1949 Act was "a decent home and a suitable living environment."

7. *Needed—a housing policy.* This country has never pursued a coherent or even deliberate total policy for applying federal subsidies to housing. For the poor, there have been different and often inconsistent programs, each reaching a somewhat different income group. They have never provided a volume that was in any way related to need.

But the Internal Revenue Code contains the largest of all housing subsidy programs, little of which goes to the poor.

It results from tax deductions (or exemptions) allowed homeowners for payments on mortgage interest and property taxes. These subsidies are highly regressive. The poor homeowner benefits little or not at all; the rich receive a large subsidy. According to Sherman Maisell, more than half of it goes to families in the upper 10 percent income bracket.

The contrast between the yearly federal housing subsidy that goes to lower-income families and the indirect (but equally significant) subsidy that goes mostly to middle-income and upper-income families is surprising. Sherman Maisell's estimates, based on the federal budget for the fiscal year 1975-1976, show $4 billion in direct subsidies to low-income and moderate-income families and $11.5 billion in indirect subsidies going to middle-income and upper-income families as tax exemptions for mortgage interest and property taxes paid. Other tax benefits (for financial institution bad debt reserves, accelerated depreciation of the value of housing owned, and deferral of capital gains on house sales) bring the annual housing subsidy to higher-income families and business institutions to $13.7 billion. Thus, over 70 percent of fiscal year 1975-1976 federal housing subsidies went to higher-income families, but less than 30 percent went to low-income and moderate-income families—about three times as much subsidy for the better-off than for the poor and near poor.

As Maisell observes, "Such a maldistribution of benefits seems to fly in the face of all concepts of equity." Beyond that, there appears to be no deliberate plan behind this distribution of housing subsidies. Maisell puts this important point succinctly: "Because little thought has been given to the purposes of [housing] subsidies or to who should have them, they appear illogical. They have grown like Topsy without any clear idea of what they cost or whom they benefit."[32]

Despite years of executive and congressional attention, we clearly have no deliberate, consistent policy for housing subsidy. The realities of where the federal subsidy money goes and the rhetoric of "a decent home for all Americans" bear little relation to each other. It is high time that the president, with help from the secretaries of HUD, Treasury, and other departments, undertook the difficult, but not impossible, job of developing a deliberate and sensible national policy for the application of federal subsidies to housing. This would require thoughtful consideration of how federal subsidies for housing can be used most effectively to achieve the national objective of decent housing for all and the elimination, as rapidly as possible, of substandard housing (judged against a realistic standard and measured with better methods than we now have). This important job should be done, not by a rapidly assembled task force in a few pressure-packed weeks, but carefully and deliberately. Then, of course, the proposed policy must be persuasively presented to the Congress and its several powerful committees with jurisdiction. Sound and enduring policies take time to develop and implement, just as effective government programs take time to mature.

HUD Secretary Patricia Harris and the director of the White House Domestic Council appear determined to give this important matter a try.[33]

We can find the ways and means to provide decent housing for those poor families who cannot afford it without government help. It is, as Barbara Ward has said, a matter of will, not money. But speeches from Washington alone will not bring it about. It can only be accomplished if the American people (and those who represent them in the Congress) rise above narrow self-interest and summon the collective compassion and the collective will to do what should be done.

The Housing Roller Coaster

We have examined the workings of local housing markets and the HUD and non-HUD programs that support them by facilitating the critical flow of mortgage credit. We have also looked at the bewildering array of HUD programs for subsidizing housing for the poor and near poor. Now we will turn to another important and damaging characteristic of the housing market—the tendency of its main crutch, housing credit, to move in cycles from plenitude to severe shortage. That is, housing credit perversely tends to become plentiful when the general economy is sagging and scarce when it is booming. This phenomenon has damaging effects on the housing market in a number of ways and also on the stability of the national economy itself.

We shall describe the record of the housing market's cyclical behavior and examine the causes. We shall then look at the unhappy consequences and discuss HUD's attempts to curb this chronic and hard-to-cure malady. Then we shall propose some additional actions that HUD and the government economic managers might take. Of necessity, this chapter is somewhat more technical than most other chapters in this book. But the matter is of great importance in a comprehensive treatment of HUD's major missions.

The Facts

Many studies confirm the cyclical character of housing starts. Since World War II there have been six clearly distinct swings in housing production. In late 1949 and early 1950, housing starts rose to over 2 million (annual seasonally adjusted rate). In mid-1950 they dropped to less than 1.4 million and stayed low until mid-1952. In 1954 starts rose again to nearly 1.8 million. By 1956, housing starts were down to about 1.1 million, only to rise again to nearly 1.6 million in 1959. In 1960 starts dropped again to 1.2 million, then in 1963 rose to 1.7 million. In late 1966, they were down again to less than 1 million. By 1969, they were up to 1.7 million, only to sag quickly in late 1969 and early 1970.[1] After 1970 another cycle occurred. In 1972 total annual starts rose to 2.4 million and dropped to 1.3 million in 1974 and 1.2 million in 1975. After 1975 another rise occurred, and by 1977 starts reached a seasonally adjusted monthly level of 1.8 to 1.9 million. There is one striking thing about the evident cyclical pattern in housing production. As former HUD Chief Economist Henry Schechter demonstrates and other experts confirm, the low points in housing production have always coincided with periods in which credit was scarce, expensive, and hard to get.[2]

Exceptions occur, most notably during the housing downturn of 1974-1975. In this period—when we were experiencing the worst general economic depression in forty years and the supply of mortgage funds was not greatly diminished—interest rates were nevertheless high. Moreover, there was high unemployment plus sometimes double-digit inflation. Although similar in some ways to other housing downturns, the most recent housing cycle was clearly influenced by several other economic factors, including some overproduction and a reduction in actual demand due to lowered family incomes in relation to house prices. In general, however, slumps in housing production have come from a lack of effective demand due to a shortage of mortgage credit, not to overproduction.

A vivid demonstration of the close relation between the availability of credit and housing production can be found in the fifteen-year period between 1945 and about 1960. We emerged from World War II with a severe housing shortage produced by two factors: the virtual cessation of home building during the war years and the return of millions of soldiers to civilian life. Postwar housing was in short supply, as those who lived through these years can verify. But during this fifteen-year period, there were at least four major downturns in housing production and an equal number of production peaks. During these postwar slumps in housing production, the problem certainly was not overproduction; neither was it a lack of families who had steady incomes and who desperately wanted housing. The problem was simply that the lack of long-term, low-down-payment credit accompanied by high interest rates periodically made it impossible for many families to purchase the housing they needed. Tight credit not only lowered housing production but also retarded the purchase and sale cf existing housing, thus affecting the performance of the entire housing market. Such periodic credit crunches occur when the general economy is booming and when the demand for credit from other users is great. Credit shortages are frequently reinforced by the Federal Reserve Board's actions to reduce the volume of credit in an attempt to stabilize a booming economy. Housing slumps thus nearly always come when the general economy is booming. Housing production and general housing market activity perform countercyclically—when one goes up, the other goes down.

Sherman Maisell, a specialist in housing finance and former governor of the Federal Reserve Board, believes that the credit-caused drops in housing activity are getting more severe. He has noted that "The last three [housing] declines average at least 40 percent deeper than any of the previous Post War drops. From the fourth quarter of 1972 to the fourth quarter of 1974, the fall in starts was almost twice as great as the average of the prior post–World War II housing recessions." He has also noted that there has been a "steady decline in housing's share of total output. New residential construction as a share of total production fell from 7 percent in 1950 to less than 2½ percent in recent periods. . . . As a nation, we are spending fewer and fewer resources on building and renewing our stock of residences."[3]

The Causes

The key factor that explains the striking relation between downturns in housing production and periods of tight credit lies in the different effect that high interest rates have on various users of credit. For a number of reasons, housing is extremely sensitive to high interest rates and to the higher down payments mortgage lenders demand during periods when credit is scarce.

Institutional Behavior

In periods of tight money, the specialized mortgage lenders—savings and loan associations and mutual savings banks—are unable to compete for savings with higher yielding investments such as U.S. treasury notes, corporate bonds, and other corporate borrowings. Their competitive weakness stems from state usury laws and from statutory ceilings on the rates specialized mortgage lenders can pay to attract savings. As a result, periods of tight money and rising interest rates produce large outflows of savings from these specialized mortgage lending institutions into direct investment in higher yielding opportunities. That is, savers, alert to relative yields, withdraw their funds from these institutions and invest directly in bonds and other instruments that provide a higher return.

When the specialized mortgage lending institutions have less money to lend, they become more selective, choosing only the soundest loans or those that produce the highest yields. They also become more conservative: they require larger down payments, offer shorter repayment terms, and charge higher interest rates on their loans. But the nonspecialized mortgage lending institutions, particularly insurance companies and commercial banks, react to tight money periods in a different way. They simply put most of their funds into loans that will provide the highest yields, not into residential mortgages. Thus, their mortgage loans decrease greatly or virtually dry up. The few mortgage loans these nonspecialized lending institutions do make during periods of tight money are also given to the best risks and require high down payments.

The Effect on Borrowers

The relationship between low housing production and tight money is greatly affected by another fact. Families seeking mortgage loans to purchase a house (and builders of rental housing too) are affected much more by high interest rates than are many other borrowers competing in the financial market. For example, the monthly payment on a $20,000 thirty-year mortgage with an interest rate of 5 percent is $107.37. The monthly payment on the same mortgage at an 8 percent rate is $146.76.[4] Add to this the other expenses connected with home purchase (maintenance, utilities, taxes, etc.), and the total monthly housing expense would probably jump from $230.00 to $272.00. Beyond that, the higher down payments and shorter terms lenders generally require in periods of tight money also have an effect. The $20,000, thirty-year mortgage we have used as an example might well cover 95 percent or more of the cost of the house when credit is readily available. Thus, the required down payment would be $1,000. But, if the lenders were willing to make only an 80 percent loan, as is often the case, the down payment on the same mortgage would become $4,000. If the term of the mortgage were also shortened, the effect of a $4,000 down payment plus even larger monthly payments would remove even more families from the housing market.

In contrast, a large corporation seeking to borrow funds in periods of tight credit is affected very little by an increase from 5 percent to 8 percent in interest rate. First, about half of the increased interest cost would be typically offset by income tax deductions. "More importantly," to quote Schechter, "financing costs constitute a small proportion of most total production costs."[5] Moreover, the large corporation, in a period of active demand, can usually pass on to consumers the added cost of a higher interest rate on borrowing. Federal Reserve Board data cited by Schechter[6] show that from 1952 to 1970, corporate borrowing actually increased during all but one of the four periods of tight credit and that in one it dropped very little. The federal government also, of course, has no trouble raising funds during periods of tight credit. Other users of credit, such as small businesses and local governments, do feel the effects of tight money. But none of them are affected as much as housing.

Almost all students agree that housing credit and housing production bear a disproportionate share of the effects of tight money and of the policies of the Federal Reserve Board that often produce this condition. The President's Economic

Report of January 1957 reported that "changes in the cost and availability of credit exerted especially severe effects on home building."[7] In 1967, the President's Council of Economic Advisers went even further when it estimated that housing had absorbed 90 percent of the Federal Reserve's credit restraint.[8] Oakley Hunter, president of the Federal National Mortgage Association, said in 1975 that "Housing . . . cannot compete for credit on equal terms with other industries and with government during periods of credit shortages. Yet, housing constitutes a basic human need."[9]

The FHA and VA programs are hit even harder: they operate with a fixed-interest rate ceiling that must be changed by administrative determination. These administrative decisions often lag behind the true market interest rate. This causes lenders to discount or charge "points" for FHA and VA mortgages. Since these points are payable in cash at purchase, they discourage both builders and home buyers from using these programs in periods of tight money. In recent years, lenders whose interest rates are not fixed by law have begun to charge discount points—in imitation of what happens in the FHA and VA programs. But there is no rational basis for this. It is simply another cost of securing a mortgage loan or a hidden device for exacting higher interest rates. If conventional lenders really need the higher interest rates, they would better serve the borrower by being direct about it and thus stretching the whole interest charge over the life of the loan.[10]

The Consequences

The extreme instability in the flow of funds to housing impairs the effective operation of the housing market, hurts would-be home purchasers, damages the home-building industry, makes a stable general economy harder to achieve, and weakens our efforts to improve the cities.

The Housing Market

Effective performance of the housing market requires adequate and steady production of new houses as well as the purchase and sale of the existing housing stock to accommodate families who move and to facilitate the filtering process.

Periodic shortages in housing credit reduce new housing construction and also inhibit the turnover of existing housing.

Home Purchasers

When funds are tight, many families who need homes cannot get the mortgage loans they need. Either they cannot get a mortgage loan, or the high interest rates and high down payments price them out of the market.

The Home-Building Industry

When mortgage funds are tight, the home-building industry suffers from unemployed resources. This means high unemployment among workers and idleness or bankruptcy of the home builder. The unevenness of home-building activity means a less efficient industry and correspondingly higher prices for homes. The effects are much the same on the manufacturers of building materials. Low levels of home building also put many architects and mortgage bankers out of work. If the production of housing could be stabilized, the home-building and related industries would be far more productive and efficient.

The Economy

Though some observers have argued to the contrary, the massive fluctuations in home building caused by periodic credit shortages contribute to the destabilization of the general economy and to general inflation.[11] Economist J. M. Clark observed over forty years ago that a depressed construction industry, particularly home building, leads the general economy toward depression.[12] A radically depressed home-building industry contributes to inflation because too few houses are produced to meet the housing demand, thereby inflating housing prices.

Social Costs

A frequently depressed housing industry "leads to failure to rebuild our cities and to replace substandard housing."[13] It is thus a formidable roadblock to HUD's mission to improve our cities.

The Remedies

What Has Been Done

The federal government has taken various steps to cushion tight credit and its disproportionate effect on housing.

1. *Direct credit infusion.* The most obvious way to support housing when its production sags is to provide government funds for the direct purchase of mortgages. This, of course, amounts to using government funds to substitute for those not supplied by private mortgage lenders. Such a step has been taken twice on a relatively massive scale. In 1958 and again in 1966, the Congress authorized $1 billion for the direct purchase of FHA-insured and VA-guaranteed mortgages for lower-cost housing. Schechter estimates that the 1958 efforts led to a 70,000-unit increase in lower-cost housing production and to a 35,000-unit increase following the 1966 action.[14] However, as with most countercyclical efforts involving construction, timing was a problem. In both cases, it appears that these actions affected housing construction only after the real crisis had passed and recovery had begun.

2. *The Tandem Plan.* Another approach to the same objective was developed in the 1960s—the "Tandem Plan." In this plan, HUD's Government National Mortgage Association (GNMA) directly purchased mortgages at interest rates somewhat below prevailing market rates and then sold these mortgages to the Federal National Mortgage Association (FNMA) or to others at market interest rates. This procedure gives much the same results as the earlier direct government purchase of mortgages. The Tandem Plan gained favor because it has less immediate impact on the federal budget than the previous approach did. That is, under the Tandem Plan, the cost reflected on the annual budget is the difference between the price at which GNMA purchases the mortgages and the price at which it sells them to FNMA or others—a difference of several percentage points. The actual long-term costs of the Tandem Plan are greater than those of the more direct approach. Indeed, the government ultimately made a small profit from its earlier direct purchase and holding of mortgages to support a tight mortgage market.

The Tandem Plan was used in the 1960s and again in the 1970s to counter what were considered excessive declines in home building.

3. *FNMA mortgage purchases.* Beyond these direct mortgage purchase approaches, FNMA can support the sagging mortgage market—simply by purchasing more mortgages than it sells when private funds are tight. However, FNMA appears to have bought more mortgages than it has sold, at least in recent years. Its consistent accumulation of a larger and larger portfolio of mortgages is inconsistent with the countercyclical impact it could have on the mortgage market. However, FNMA cannot be accused of acting irresponsibly. Recent, curious economic developments—in which recession was accompanied by unemployment, inflation, and continued high interest rates—made it practically impossible for a private FNMA to sell mortgages without experiencing a loss when, from past experience, it should have been able to do so.

The recently created Federal Home Loan Mortgage Corporation can also cushion the impact of tight money on home building—by buying mortgages when private credit is scarce and selling them when it is plentiful. But FHLMC, like FNMA, can scarcely have been expected to perform this role very well in recent years.

4. *FHLBB advances to member savings and loans.* FHLBB, through its power to make advances to savings and loan associations, can also cushion the impact of private credit stringencies on housing. The National Commission on Urban Problems was quite critical of the FHLBB's actions in this regard:

> The Federal Home Banks could provide at all times, including periods of extremely tight money, a more reliable and dependable channel to the money and capital markets for homebuyers and homebuilders than their individual banks can provide. They have not done so, even though this is the purpose for which they were created. Instead of making funds available to members when such funds are needed for mortgage lending, the Home Loan Banks have generally performed in an opposite manner, lending more freely when they were not needed and restricting lending when needs were greatest.[15]

The commission's report was published in 1968. Since then, the FHLBB has performed much better than the commission pictured it. (Some students, including UCLA's Leo Grebler, believe the FHLBB's record was never so bad.) Indeed, during 1975-1976, the FHLBB used its advances to support mortgage lending by savings and loan associations until it was forced to curtail its support for reasons similar to those that inhibited FNMA.

One fact weakens the total impact of the federal government's existing instruments capable of modifying the frequent ups and downs of housing production caused by fluctuations in the supply of mortgage credit. Namely, these instruments are widely dispersed in several government agencies, and one of them (FNMA) is a private corporation, making coordination and coherent policy hard to achieve. The National Commission on Urban Problems wrote, "It is difficult to accept objectively the proliferation of housing financial policies among HUD, the Federal Home Loan Bank Board and the now-to-be private FNMA."[16] There is little evidence that HUD has been able to exert much influence over the FHLBB. Neither has HUD had much influence on the federal agencies that make general economic policy—the Office of Management and Budget, the Treasury Department, the Federal Reserve Board, and the Council of Economic Advisers. General economic policy affects urban conditions, not only with respect to housing finance and production, but in many other crucial ways as well. On this important matter, the National Commission on Urban Problems observed, "The interrelations of these responsible agencies need rethinking, and perhaps reshaping to fit the needs of society."[17]

One conclusion seems inescapable. Although the government probably does not have all the tools it needs to stabilize the violent and harmful fluctuations in the flow of mortgage funds, the tools it does have are fragmented, and their policies are sometimes contradictory.

What More Can Be Done?

The most fundamental method by which government could reduce the steep ups and downs of housing credit is also the most difficult: namely, to make more use of fiscal policy (increases and decreases in federal expenditures through changes in taxes or in public expenditures or in both) and to make less use of monetary policy (use of the various powers of the Federal Reserve Board to reduce or expand the supply of credit). As Charles L. Schultze has pointed out, "In the context of efforts to moderate inflation, the greater the fiscal restraint on the budget, the less the need for restrictive monetary policies."[18] Schultze also agrees with nearly all students of housing economics that a restrictive monetary policy is principally responsible for the sharp reductions in the availability of housing credit and housing production.

The hitch in the use of fiscal policy as a means of housing stabilization is that administrations and the Congress have always found it easier to stimulate the economy through public expenditures and reduced taxes than to restrain it by doing the reverse. This is the prescription for economic stability articulated by John Maynard Keynes. But both sides of the Keynsian formula have rarely, if ever, been used. The political reasons for this failure are not hard to see. As the President's Commission on Mortgage Interest Rates put it, "even when the need for economic restraint is widely acknowledged, the administration and the Congress have generally been unwilling or slow to take the necessary fiscal actions—to curb inflationary forces. In such situations, monetary policy has little choice but to take up the slack."[19]

After reading a draft of this chapter, housing economist Henry Schechter made an observation that is worth noting here:

> The inflation of the last few years [up to 1977] probably could not have been stopped by any reasonable Federal fiscal policies. Certainly, the price rises of oil and grain, which permeated through the economy, could not have been stopped. Nor could fiscal policy have stopped the loose credit extended for beach-front condominums, the overbuilding of 747 airliners and tankers, the speculative hoarding of industrial inventories in 1973-74, or the speculative recreational land development.[20]

Schechter makes a valid point. He underlines the way

inflation, once started, stimulates speculation in anticipation of further inflation. He also makes clear the increasing interdependence of the economies of the nations of the world. Both developments make it vastly more difficult to stabilize our economy. If this is so, then it becomes even more difficult to stabilize housing production. We must hope, however, that neither becomes impossible.

Other proposals for relieving periodic credit stringencies and disproportionate effects they have on home building have been advanced. They include (1) creation of a national development bank (to insure private loans or make direct loans when necessary); (2) selective credit controls (the Federal Reserve Board would use its powers in such a way as to restrain the flow of credit to some less vital sectors of the economy while protecting housing credit from unnecessary restraint); (3) direct government loans; and (4) the government as "builder of last resort" (when housing production is affected adversely by stringent credit conditions, the government would build housing directly and finance its building). None of these alternatives have gained much support.

Still other proposals include strengthening the specialized mortgage lending institution (savings and loans, especially) by giving them more freedom to make installment and other types of nonmortgage loans. There is wide disagreement over whether such a step would increase or decrease the volume of mortgage loans these institutions would make. Ironically, the savings and loan associations, long supported by the government as a source of mortgage loans, now want to become much more like general banks, presumably with the same government benefits they have long enjoyed because they were exclusively mortgage lenders.

Conclusions

The experts disagree on the merits of most additional approaches to housing credit stabilization. But several tentative conclusions can be offered.

1. Greater reliance by the economic policymakers on fiscal, rather than monetary, policy as an economic stabilization tool (in spite of its limitations in current circumstances) is still

the most obvious way to relieve housing of its cyclical burden.

2. All agencies of the government related to housing finance should be required to coordinate their efforts toward the desired end.

3. The Federal Reserve Board should make a serious effort to develop and use methods for assuring that the major impact of monetary restraint, when it must be used, does not fall on housing.

4. The various other devices that economists are now debating should be studied further, and even tested, to discover their practical usefulness.

5. At cabinet meetings and elsewhere in the government's policy-making councils, HUD should articulate the important effects that general economic policy decisions have on the volume and stability of housing production and on many other aspects of the urban problems for which HUD is responsible. It should also seek participation with the President's Council of Economic Advisers, the Treasury Department, the Office of Management and Budget, and with the Federal Reserve Board on economic policy decisions that affect housing production and its other important missions.

President Carter's HUD secretary has publicly committed herself to a stable production of housing, and so has the director of Carter's Domestic Council, Stuart Eizenstat. This is a step in the right direction. It is not easy, but it certainly needs doing.

10
Reducing Housing Costs

This chapter will deal with a disturbing urban problem—the rapid escalation of housing costs. It will evaluate HUD Secretary George Romney's effort to halt, or at least slow, rising housing costs through Operation Breakthrough—a much-publicized program to industrialize housing production and thereby to improve its efficiency. It will also discuss an effort of the same kind, conducted over twenty years earlier by one of HUD's predecessors. Then it will show that housing costs come from many factors other than the cost of the house itself. It will be argued that a successful assault on housing costs must be a many-sided effort that deals with all of these factors, many of which are not under the direct control of HUD, but which HUD can influence directly or indirectly. In conclusion, some recommendations will be proposed to deal with the problem of housing costs.

HUD's Charter

The Congress has repeatedly ordered HUD and its predecessors to do something to arrest rising housing costs. Since 1945, nine major laws have addressed the problems of housing costs. In 1965, President Johnson's Message on the Cities proposed an institute on urban development, among other things, to provide research grants aimed at reducing the costs of building and home construction through the development of new technology.[1] At least three presidential advisory committees noted the increase in housing costs and recommended actions to reduce them.

The Upward Leap in Housing Costs

For over two decades, the cost of housing has been rising faster than general living costs. After World War II, a family could purchase a perfectly decent new home for about $7,000. By 1965, the median price of a new home had reached $20,000. By 1975 the median price of a new home had climbed to $44,200, over six times the price the returning veterans paid in 1945. The price of an existing home has risen at about the same pace, and it was only a few thousand dollars less. At the same time, family incomes increased correspondingly during the past twenty years. Consequently, most families were able to improve the quality of their housing. In fact, the typical new house built in 1977 was larger and had more bathrooms and other amenities than the typical house built twenty years before.

To the home buyer, of course, the important thing is the relation between his after-tax income and the total cost of paying for a house—mortgage payments, property taxes, heat and utilities, home maintenance, and related costs. When all these costs are taken into account, the picture looks somewhat different. During the past twenty years, housing expenses have increased each year by about 7 percent, but disposable, after-tax family income has risen slightly over 5 percent. As the typical American family was improving its housing and demanding even larger and better-equipped homes, the adverse relationship between spendable income and total housing expenses was gradually requiring it to spend a higher percentage of its income for housing.

Between 1970 and 1976, the gap between total housing costs and disposable family income increased more and more sharply. During this seven-year period, expenses rose at an annual rate of nearly 12 percent, and disposable income rose less than 7 percent. Between 1975 and 1976, housing expenses jumped nearly 15 percent, and disposable family income rose slightly over 7 percent.[2] The principal reasons for this recent, serious deterioration of family income in relation to housing costs are increases in interest rates, increased land and utility costs, greatly increased property taxes, and higher income taxes. As a result, most families paid a very high proportion of their income for housing. Many were priced out of the housing market entirely.

This state of affairs is particularly hard on the family purchasing its first house, particularly the newly married couple. Those who purchased their homes some years ago suffer less—because the value of their investment has increased—and are also in a better position when they move or decide to purchase another house. Renters are also feeling the pinch of rising housing costs, though rents have not gone up as fast as house prices. Most experts think rents must go up at a faster rate if we are to avoid a rental housing shortage.[3] The reasons that house purchases were as high as they were in 1977 is that more wives are working, mortgage terms have been extended, and families are paying a much higher portion of their incomes for housing.

Oakley Hunter, president of the Federal National Mortgage Association, has depicted the seriousness of our present plight: "Twenty-five years ago two-thirds of all American families could afford to make monthly payments on a median-priced new single family home and one-third could not. Today the situation is reversed; two-thirds cannot and one-third can."[4] These figures accurately reflect the recent, alarming escalation in housing costs, but they exaggerate the situation, as Anthony Downs, who made the calculations on which Hunter based his statement, is fully aware.[5] The reason is that the calculations are based on the median-priced house. By definition, about half of the new houses are sold at prices below the median. It is accurate to say that only one-third of American families can afford a median-priced house, but it does not follow that two-thirds of our families cannot afford to purchase any new house at all. Downs made later calculations that took the limitations of his previous estimates into account. He now estimates that in 1974 "about 46 percent of all households could afford *some* type of newly built home."[6] Nonetheless, recent trends in housing costs in relation to family income are still serious and getting more so.

Some observers have suggested that the current rapid rise in housing costs is but temporary, a reflection of the unusual conditions of "stagflation" in the national economy. But Downs, who is one of our most qualified students of such matters, is not convinced that such an optimistic view is justified. He argues that we "simply do not know" how long current trends in house prices will persist. He sees about as much evidence that the trend will continue as that it will not.[7]

Damaging Consequences

This drastic rise in housing costs has damaging results. Rising housing costs make it more difficult for many families to afford good housing. High housing costs hurt the poor and the near poor most severely. They also hurt families of moderate income, especially newly married families. By driving families out of the housing market, rising rents and rising sales prices also damage the housing producers, decrease their efficiency, and produce unemployment in one of the country's most labor-intensive industries. Not only does a depressed housing industry produce unemployment in the building trades, but it also affects the general economy. Residential construction is a strategic factor in business cycles, and low levels of construction can lead the general economy into depression. This is why economic policymakers give much attention to present and anticipated levels of housing production. Beyond all this, housing prices greatly affect public expenditures on subsidies for housing. As housing prices rise, more and more families need and become eligible for housing subsidies.

For all of these reasons, John Lindsay, in the preface to a 1972 book on housing, identified "soaring construction costs as one of the four major failures of government in dealing with the housing crisis."[8] Controlling housing costs is one of HUD's most important missions. Yet it is also a difficult and complex job, and HUD has no direct control over many of the forces involved. Hence, HUD's efforts have been considerably less than successful so far.

The Favored Remedy

HUD's efforts to control housing costs have been directed

largely at making the home-building process more efficient through the application of mass production methods. This is, after all, the thing for which American industry is most renowned and from which we have come to expect miracles. Henry Ford and his $500 Model T have become a legend. That such miracles of mass production are still possible is shown by the astonishing development of electronic calculators. What cost $500 or more fifteen years ago can now be purchased for $9.95. Besides that, the cheap calculators of today are small enough to fit into one's pocket and will perform mathematical feats of complexity previously unavailable to a layman.

With these very American wonders before us, it is not surprising that HUD's and Congress's impulse has been to tackle the cost problem by trying to build homes like we build automobiles and many other things. Second, another fact has reinforced this impulse. As everyone knows, houses are built today much like they have been for two centuries or more. On the other hand, there have been significant evolutionary improvements in the traditional process of home building. Many elements used in home construction are now prefabricated in a factory, including windows, doors, roof trusses, and many others. Third, there is another reason why home building seemed a good place to apply mass production. The industry is highly fragmented. The average firm builds fewer than 200 homes a year. The few that build several thousand annually are comparative giants. Made up of thousands of small entrepreneurs, the home-building industry appears antiquated and inefficient, indeed, when compared with General Motors, General Electric, and other industrial mammoths.

Operation Breakthrough

Shortly after he took office, HUD Secretary George Romney announced with characteristic fanfare the launching of Operation Breakthrough. It was May 1969. The announced purpose was to stimulate the development of techniques capable of producing housing in volume and at costs that would rise more slowly for all income groups. Through Operation Breakthrough, with one bold stroke, Romney hoped to solve the tenacious problem of rising housing costs.

Because Romney was once president of American Motors, many thought this plan to turn out houses on the production line was intuitive, even inevitable. This is not quite so. He undoubtedly did harbor some dream about mass producing housing. But, like any dream, it was ill defined. Operation Breakthrough's concrete conception was developed by others in HUD and sold to Romney only after tortuous, sometimes testy, examination and reexamination. When Romney embraced the idea, he plunged into its promotion with fervor and directed a whirlwind series of meetings in Washington and throughout the country reminiscent of the sales plan for a new model automobile.

The Plan

Operation Breakthrough involved five steps:

1. to invite the creation and submission of promising ideas for the volume production of housing
2. to screen each proposal for design, engineering soundness, mass production potential, livability, and cost-saving potential
3. to finance and guide the further design and development of the systems selected
4. to demonstrate the product of the new production systems in several real residential settings to persuade local code authorities the houses were satisfactory even though they might violate some specific code provision; to persuade the public that factory-built housing was as good as or better than conventional housing; and to generate zoning flexibility
5. to provide an initial market sufficient in volume to begin to realize the economies under each system of mass production

Response and Selection

The official invitation for submission of proposals under Operation Breakthrough was made public in June 1969. Over 600 proposals were submitted to HUD, involving over 1,000 organizations. After careful analysis by teams of experts, twenty-two building systems were selected. Among them were systems proposed by the Aluminum Company of America (ALCOA), General Electric, and Republic Steel. Also represented were already established prefabricated home manufacturers such as National Homes. Some conventional home builders were also included. Among these were Levitt and the Rouse-Watts Company. There were three basic approaches to industrialized housing: complete modules, panels, and component subassemblies. Systems for single family homes, a town house, and apartments were included. Materials used included concrete, metal, wood, and plastic. Following selection, most systems were refined and developed with HUD's financial support.

First-rate architects and engineers from HUD and the National Bureau of Standards as well as from the sponsors were used to refine the systems.

Public Display

In accord with the original plan, the products of the various systems were constructed on nine sites selected through competition to represent a wide range of geographic, climatic, and marketing conditions and wide range of sizes (from fifty acres to less than two). The building sites were carefully planned by selected site planners to provide a good living environment. HUD paid the necessary costs for site development and provided mortgage financing for construction of the units and subsidies where needed. Over 2,500 homes and apartments were built on the nine sites. When completed, they were rented or sold along with the sites. Thus, as Romney had planned, the new housing systems—their appearance, performance, and livability—were displayed publicly all over the country.

Results

Without doubt, Operation Breakthrough failed to achieve its cost reduction objectives. It neither generated the mass production of housing nor demonstrated that the building systems it chose could produce housing at lower costs than housing built by conventional methods. The cost-saving

potential of Breakthrough's systems was probably never really
tested because neither the manufacturers nor HUD managed to
generate the sustained, large-volume demand so indispensable
to the achievement of economies of scale. Indeed, seven years
later, only one of the Breakthrough systems is being produced
in the United States, and that on a small scale. A few are selling
their systems in the oil-rich, but underdeveloped, countries of
the Middle East.

Studies of Breakthrough's results are revealing. On the
whole, the houses it produced were well built, attractive, and
livable, as studies by the National Bureau of Standards reported. NBS studies also found that the families who occupied
the units were no less satisfied than they would have been with
good, conventionally built housing of the same type and that
these families did not object to the housing simply because it
was built by nonconventional methods.[9] But a study made by
the private Real Estate Research Corporation reached a different conclusion on consumer acceptance: it found consumers to
be still skeptical about factory-built housing. All those involved agreed that construction labor, long opposed to the industrialization of housing production, offered no significant
resistance to the new systems, a positive result. There are differences of opinion on the impact of Operation Breakthrough
on local code officials. The Real Estate Research Corporation
found no major change in the negative attitude of local code officials, although it noted a slightly broader acceptance of
plastic pipe and single-stacked plumbing.[10] On the other hand,
Dr. Robert Wehrli of the National Bureau of Standards believes
Operation Breakthrough had a major impact on building code
officials and on their willingness to accept performance
standards as opposed to the prevalent detailed specifications of
required materials and components.[11] The Real Estate Research Corporation study concluded that because of Operation
Breakthrough, mortgage lenders found industrialized housing
somewhat more acceptable but that no significant financing
mechanisms were developed and tailored to the special requirements of industrialized production.[12] Harry Finger, then a
HUD assistant secretary, who directed the program, disagrees.
He reports that bond warehousing and related financial

arrangements were used to pay for housing not yet on the construction site.[13] A very positive result was the impetus given to the enactment of standard building codes in thirty-three states.

All observers agree that Operation Breakthrough suffered from the cost and difficulty of transporting the modules from the factory to the building site. Transportation of modules proved so expensive that a factory could efficiently serve marketing areas of 300 miles or less. Harold Denton, an expert in industrialized housing, has made another significant observation, namely, that Operation Breakthrough produced no truly new approaches to home-building technology. All the systems employed had been in existence a long time, though they may have been put together in fresh ways.[14]

Operation Breakthrough is difficult to evaluate, primarily because its objectives were perceived differently by the public, the participants, and the government officials involved. Its objectives also seem to have changed over time. In its early stages, much stress was put on industrialization and cost reduction. Later, social objectives were introduced, such as demonstrating good land use, flexible zoning, and a mix of income levels in a single community—the demonstration site. This latter, though important, hardly seems to justify Operation Breakthrough's massive effort—for they had all been tested before. For example, flexible zoning (called "planned unit development") had been demonstrated with considerable success several years earlier. The mixing of income and racial groups had been tested in Pittsburgh and was a major feature of Columbia, the new town developed by James Rouse.

But one thing is clear. Operation Breakthrough neither reduced housing costs nor industrialized the home-building process.

Breakthrough's Forgotten Predecessor

As World War II drew to a close, President Harry Truman realized the country was bound to face a severe housing shortage: little housing production had been permitted during the war, and thousands of soldiers would be returning to civilian life. A great increase in housing production was clearly needed. To do something about this, Truman called on Wilson Wyatt, the energetic and eloquent former mayor of Louisville. Wyatt came to Washington and became the nation's housing expeditor; armed with the power granted by the Veterans Emergency Housing Act of 1946, he charged all the housing production barriers in sight.

Wyatt decided it was necessary to stimulate the mass production of housing in order to increase production volume and reduce costs. He therefore sought out firms with promising and innovative ideas. From many applications, he selected twenty. To help them mass produce housing, he provided federal capital and development loans to support the tooling-up process. To support the high volume necessary for efficient mass production, Wyatt negotiated guaranteed market contracts with his chosen producers. These contracts guaranteed each producer an annual market of about 30,000 units. The effect of the guaranteed market contract was to make the federal government the potential purchaser of last resort. Each producer was expected to devise ways to market his houses. But if he failed to reach the volume agreed upon, the government was committed to buy the rest.

Various existing producers of prefabricated housing participated in the Wyatt program, and new ones were created. The most striking new entry was the Lustron Corporation. It leased a vacated aircraft factory and designed a house that could be manufactured on an assembly line at the rate of 100 a day. The Lustron house was a good one. Thirty years later, some are still occupied and in excellent condition. But the company could not sell enough houses to keep its production line going at full capacity and to repay its capital loan. Wyatt's market guarantee helped, but other problems developed. Finally, after much negotiation, the government withdrew its loan for capital expenses. Lustron collapsed. In a few years, most other producers also disappeared. Only one of these pioneers in housing mass production still survives, and it has drifted away from factory, assembly-line production toward a conventional house, some elements of which are preassembled and put together on the site.

All the lessons of Operation Breakthrough were vividly

learned through the Wyatt effort thirty years before—plus a few more. For example, the Wyatt program demonstrated that successful marketing of factory-built housing requires financial devices quite different from those used by traditional home builders. What was needed was some kind of inventory loan, like that used in the automobile industry, which relieves the manufacturer of the heavy costs involved in supporting numbers of houses during the long period between the time the house rolls off the production line and the time it is placed on a site. In addition, no one has figured out what kind of business entity erects the factory-produced house on the site. The traditional home builder is unlikely to be interested because the work is relatively minor. Besides this, he would be helping his competitors. There were no solutions to these problems in 1948, and despite Operation Breakthrough, there are none today.

All of this raises an important, and sad, question. Why must the federal government continue to reinvent the wheel? When George Romney committed so much energy and money to Operation Breakthrough, he did not bother to find out whether the same thing had been tried before. When he later found this out and was offered the benefits of the Wyatt experience, he brushed the offer aside.[15] This is one of the most unfortunate compulsions that afflict federal executives. Anthony Downs has come close to describing this in his "Law of Compulsive Innovation."[16] An even closer description might be the "Law of Repetitive Error."[17]

The Multiple Causes of Housing Costs

HUD has tried to reduce housing costs primarily by mass producing the house itself. Mass production of housing is important, and someday it may be achieved. But HUD's approach is too narrow: the cost of the house itself is by no means the main reason why housing costs are rising at such an alarming rate. Many factors make up the cost of owning or renting a place to live, and they themselves are affected by many different forces. Thus, when it focuses on mass production and improved building technology alone, HUD is looking only at the tip of the iceberg.

Let us look at the elements of housing costs and the forces that influence them.

Production Costs

1. *Land.* The cost of land is influenced by many factors: population increases; distance from the central city; access to transportation, shopping, and other essential facilities such as roads, major water lines, and sewers; zoning restrictions; and the quality of the neighborhood. In 1949, the cost of the land was 11 percent of the cost of the typical house. By 1977, it had risen to 25 percent.

2. *Site improvements.* These include clearing, grading, excavation, landscaping, and connective plumbing. They may also include streets, sidewalks, curbs, and other facilities required by subdivision ordinances if the houses are built in a new suburb.

3. *Structure.* This includes the cost of foundations, frame and shell, interior finish, mechanical equipment, and major appliances. Structure cost is made up of labor and materials, each of which is influenced by quite different forces. Labor costs depend on the skill required, the extent to which labor is unionized, the demand for construction labor, and other factors. Materials costs depend to some extent on supply-demand relationships in the market, but also on the pricing policies of large materials manufacturers and on natural forces such as the supply of timber and other basic structural materials. In 1949, the structure accounted for 69 percent of total house cost. In 1977, it accounted for only 47 percent. Obviously, structure costs have not gone down—other cost components have risen faster.

4. *Construction financing.* This is related to the cost of borrowed funds and reflects not only the demand-supply relations in the money market but also federal economic policies. In 1949, the financing cost was about 5 percent of the total sales price. Now, it is 11 percent.

5. *Profit, overhead, and fees.* A builder will not work unless he expects a profit, usually a profit of 15 to 20 percent of gross sales. Fees, such as architects' fees, vary but are not low. According to the home builders, overhead and profits increased

on the average from 15 percent in 1949 to 17 percent in 1977.

6. *Marketing.* The marketing costs include salesmen's fees, advertising, and related items.

7. *Miscellaneous.* Time is a very important part of a builder's cost. It takes time to get the numerous and increasing approvals required by local governments—building permits, zoning changes, environmental impact approvals and the like. It also takes time to apply for and secure financing—which can greatly add to costs, especially if the builder uses HUD-supported financing. The costs of financing have risen substantially in recent years. Another element of housing cost is the cost of closing the mortgage loan to the purchaser. Closing costs include title search and legal fees. These costs vary widely from place to place.

Operating Costs

1. *Financing costs.* These include payments to principal and interest on a mortgage. Financing costs reflect not only the percentage of the purchase price financed but also the rate of interest charged. The rate of mortgage interest, like the cost of construction financing, reflects supply-demand conditions in the money market as well as government economic policies. In the last twenty years, financing costs for a family of four have increased $2,222, or 497 percent. (In the early 1950s, mortgage interest rates were about 4 percent.)

2. *Property taxes.* An important element of the cost of owning a home is property taxes assessed by the county or some other local jurisdiction. Since local governments rely heavily on them as a source of revenue, property taxes are usually high and keep going up. Between 1975 and 1976, average real estate taxes jumped 20 percent.

3. *Heat and utilities.* These essential operating costs have increased rapidly in recent years and can be expected to increase even more in the future as energy shortages threaten the country. In the past few years, the costs of gas, oil, and electricity have climbed rapidly—between 1975 and 1976, by about 20 percent.

4. *Maintenance and repairs.* It has long been estimated that maintenance and repairs amount annually to about 2 percent

of purchase price. They have been rising rapidly and will probably continue to do so.[18]

General Economic Inflation

In recent years, this country has been plagued by a rapid rate of inflation, even during periods of unemployment. General price inflation influences every element of housing cost. Beyond that, the expectation of an inflationary trend in house prices reinforces that very inflationary trend.

Each of these housing cost components varies widely, depending on the type of housing, location, general economic conditions, and other factors. Thus, its impact on the total cost of a house varies widely. Mortgage interest rates are a striking example. A decrease of three points in current mortgage interest rates would reduce total monthly housing costs on the median-priced $39,000 new house (financed with a 90 percent, thirty-year mortgage) by about twice as much as would a reduction of 15 percent in the cost of the house itself. This fact reflects rather dramatically the limitations of HUD's previous preoccupation with attempts to reduce housing costs through mass production alone.

The factors affecting the total cost of housing are not only many; they are also immensely varied, complex, and the result of many quite different influences.

HUD and Housing Costs

As we have seen, HUD and its predecessors have tried primarily to reduce only one of the many components of housing costs. Whatever their beneficial side effects, they have failed to reach their main objective. HUD has made a few passes at other aspects of housing costs, for example, at closing costs. But these efforts have produced more studies than results. True, mortgage lenders must now disclose the closing costs to each purchaser. This is a step in the right direction, even if its benefit is only to make the purchaser aware of them at closing rather than to lower them. Likewise, HUD has taken various steps— direct and indirect—to do away with the anarchy of local building codes. Operation Breakthrough was one such step, and some small successes have been won. But HUD has hesitated to attack the building code problem directly—by creating a national building code. First, building codes are promulgated by local jurisdictions, whose freedom HUD must respect. Second, local building codes are surrounded by numerous interests and pressure groups. HUD has studied but never acted to influence local property taxes and the numerous time and money consuming local approvals builders must receive before building. Neither has it been able to keep its own processing of applications for mortgage assistance simple and fast. Rather, the trend has been in the other direction. Other elements of housing costs—notably energy costs, mortgage interest rates, and general inflation—lie beyond HUD's direct influence. But the HUD secretary can, at least, make known to those with influence over such matters the devastating impact that these elements have on housing costs. That is one of the reasons cabinet meetings are held.

What HUD Could Do

First, HUD must recognize that the rise in housing costs results from many complex factors. A single bold stroke, such as Operation Breakthrough, is not enough. What is needed is a sustained, comprehensive strategy aimed at all of the many causes of housing cost increases. No element is too trivial to be ignored. HUD can deal directly with some housing costs. Others it must approach indirectly: through the conditions it attaches to its program benefits, through wide dissemination of the facts and their consequences, or both.

A HUD strategy for reducing housing costs might include the following actions.

Construction Costs

Despite past failures, the search for a way to reduce construction costs should be continued. We need a sustained program of research and testing to discover ways to improve productivity in home building. Whether this research will lead to production-line, mass-production methods, or some other approach cannot be predicted. The important thing is that the search continue.

Land Costs

As already noted, the cost of land makes up a large and rapidly increasing proportion of housing costs. HUD could take several approaches to deal with this problem.

The President's Commission on Urban Problems asserted, "The imposition of new taxes on land (as distinguished from the house and the land) would be one of the most comprehensive approaches governments might take to retard or reverse the rise in land prices."[19] A land tax could provide new revenues for already heavily burdened municipalities and help decrease the reliance of local governments on the property tax. One of the principal ways in which a land tax could reduce urban land costs is by discouraging owners from retaining vacant land for speculative purposes. Some form of land taxation is widely practiced in western Canada, England, Australia, New Zealand, South Africa and some Latin American countries. In this country, special or differential land taxation is used in Pittsburgh, Pennsylvania; Arden, Illinois; and Fairhope, Alabama. A land tax might take several forms, as the President's Commission on Urban Problems has suggested:

1. differentially higher taxation on the land portion of values subject to general property taxation, possibly extending to final exemption of structural values
2. a separate, recurrent tax on land values as such
3. a separate tax on land value increments, primarily through a transactions tax procedure[20]

The most politically acceptable approach is probably to leave existing land values undisturbed but to tax an increment of any future increase in land values. This can be done either through the federal income tax (a special supplement rate on capital gains on land) or through state income taxes.

Another approach is land banking. Land banking, as advocated by many students of the problem, involves federal financial assistance to state or metropolitan bodies to acquire land (through eminent domain, if necessary) that is in the path of future urban growth, to hold it, then to sell it for public or private uses in accordance with a general plan. Land banking could help lower land costs. It could become an important tool for controlling the timing, location, type, and scale of urban development. It could deter the costly "leap-frogging" resulting from private land speculation and thus reduce costly urban sprawl. Federal financial aid to land banking need not be costly in the long run, for the public capture of the "unearned increment" could be used to reimburse the federal government over time as land is sold. Land banking has made possible Stockholm's much admired planning.

Mortgage Interest Rates

As we have seen, mortgage interest rates are a signficant part of total housing costs. But they influence housing costs in yet another way. Because of the notorious instability in the flow of mortgage funds, housing production is inefficient and fluctuates widely from year to year. As a result, housing prices skyrocket. If there were stable flow of mortgage funds into housing, then the home production process would be cheaper and far more efficient. If there were a stable flow of mortgage funds at low interest rates, housing costs would be reduced even more. The difficult problem of stabilizing the flow of mortgage funds and lowering interest rates has been discussed in chapter 9.

Closing Costs

Mortgage closing costs consist of several different charges— e.g., title insurance, prepaid taxes and insurance, settlement fees, transfer taxes, and lender's service charges. They vary widely from place to place, although nearly all experts believe they are higher than necessary. One of the largest closing costs is title search and insurance, which results, to a large extent, from the fact that local land transfer records are poorly kept and difficult to trace. HUD could encourage and assist localities to make major improvements in their systems of land records, including centralization and computerization. It could also encourage state legislation limiting unreasonable and un- necessary closing costs and put pressure on bar associations and title companies to reduce closing fees in areas where they are exorbitant.

Property Taxes

It is well known that local governments rely heavily on property taxes for revenue. It is perhaps not so well known just how high property taxes are. As Dick Nitzer wrote in a study prepared for the President's Commission on Urban Problems, "It is simply inconceivable that, if we were starting to develop a tax system from scratch, we would single out housing for extraordinary high levels of taxation. More likely, we would exempt housing entirely from taxation, just as most states exempt food from sales tax."[21] The property tax is also regressive and puts a special burden on the poor. HUD's objectives should be to encourage states and localities to improve tax assessment administration and to make the property tax fairer. It could encourage localities to assess both land and buildings at market value rather than underassessing land. In order to reduce the heavy reliance on property taxes, HUD should encourage localities to make greater use of user charges for highways, parking, recreational facilities, and other public services.

Zoning, Subdivision Regulations, and Building Codes

These three forms of local regulation have a substantial effect on housing costs. For example, large-lot zoning drives up the cost of land and site improvements, as well as the cost of the house itself. Zoning that excludes apartments increases housing costs by preventing more efficient use of land. The prohibition of planned unit developments increases housing costs by reducing the efficiency with which land can be used without reducing amenities. Subdivision requirements that establish precise specifications for site improvements and for the amount of land that can be devoted to housing can add significantly to housing costs. Building codes increase housing costs because they are inconsistent from place to place, thus requiring builders to modify their structures at substantial cost when they build in several jurisdictions. Many building codes prohibit the use of new, more economical products and practices and contain requirements greater and more costly than needed to assure good housing standards.

Once again, HUD must proceed indirectly—through encouragement and incentives. Through its financial support of local planning, HUD can influence zoning and subdivision regulations. By carrying out and disseminating research to improve building codes and by promulgating model regulations and codes, it can influence building codes. It can also exert pressure for interjurisdictional uniformity in codes and regulations. Another useful tool, applicable to some of these issues, is a demonstration. Some years ago, through demonstrations it carried out in cooperation with states and localities, FHA had some impact on local acceptance of planned unit development (a form of flexible zoning).

Restrictive Labor Practices

There can be little doubt that restrictive labor practices incorporated in agreements between labor and builders increase housing costs: they inhibit the efficient use of manpower and retard the adoption of new, more economical materials. Although many home builders, especially those building single-family homes, employ nonunion workers, they often pay the same wages and apply the same work rules that apply to unionized labor in the same locality. HUD's laws require "prevailing wages," as determined by the Department of Labor, to be paid to workers on all multifamily housing it assists. As a result, wage rates on apartment construction are the same as those negotiated by unions for heavy construction (office buildings, for example) rather those those that normally apply to light construction. It should be remembered, however, that labor's demands are prompted not only by the desire for higher wages but also by concern for safety and by the fact that construction work is seasonal and highly intermittent.[22]

HUD's action and leadership are needed to reduce the impact of labor's restrictive practices and the prevailing wage requirement. HUD should use its influence and its pressure to keep housing construction wage rates down to a reasonable level. It should exert pressure to use federal and state construction to reduce the seasonality of construction and thus to maintain a steady demand for construction labor and reduce pressures for higher money wages intended to compensate for seasonal unemployment. HUD-assisted state and local agencies should be influenced to negotiate labor-management agreements that eliminate restrictive and ineffi-cient work practices yet retain those needed to protect the workers and the quality of construction. HUD can also collect wage data and thus enable the Department of Labor to establish realistic prevailing wages for housing construction. HUD has taken some steps in this direction, but it should do more.

If these proposals appear to be a large and difficult undertaking, they should be weighed against the alternative— more and more federal housing subsidies as house prices exceed the ability of more and more Americans to pay.

11
Equal Housing Opportunity

This chapter will deal with a HUD mission of singular importance, namely, the achievement of equal opportunity for all races to live in decent housing whenever and wherever they choose. First, we will discuss the laws and executive orders that give HUD this responsibility and provide some authority to carry it out. Then we will assess HUD's performance and the disappointing results. Some reasons for HUD's limited accomplishments will be identified. We will discuss the views of some who have concluded that government cannot do much about racial equality. We will conclude with a discussion of some ways in which HUD's capacity can be strengthened to accomplish the job Congress has given it.

HUD's Mission

In essence, HUD's mission is to use all of its programs and the direct authorities that civil rights legislation gives it to (1) eliminate racial discrimination in housing, and (2) promote integration of the races. HUD's responsibilities and authorities derive from a series of executive orders and laws that have become broader and broader in scope. The first was President John Kennedy's Executive Order 11063 of November 1962, which prohibited racial discrimination in housing financed by FHA-insured or VA-insured mortgages and in federally assisted public housing. The Kennedy action was therefore quite limited, that is, the great bulk of housing was conventionally financed (non-FHA or non-VA) and thus exempt from the order. Some lawyers, especially those with the U.S. Commission on Civil Rights, believed the president's authority was broad enough to cover loans made by savings and loan associations receiving support from the Federal Home Loan Bank Board. In such matters, however, the views of the Department of Justice are decisive. Moreover, FHA and VA housing was affected only if it was financed after the executive order was issued. Two years later, the Civil Rights Act of 1964 was passed. Title VI of this law prohibited racial discrimination in housing or in any other construction receiving federal financial assistance. In housing, the law extended coverage to that constructed in urban renewal areas and to all public housing, no matter when it was initiated. But the great bulk of housing financed in the country still remained unaffected. Finally, Title VIII of the Civil Rights Act of 1968 prohibited racial discrimination in the sale, rental, and use of nearly all housing (about 80 percent) as well as in mortgage lending, sales, and advertising practices. The responsibility for administering these prohibitions was given to the secretary of HUD, and creation of a new HUD assistant secretary was authorized with these responsibilities in mind.[1]

The Housing and Community Development Act of 1974 prohibited discrimination against women and also included, as one of its major objectives, reduction of the isolation of income groups and the promotion of diversity within neighborhoods. Through this gradual extension of authorities, HUD was given the broad mission of prohibiting racial discrimination in nearly all housing and also of promoting racial integration in living patterns.

The Importance of HUD's Mission

As it deals with the problems of urban America, HUD has many awesome challenges. But its responsibilities for fighting racial discrimination and segregation may well be the most awesome of all. Foreign visitors often see us more clearly than we see ourselves. In 1840, for example, Alexis de Tocqueville wrote, "The most formidable of all the ills that threaten the future of the American Union arises from the presence of a black population."[2] One hundred years later, the Swedish scholar Gunnar Myrdal depicted in grim detail America's pattern of systematic racial discrimination—something that made a caricature of our credo that all men are created equal.[3] Even as late as the 1940s, most Americans were trying hard to ignore this self-evident proposition. America's ambivalence is perhaps best illustrated by Abraham Lincoln, who signed the Emancipation Proclamation and fought a civil war over slavery—and once said that Negroes were an inferior race and should not be allowed to associate too intimately with whites. In 1896 the Supreme Court reinforced this view in its "separate but equal" doctrine in education. Over fifty years passed before the court reversed itself and started the country on the painful road to equality for all citizens.

This sad chapter in American history needs no elaboration here. However, one important fact does need emphasis. Racial discrimination in housing is closely linked to some of our most bedeviling urban ills—poverty, crime, slums, unemployment, central city insolvency, distorted patterns of growth, and the racial apartheid that casts an ominous shadow over the future of our metropolitan areas and of American society itself. The famous Kerner Report of the 1960s spoke with chilling truth when it asked whether this country could long survive as "two nations, separate and unequal."[4] So long as discrimination in housing persists, it will be difficult, if not impossible, to reach full equality in education and employment. Where people live is of prime importance. School busing—now our most visible effort toward racial equality—is basically an effort to counteract the effects of racial polarization in housing. Equal access to jobs is also greatly influenced by where people live.

In view of the crucial role housing plays in many aspects of racial discrimination, it is curious that the authority to ban racial discrimination in housing came fourteen years after the famous Supreme Court decision to ban racial segregation in schools.

During the 1960s, under Robert C. Weaver (first as HHFA administrator, then as HUD secretary), the federal government had a strong commitment to racial equality in housing. Until 1968, however, Weaver had to work with limited powers.

Despite this, he made progress. Significant strides were made in eliminating racial segregation in public housing. The FHA changed its earlier attitudes completely. It became deeply involved in providing housing for the poor and the minorities. It also took the lead in the effort to encourage private mortgage lenders to change their practice of boycotting the run-down neighborhoods where most of the minorities live—a practice called "red-lining."

George Romney, who succeeded Weaver, was also dedicated to the elimination of racial discrimination. Armed with more powers than Weaver had possessed, Romney not only made every effort to enforce the antidiscrimination provisions of the 1968 Civil Rights Act, but he also added to HUD's subsidy programs two new sets of standards for the approval of applications. The Project Selection Criteria, made effective in 1972, established eight additional standards to be used in determining the acceptability of applications for housing subsidy. Applications were to be given higher priority if, among other things, proposed projects (1) "provided minority families with opportunities for housing in a wide range of locations and contributed to decreasing the effects of past housing discrimination," (2) "avoided concentrating subsidized housing in one section of a metropolitan area," and (3) "were located in such a way as to provide opportunities for business concerns owned in substantial part by minority persons."[5]

Romney's second tool—the Affirmative Marketing Regulations—prohibited advertising or sales tactics with respect to HUD-aided housing that were in any way discriminatory, defined these various practices, and required each applicant to submit a marketing plan showing the ways in which the seller would inform minority families that the house or apartment was to become available.[6]

In recent years, HUD's formal efforts to enforce racial equality in housing and to promote racial integration have by no means been half-hearted. This contrasts sharply with the previous record of most of the government's housing agencies. From 1934 to 1948, the FHA actively encouraged racial discrimination and often exclusion in new suburban housing through use of a covenant in the deed of sale—that is, the buyer and the seller signed a written agreement in which the buyer promised not to sell, rent, or transfer his property to families of a specific race or religion. Although these agreements were private, they achieved the status of law through enforcement of state laws governing private contracts.[7]

The FHA's underwriting manual justified and extolled this practice on the grounds that house values, the ultimate security behind the mortgage risks FHA insured, would remain more stable in a neighborhood that was "homogeneous" in income, race, and other population characteristics. Frederick M. Babcock, who wrote the original FHA underwriting manual, was simply reflecting the traditional "wisdom" of real estate appraisers of the time (many still hold it today). It must also be remembered that FHA was initially conceived as a government insurance company responsible for relating the risks it took to the premium income it earned and to the reserves it accumulated in a businesslike fashion.

In the wisdom of hindsight, it is easy to see that these actions were clearly against public policy. But the FHA was not alone. It reflected the racial attitudes of the nation itself. What early FHA policy failed to do was to see beyond, as the Supreme Court was later to do, the errors of society itself.

The early record of public housing was quite different. From the beginning, it was more receptive to blacks. It had an affirmative equal participation program with respect to admissions, equality of facilities, management, and even employment in project construction. As a result, Gunnar Myrdal reported that public housing proved "a God-send for Negro Americans." Until 1940, from a third to a quarter of public housing tenants were black.[8] The racial policies of public housing were well ahead of the general attitude of the times. However, public housing was locally owned and administered, and the federal agency that subsidized it could do little to break down racial segregation. "In only a few [projects did] Negroes and whites live together without any kind of segregation."[9]

In the early public housing program, there were black racial relations advisers (the first of whom was Robert C. Weaver) who had real influence and were firmly supported by their white superiors. But when public housing was made a part of the National Housing Agency, and later the Housing and Home Finance Agency, the racial relations advisers lost status and influence. Their authority to influence actions rested not on clear-cut rules but on their own powers to persuade. During the 1950s, their influence was nominal at best. In the 1960s, when Robert Weaver became HHFA administrator, they had more influence but less status. But this was less important, in view of Weaver's own interests and powers.

Limitations on HUD's Power

The 1968 Civil Rights Act gave to HUD's secretary broad power and responsibility to combat discrimination in nearly all housing and an assistant secretary to exercise and enforce them. However, HUD's efforts in this respect encountered three serious limitations. The first were limitations in the law itself. The second was the less than perfect administration of HUD's powers. The third was the nature of the housing market.

Legal Limitations

HUD's power to control various forms of housing discrimination rested on its authority to investigate complaints from persons who claimed they had been discriminated against on racial grounds. To assist in investigating such complaints, HUD could issue subpoenas for the appearance of witnesses at hearings and for the provision of documents. If it met resistance, it could refer difficult cases to the Department of Justice. Moreover, it could help aggrieved persons to file a civil suit in the courts.

The 1964 Civil Rights Act gave HUD rather limited tools to force compliance with the sweeping provisions of the law. It could not initiate a court action itself. It had to rely on complaints made to it by aggrieved parties. Thus, HUD's enforcement role was largely limited to persuasion and voluntary compliance with the law. Both a HUD assistant secretary for Equal Opportunity under President Ford and the U.S. Civil Rights Commission have noted with dismay the weakness of HUD's enforcement powers under the 1968 Civil

Rights Act.[10] Those who have served as HUD assistant secretaries for equal opportunity have usually been zealous and energetic. But they have been frustrated by their limited powers of enforcement.

Ineffectual Administration

If HUD's enforcement powers were weak, its use of even these powers has left much to be desired. According to the U.S. Civil Rights Commission, which studied nearly 2,000 complaints received by HUD during 1972 and 1973, HUD has not pursued effectively—largely because of understaffing—many of the complaints it has received. Barely more than one-fifth of these complaints reached the conciliation stage, and four-fifths were dropped without any relief to the complainants. Furthermore, the commission concluded that many of the unpursued complaints did not lack merit; they were simply neglected.[11]

The Housing Market

In 1975, the U.S. Civil Rights Commission stated flatly that "HUD's efforts have so far had minimal impact on curbing housing discrimination."[12] If this is so, and it probably is, it is due not only to legal weaknesses in the enforcement and ineffectual administration. It is also due to a far deeper cause, namely, the fact that racial discrimination in housing is perpetrated by many people in many ways. Most of these discriminating tactics are subtle, hard to discover, and harder to prove. Some have the effect of racial discrimination without necessarily being so intended. Suburban zoning commissions, in order to increase tax revenues, often zone residential land in such a way as to bar all but the most expensive homes. This effectively bars most blacks—whether deliberately so or not. In the purchase and sale of new and existing homes, real estate agents deal personally with both buyers and sellers. Under these circumstances, it is not hard for an agent to prevent a black family from purchasing a home in a given neighborhood without leaving any tangible evidence that discrimination has occurred. Such families can be "steered" with any number of purely verbal ploys. If the sales agent does not discriminate, the mortgage lending institution may by turning down the family's application for a loan. In this case, too, it will be hard for the applicant or for HUD to prove that racial motives alone prompted the rejection.

"Red-lining" is another form of racial discrimination practiced by lenders. In effect, the lending institution draws a red line around certain run-down city neighborhoods and refuses to make loans in these areas. The motive is often simply economic. Many older, blighted neighborhoods involve higher than normal risks both because house values may be declining and because incomes of house purchasers are low or uncertain. The lender's motive may be—and generally is—purely a proper concern about the soundness of a loan in such a neighborhood. But the effect is to make it hard or impossible for even creditworthy residents of the red-lined neighborhood to get a loan to sell or improve their houses.

For these and other reasons, the enforcement of antidiscrimination laws in housing is much more difficult than in public accommodations, transportation, education, and jobs. The eradication of racial discrimination in housing is very basic; it is also very, very difficult.

What Has Been Accomplished?

Since the Supreme Court handed down its historic decision in 1954, few would deny that blacks and other racial minorities have generally made significant strides toward the full citizenship the Constitution guaranteed to all almost two hundred years ago. Progress toward racial equality, however, has been halting and uneven. Much remains to be done.

The federal government (as well as state and many local governments) is now an active partner in the black man's fight for equal opportunity. Restaurants, theaters, and stores are open to blacks, although, of course, these are meaningful rights only for those who can afford them. Blacks vote in as high a proportion as whites. Thousands of blacks hold public office, although their relative numbers still remain small. Several large cities have elected black mayors. There are a few black congressmen, black cabinet members, and a black Supreme Court justice. Black athletes dominate some of the country's most popular sports. There has been an amazing transformation in the South. A southerner is president of the United States, elected with the support of a large proportion of black voters. Thousands of blacks have "made it" into the middle class.

In housing, progress has been made, too. As the economic status of blacks in general has improved, so have their housing standards. Opinion surveys show that from the middle of 1942 to the middle of 1968, the percentage of whites who objected to a black family (of equal income and education) living next to them dropped from 62 percent to 21 percent.[13] There has also been more effective federal intervention to reduce discrimination. But the extent of progress should not be exaggerated. Much less progress has been made in housing than in jobs and education. In some important housing-related aspects, we have actually lost ground.

Housing Discrimination

Racial discrimination in housing is still a reality. Some real estate agents practice subtle forms of discrimination—such as "steering." Mortgage lenders still practice red-lining, though it is now less common. Suburban zoning boards still take actions that discriminate against most blacks. In general, the attitude of most prosperous middle-class suburbs is one of real, if unspoken, resistance to blacks, particularly to low-income blacks.

Racial Segregation

Despite HUD's Project Selection Criteria and despite the polls that show whites to be more receptive to black neighbors, the blacks are more segregated (in where they live) than they were in 1960. Doris Holleb analyzed the latest census data and concluded, "Since 1970, apartheid patterns of settlement have persisted, and the white population in central cities has declined sharply."[14] A recent publication of the Urban Institute has concluded from its segregation indexes that racial "segregation generally increased between 1960 and 1970."[15] In uniting the two races, housing is the last and most intractable barrier.

Slums

The ugly problem of the central-city slum remains. Despite HUD's efforts at slum rehabilitation and its high levels of subsidized housing production in the early 1970s, the slums have, if anything, deteriorated. The relatively new phenomenon of housing abandonment has made the slums less densely populated but more hideous, dismal, and dangerous. Whites and better-off blacks, helped by a general increase in income, have escaped to the suburbs or to better parts of the central city. Census figures show that a high proportion of black slum residents have lived there for three generations.[16] High unemployment, especially among youth, is a reality—as is vandalism, dope addiction, and crime.

The Discouraged

In this decade of disillusionment, some formerly ardent advocates of civil rights now question whether government can really influence events and whether the fight for equal opportunity has not gone too far.

Professor James S. Coleman, whose original study of schools provided the "scientific" rationale for the desegregation decisions of the courts and the busing that followed, is now expressing second thoughts. He is no longer so sure that school busing has actually achieved true racial integration, except perhaps in the South. In many places, Coleman thinks that court-ordered busing has led to more racial isolation rather than less.[17] Many reputable educators believe Coleman's original findings, as well as his later recantation, are superficial.

The signs suggesting a deterioration in the quality of secondary and higher education are well known. Nearly all educators view with alarm the progressive drop in academic achievement test scores, the escalation in grades, and the growth of elective courses considered "relevant" by students and the corresponding decline of courses requiring intellectual discipline. Some of the decay in educational content and standards can be blamed on the youth revolts triggered by the war in Vietnam. But some, too, has grown out of the zeal of administrators and teachers to open up educational opportunities to blacks. This neither helps blacks themselves nor serves education in general. A recent report of the U.S. Civil Rights Commission, which concluded that the quality of education has not suffered from busing, caused many of its own professional staff to resign in protest over what they considered the determination of the commission to prove a preestablished conclusion.[18]

These are very difficult issues: they are not yet settled nor even fully understood. Such controversial circumstances produce premature, absolute positions on both sides. Those who denigrate "quotas" in education for racial improvement tend to forget that such devices are not new. Most of our more prestigious centers of higher education have for decades done the same thing for athletes and for the sons of their alumni.

One of the great achievements of the civil rights movement has been the improvement of job opportunities for blacks. Obviously, this has great social value. However, many now feel that the job quota system has placed many black people in jobs for which they are ill qualified, that whites of equal or superior qualifications have been given less than an equal opportunity, and that we have paid a price for this desirable achievement in reduced organizational efficiency. All this has undoubtedly occurred, but it does not prove that the use of job quotas is wrong. It simply shows that this tool, like any other, can be misused.

This disillusionment has spilled over into the field of housing. Some now question the wisdom of federal efforts at housing desegregation. Nathan Glazer, for example, doubts that housing desegregation would improve either the housing or education of blacks. He also disputes the validity of the job mismatch theory and goes so far as to state that affirmative action aimed at racial dispersion is unconstitutional—a form of reverse discrimination. On this last point, he differs with the Supreme Court. Glazer believes that the integration of blacks will proceed at a pace more related to their rise in income, because racial segregation is based more on income and occupation than on racial discrimintion.[19] According to this view, we no longer have a race problem, but simply a class problem. That is, the middle class refuses to live in the same neighborhoods with blacks, not because blacks are black but because they are poor and behave differently. There is some truth in this. Middle-class and upper-class families often resist living near families of a lower economic class than their own— precisely because of class rather than race. But race is a greater reason for exclusion than class alone.

There is another argument for doing nothing. According to this argument, many immigrant groups of various ethnic origins once lived in big city ghettos, for a generation or so, only to escape when they took on middle class values, behavior, and motivation.[20] Since this happened with other immigrant groups, it is argued, it will happen to blacks, too. The flaw in this argument is that the previous ghetto residents moved out not after but as they achieved upward mobility.[21] Because of racial discrimination, blacks cannot move as freely as their predecessors in the ghetto. Both with respect to jobs and residence, their options are more limited. This makes their escape much harder.

There is a good deal of this kind of defeatism among the disenchanted liberals of the 1960s. It is an overreaction. Two hundred years of social injustice will not be erased overnight, nor will racial integration be accomplished easily or quickly. Anthony Downs, who has outlined a strategy for achieving racial integration in housing, concedes that the people are not yet ready for it.[22] This is one of the many HUD missions that ultimately rest on public consensus and the capacity of government to unite and carry it out. If we, as a country, have committed a gross injustice—and we have—then we should be prepared to pay a large price to rectify that injustice. Perhaps we cannot redress the injustices inflicted upon the minority without inflicting some injustices on the majority. But this is a price we should be prepared to pay—unjust as it may appear in the short run. But in this effort some balance is required too. Flagrant misuse of legitimate tools will only generate resistance to the larger purpose.

With regard to crime in our slums and ghettos, we must have a balanced assessment of the problem and a balanced understanding of its causes. Blacks in the ghetto—as opposed to other blacks—have benefited least from the progress we have made toward civil rights. Here is where the much publicized crime and drug use largely exist. But earlier groups who have experienced the same pressure and poverty have behaved similarly. Not only that, relatively few commit violence. Most ghetto families are peaceful and law-abiding. They, too, are terrified by the violence that surrounds them; in fact, they are more likely to be its victims. Also, violence is by no means confined to blacks or even to the ghetto.

If balance is required of the white majority, it should also be expected from black people themselves. As Richard Kluger has put it, "once these rights were won, the black man's obligations as a citizen are plain. Equal protection of the law is a two-way street."[23] No longer is it realistic for a black to flout society's normal restraints or to respond to life's disciplines and disappointments with the automatic and unthinking cry of "racism." Blacks must also realize, as others have, that "equal opportunity does not necessarily mean equality of results."[24] That is, results, in the sense of achievement, are produced not only by equal opportunity, but also by inherent talent, effort, and a considerable amount of luck. Not every businessman, whatever his or her race, will become a millionaire, nor will every student become an Einstein. The proper goal of equal opportunity is to give every American citizen the chance to achieve his full potential, whatever that may be.

Conclusions

There are a number of things that HUD can do, or urge to be done, toward accomplishment in this most vital of its missions.

1. *Stronger enforcement provisions in the Civil Rights Law.* As we have seen, HUD's enforcement powers under Title VIII of the 1968 Civil Rights Act are weak. It should seek amendments to the law to give it the power to issue cease and desist orders "both to preserve the *status quo* while a complaint is under consideration and to prevent the continuation of proven discriminatory conduct."[25] HUD should also be given specific authority to make rules and to set objective guidelines for nondiscriminatory activity in the housing industry. Such regulations should be given the force of law.[26] This would

greatly strengthen HUD's hand in dealing with the many and elusive ways in which discrimination is practiced in the housing market.

2. *Better enforcement.* HUD should acquire additional staff, or improve the efficiency of its present staff, to investigate thoroughly all complaints it receives. Those who discriminate stand little chance of being called to account and are, of course, aware of this fact.

3. *Better use of the Housing Assistance Plan.* The Housing Assistance Plan, required of localities as a condition for block grants under the 1974 law, provides an excellent vehicle for HUD to exert leverage toward the dispersal of subsidized housing for low-income families and thus for racial dispersion.[27] HUD, under the Ford administration, approved Housing Assistance Plans with little or no serious review. This policy should be changed, and particular attention should be given to the racial implications of such plans.[28] Under new HUD Secretary Patricia Harris, HUD has recently used its powers to refuse block grants to several localities whose housing assistance plans were found to be inadequate. It should be remembered, however, that HUD-subsidized programs are a weak tool for achieving racial dispersion. Anthony Downs has estimated that no more than 12 percent of low-income and moderate-income families lived in subsidized housing in 1974. The rest lived in units they had purchased in the nonsubsidized housing market—which is, of course, not susceptible to HUD's dispersal policies.

4. *Slum improvement.* In addition to using all its powers to encourage open housing, HUD should not neglect the rehabilitation of slums and ghetto neighborhoods. This is discussed in chapter 5. Upgrading the ghetto and racial dispersal are not opposing approaches; they are complementary, and both should be pursued. The fact that both are difficult is no justification for neglecting them.

5. *Jobs.* Robert C. Weaver, with the insights provided by years in the civil rights movement and in the HUD secretaryship, thinks that the single most important step the government can take to improve ghetto conditions is to provide jobs. (As he has reminded the writer, this should not be

construed to mean that he does not also favor affirmative action to achieve open housing.)[29] The late Julius Hobson, who also devoted his life to improving opportunities for his race, mostly in the nation's capital, shared this opinion. A productive job brings self-respect, dignity, a sense of participation, and reduces alienation. Improvement of job opportunities for minorities is not a job for HUD, but one for the president and his economic advisers.

12
Urban Research

This chapter deals with research, that is, HUD's and its predecessors' efforts to gain a better understanding of the intricate problems with which it deals and thus to improve its programs. We will discuss HUD's current research efforts and the brains it taps. HUD's relatively small research funds compared to those of other departments will lead us back to an examination of HHFA's short-lived research program of the late 1940s and the long dry period that followed. We shall discuss the resurrection of HUD's urban research program, a resurrection engineered largely by HUD Under Secretary Robert Wood. Then we shall attempt to evaluate the quality and impact of HUD's research program. Finally, we shall offer some proposals on the directions HUD's urban research should take and how it should be managed.

HUD's Research Mandates

From 1948 through 1974, the major laws relating to HUD and its predecessors have been replete with authorities and directives to carry out the demonstrations and research. Some have stressed improvements in home building technology and other specific objectives. Others have authorized general research in urban and housing programs. A 1949 law authorized a program of research in housing technology and economics. A 1964 law gave HHFA the authority to carry out research in urban mass transportation. A 1968 law authorized a broad program of urban research and demonstrations. The 1974 law directed research into such matters as solar energy, housing design, housing for the handicapped, and various methods of housing financing. It also authorized a National Institute of Building Sciences. Research on urban problems to improve understanding and program performance must be considered a major HUD mission.

HUD's Current Research

Subject Matter

HUD's current research covers a broad range of subjects related to its various programs. This incomplete list is representative of HUD's research in recent years.

1. *Housing*
    a) Housing demand and the behavior of the housing market
    b) Housing services
    c) Housing rehabilitation and neighborhood preservation
    d) Housing for the elderly
    e) Management of housing for low-income families
    f) Housing allowances as a subsidy device
2. *Land Use*
    a) Zoning
    b) Land banking
    c) Effect of taxes on property location
    d) New communities
3. *Local Government*
    a) Management systems
    b) Efficiency of administration
    c) State and local property taxes
    d) General revenue sharing
    e) Local government finance
    f) Local government services
    g) Public safety
    h) Metropolitan government
4. *Racial Discrimination*
5. *Urban Social Problems*

6. *Technology*
    a) Communications technology
    b) Solar energy designs
    c) Applications of solar energy
    d) Housing technology
    e) Evaluation of industrialized housing systems
    f) Mass transportation methods
7. *Program Evaluation*
8. *General*
    a) Urban indicators
    b) Policy research agenda

Research Resources

To carry out its research agenda, HUD makes use of the three sources of knowledge and skill.

1. *In-house staff.* HUD has built up its own staff of researchers. This staff is modest in size (compared with those of many other departments) and consists largely of economists, architects, engineers, and people with special knowledge of HUD's various programs.

2. *The Urban Institute.* This nonprofit "think tank" was, as we shall see, established largely at the instigation of HUD in the 1960s. It is staffed by research specialists in the various disciplines related to urban affairs. Its talents are used by HUD and by several other departments.

3. *Other outside sources.* HUD also uses the skills of many outside sources, including universities, various private research organizations (both profit and nonprofit), and other departments of government.

Limited Funds

To finance research on the important subjects with which it deals, HUD's funds amounted to $65 million in 1973 and $65 million again in 1975. HUD's own budget requests for research have never exceeded $80 million—a paltry sum in comparison with the research funds granted many other federal departments and agencies. In 1976, for example, HEW spent $2.5 billion on research, the Department of Agriculture $460 million, the federal government, as a whole, over $20 billion on research and development. But HUD spent only $54 million on research in 1976. In 1976, in fact, a law was passed limiting the funds authorized (not appropriated) for HUD research to $65 million a year.

In this age when research is so revered and Congress is so generous in voting research money on almost every conceivable subject, HUD has been almost left out. Congress's unwillingness to vote funds to discover more about the problems of the cities in which nearly all of us live contrasts dramatically with the vast sums provided for research in space, defense, health, and welfare, to name just a few. In the 1950s, Professor Ernest Fisher remarked that "we spend more money in research to improve the sugar beet than in the entire field of housing and urban affairs." Though HUD is now less starved for research funds than it was when Fisher made his remark, his point remains valid.

There appear to be a number of reasons for the relatively paltry sums made available to HUD for research. The conquest of space and exotic weapons of destruction are certainly more dramatic than curing slums. In contrast, the social sciences produce less tangible results, especially when applied to the appalling complexities of the urban environment. Yet this in itself does not completely explain HUD's meager research budget. Other domestic departments spend large sums researching equally elusive knowledge. One fact has been apparent for many years. The House Appropriations Subcommittee, which controls HUD's funds and controlled those of HUD's predecessors, has been skeptical, if not cynical, about the value of urban research. HHFA's brief, unhappy venture into research some twenty-five years ago certainly reinforced the doubts of an Appropriations Subcommittee that was already reluctant to make appropriations in many fields.

An Early Aborted Effort

The first modest venture into research on housing quality and cost grew out of provisions in the 1948 and 1949 legislation. The 1948 act authorized the HHFA administrator "to undertake technical research and studies on the development and promotion of standardized building codes and regulations, and standardized dimensions and methods for the assembly of home-building materials and equipment."[1] The 1949 legislation broadened this narrow research charter; namely, it authorized the HHFA administrator to conduct technical research and studies which will promote reduction in housing construction and maintenance costs and stimulate the increased and sustained production of housing.[2] Between 1948 and 1953, about $3 million was appropriated to carry out this research.

Richard U. Ratcliff, a professor at the University of Wisconsin and respected land economist, was recruited to direct the program. A small staff of housing economists, architects, and engineers was assembled. The program was carried out almost entirely through contracts with university professors. Some of the contracts reflected subjects the HHFA research division had conceived. Others were responsive to proposals submitted by researchers themselves.

The results of the completed research were, on the whole, disappointing. In 1950, few universities had faculty members with real competence in housing construction or in housing economics. The research HHFA supported reflected this fact. Too often, the reports read like a master's thesis (many of them were); HHFA's own staff could have done much better.

If federal funds had remained available, the academic expertise might have developed. If this first venture into urban research had been more carefully developed and more skillfully executed, it might have gained the needed momentum. The program's chances were not helped by a good deal of scathing publicity given to one report dealing with the efficiency of chimneys. For reasons that are obscure, this report and the topic it treated were widely and wrongly derided as the height of folly. In 1953, the House Appropriations Committee decided to terminate the program before it had really begun. The late Congressman Albert Thomas, the powerful chairman of the Appropriations Subcommittee dealing with HHFA's budget requests, had no faith in the practical results of the HHFA's research, and he looked with equal skepticism on the professors who were doing the research. The formidable Mr. Thomas was a shrewd man. He had supported other research programs, notably that of the space program. He was probably right in his skepticism of HHFA's ill-conceived and poorly executed maiden research effort. He probably saw that the required research capacity did not exist in the universities or anywhere else and that HHFA was not equipped to design and manage such an effort. The time for serious, productive urban research had not yet come.

The Dry Period

After the demise in 1954 of HHFA's first plunge into urban research, nearly a decade passed before a single dollar was appropriated for this purpose. During this period, HHFA's people marched up to the Capitol each year to request funds, often as little as $50,000. Each time they were politely but firmly turned down by Congressman Albert Thomas and his committee. By a strange quirk of fate and politics, the only research funds HHFA received during these dry years were forced on it. These funds were for a small research project in the field of agriculture. A member of Congress was annoyed because the Department of Agriculture had not carried out the project at the land grant college in his district, and he contrived to have the project's funds given to HHFA. Finally, in 1961, the Congress relented slightly and appropriated $375,000. In the year HUD was created, its annual appropriation for research was the modest sum of $750,000.

A Minor Miracle

Robert C. Wood, HUD's first under secretary, had been for years a professor of political science at MIT and chairman of its political science department. A forceful, energetic man, he believed in big ideas and was undaunted by difficult problems. Soon after becoming under secretary, he undertook to do something about the paucity of HUD's research funds.

His first move was to gain the cooperation of the White House Office of Science and Technology. Together, they sponsored a three-week summer study on science and urban development, held in June 1966 at the National Academy of Science's Summer Study Center in Woods Hole, Massachusetts.

To this conference he invited about fifty eminent scientists and urban specialists. The chairman was MIT Professor Walter Rosenblith, a specialist in the study of electrical impulses in the human brain.

The scientists who attended came from some of the country's most prestigious universities and research centers, including the Oak Ridge National Laboratory, the Institute for Defense Analysis, the research arms of General Electric, IBM, and the Ford Motor Company. One participant, Thomas Paine, of General Electric, was soon to become head of NASA. Among the prominent students of urban problems attending were John Bebout of Rutgers, Glenn Beyer of Cornell, Anthony Downs, Ezra Ehrenkrantz, Hortense Gabel of the Ford Foundation, Wilfred Owens of The Brookings Institution, and Harvey Perloff of Resources for the Future.

This glittering assembly of scientists and urban experts discussed at length the application of modern science and systems engineering to the rehabilitation of slums, new housing construction, environmental engineering, transportation, and health services. After some days, this disparate group of hard scientists and urban experts began to communicate, even to understand one another. During the stimulating exchange, Chairman Rosenblith made a significant remark. He observed that "sending a man to the moon was easy compared with the improvement of cities because, in the former case, scientists were dealing with a closed system while the problems of the cities represented 'open systems.' " As this remark indicates, Rosenblith recognized that the moon mission involved complex, but quantifiable, variables but that improving the cities involved many intangibles. He might have added that lines of authority and decision making are considerably more diffused in urban areas than they are in the space program.

Despite Rosenblith's warning, the scientists emerged from the session hopeful and convinced that science could indeed be applied to urban problems and that with sufficient research, the urban environment could be greatly improved and many efficiencies achieved.

Under Secretary Wood did not allow the three-week

discussion to become another conference. His objective was to change the atmosphere toward urban research in Washington, particularly in the Congress. His next step was to make the substance of the Woods Hole Conference generally available in easily understood book form. For this purpose, he persuaded NASA Administrator James Webb to lend him a writer. The choice was a fortunate one. The writer was skilled in translating scientific obscurities into plain English and, at the same time, cloaking them in the glamour of space flights and other modern scientific achievement.

The result was a persuasive, easy-to-read pamphlet called *Science and the City*.[3] It was published by HUD in 1967, less than a year after the Woods Hole Conference. It contained a quotation from the president, an introduction by HUD Secretary Weaver, and numerous dramatic photographs, which, along with the beautifully written text, suggested that the cities could be saved by the magic application of science. In his introduction, Secretary Weaver said, "The kind of forced-draft technological effort that has characterized the development of space and weapon systems needs now to be applied to the urban task."[4] Wood saw that this shining, well-packaged promise was widely circulated in the places where it counted. It did, indeed, change the Washington climate on research in urban problems—with a big assist from the urban riots of the 1960s and President Johnson's legislative skills. Wood's minor miracle soon produced three important results.

More Funds

The year after the Woods Hole Conference (1967), HUD's research funds jumped twentyfold, from $500,000 to $10 million. By the time Secretary Weaver and Wood left office, they had climbed to $23 million. By 1974, they had reached $65 million. They have never exceeded this amount.

A New Assistant Secretary

In 1968, the Congress authorized an additional assistant secretary, a position that was to become HUD's first assistant secretary for research.

A Think Tank for Urban Affairs

The Woods Hole effort also produced presidential support for the creation of a private "think tank" on urban affairs modeled after the well-known Rand Corporation, generated long before by the Department of Defense. This new organization was named the Urban Institute. President Johnson addressed its Board of Trustees at the White House in April 1968 and announced its incorporation.

As often happens in government, it fell to the Nixon administration and HUD Secretary George Romney to administer what Wood had wrought. The only problem of significance growing out of the change of administrations was the suspicion with which Romney at first looked upon the fledgling Urban Institute. In time, this suspicion was overcome, and constructive relations between HUD and the Urban Institute were established, principally in the field of housing.

A More Mature Urban Research

In contrast to the very disappointing research that HHFA's brief effort produced in the early 1950s, there can be no question that HUD's revived program nearly two decades later produced much more sophisticated research. There are several reasons for this improvement.

A New Generation of Urban Experts

Between 1950 and 1965, a whole generation of urban specialists had been developed, largely in universities. In 1950, there was but a handful of academic specialists in urban matters, mostly in housing and urban planning. By 1965, academic attention to urban affairs had grown remarkably. Few large universities did not have some faculty devoting full time to this subject, and many small schools were following suit. Harvard-MIT had a well-established, interdisciplinary Joint Center for Urban Studies. Cornell, Pennsylvania, North Carolina, Rutgers, the University of California at Berkeley, and at Los Angeles had interdisciplinary urban study centers. Washington, D.C. also had an urban study center, loosely affiliated with several of its local universities. A study of this subject in 1971 counted no fewer than 300 urban study research centers at universities. Nearly every campus had one or more serious students of urban affairs. For example, an urban studies center was established in 1975 at the College of Charleston (S.C.), a relatively small liberal arts institution. It now publishes a journal on urban affairs.

Thus, the second wave of HUD research was better—simply because there was more talent to draw on. But much more is needed. "A solid infrastructure still remains to be built in this area."[5]

A HUD Assistant Secretary for Research

Shortly after his appointment, President Nixon's secretary of HUD, George Romney, chose Harold Finger as HUD's first assistant secretary for research. Finger was an able science administrator recruited from NASA. The prestige of his rank, as well as his skill in planning and carrying out a broad, coherent program of urban research and experimentation, greatly improved HUD's efforts.

The Urban Institute

HUD's research has also received useful support from the Urban Institute. A stable of readily available experts can greatly support a department's research efforts. The list of the Urban Institute's many publications reflects intelligent planning and covers most important aspects of the urban condition. Its staff is, on the whole, competent. Its publications are priced low enough to be available to serious students, a pleasant surprise in this day of inflated book costs.

However, even after a decade, the Urban Institute can boast of no urban scholar of national renown. The most respected "names" in urban scholarship are still in universities. This could well result from the constraints under which the institute works, that is, from the fact that most of its funds come from HUD, HEW, and a few other government agencies—all of which exercise substantial control over the work the institute can do—and from the fact that federal funds for specialized research tend to dry up as federal priorities change. Such conditions are hardly likely to attract the most brilliant, original scholars. Even in the 1960s, few people fit this description.

Has HUD Research Made a Difference?

The Quality of Social Research

HUD's research has produced interesting and helpful information on the various urban problems with which HUD deals. In at least two cases, it has produced quite valuable assessments of the performance of specific HUD programs (Operation Breakthrough and Block Grants for Community Development). A pre-test of one program idea—housing allowances as a means of subsidizing poor families—is nearly completed. This is an old idea, however, which has been studied many times before, and preliminary reports on the test results suggest that no very surprising conclusions are likely to be produced. Some useful work has been done on management of housing for the poor. The newly started studies on the use of solar energy to heat houses may produce useful results—they are certainly worth a try.

Undoubtedly, what has been done has value. But we are still only a little closer to an understanding of the most basic and difficult problems of cities. Nor has research produced any dramatic improvements in HUD's programs. We still do not understand the social and physical causes of slums, and we are almost as far as ever from possessing the cures. We do not fully understand what causes some poor families to be upward-mobile, frugal, and ambitious while others are not. Therefore, we do not know how to generate this motivation. We understand neither the causes of mindless crime, as former Attorney General Elliot Richardson has stated,[6] nor the roots of vandalism and other antisocial behavior. We do not know how to achieve metropolitan government. We do not know the full effects of HUD's programs and how to make the delivery of its services more effective. We have not yet conceived a coherent and consistent housing policy. We have no sensible policy on urban land and its uses. Orderly urban planning is still a distant dream. Housing costs still soar. These and many other matters discussed in this book are the gut questions that HUD and the country face.

HUD's research effort has not contributed many answers to these very urgent questions. Is this too much to ask of research? The problems are certainly complex. Beyond that, they are not easily isolated. Many forces operate on them—some within HUD's purview, many not. Political realities often intervene to compromise the thinker's best ideas.

It is no secret that much of the social research the government has supported in recent years has not always been of a high order. It parades as social research, but it is often sheer banality, dressed up in pedantic verbiage studded with lengthy tables of data. If it is not too bad, it painfully reaches fairly obvious conclusions. An executive of HEW, a department that spends millions on social research, once showed this writer a room crammed with such studies. With an impatient expression she said, "Most of it is trash. And besides that, nobody ever reads it."[7]

On the other hand, a good deal of HUD's social research is professional, if rather pedestrian. For example, the famed Arthur D. Little Company prepared a study of residential rehabilitation for HUD. It was a competent description of HUD's efforts, but it reached the conclusion that HUD had proved that volume rehabilitation was possible. This was a premature conclusion, and thus the research could not be called truly penetrating. It missed the key truth that the success of rehabilitation can be judged only much later, when the lasting improvement of a neighborhood can be judged. Because HUD contracted for so early a study, it, too, must be blamed for not grasping that rehabilitation completions are no true measure of success. But the Little firm, by concentrating almost entirely on immediate physical improvements, displayed little understanding of the real objectives of neighborhood rehabilitation.

But some social research provides deep and original insights. This is true of the work of a few distinguished academic scholars and some of the work of such organizations as the Brookings Institution. But good social research cannot be mass produced. It requires great minds and years of study. Most often it is produced by scholars of breadth, not by the narrow specialists our universities so often produce. The penetrating insight, the sweeping revelations do occur—but not often.

The Urban Institute, ten years after its creation amid high hopes and strong rhetoric, is now surprisingly humble about its capacity to penetrate the mysteries of the urban condition. A 1976 book, *The Urban Predicament*,[8] starts on a note of extreme modesty and, after some competent but unsurprising chapters, ends with a few mild, hardly fundamental, recommendations. This is a far cry from the lofty promises of Robert Wood's *Science and the City*, which started the whole thing. From "science can solve all our urban problems" to "we really don't know many of the answers" is quite a swing within a ten-year period. When this new humility was mentioned to Charles L. Schultze, then vice chairman of the Institute's Board of Trustees, his reply was a cryptic "It's about time."[9] One cannot be certain, but Schultze probably meant no disrespect for the staff or leadership of the Institute. More likely, he recognized that the problems of urban America are far more complex and intractable than was so cheerfully supposed just ten years before. On the whole, this is a step toward realism. Schultze and his fellow economists know the same thing is true of the nation's economy, the management of which President Carter has recently entrusted to him.

The Hazards of Scientism

One other pitfall in social research needs mentioning. The Woods Hole Summer Study of 1966 and the events it precipitated were replete with high hopes that the same scientific minds who had put a man on the moon could apply the same scientific method to the problems of our cities and perform similar marvels. Wood and Weaver were profoundly right when they asserted in 1968 that the problems of the cities need a massive application of the nation's best brains, just as the space effort had received. But if they thought, which the author doubts, that urban problems could be unraveled by the same brains using the same methods, they were making a very dubious assumption. There is, as Woods Hole Chairman Rosenblith has quickly perceived, a vast difference between closed systems and open systems.

It is not at all clear whether the methods of the natural

sciences—which analyze quantitative, measurable, and predictable events with remarkable results—can be successfully applied to the most basic social problems of human settlements. Transportation, sewage disposal, and other such physical systems seem most susceptible to the scientific method of the physical sciences. But even these are subject to market or political forces that are not easily quantifiable, much less predictable. The most basic of our urban problems are inextricably related to people and their tastes, hopes, despairs, values, virtues, and vices. These very real things escape the microscope and are placed in a computer only at great danger of distortion or deceptive oversimplification.

Some students of urban issues display an unrealistic impulse to imitate the comfortable certainties of the physical sciences, forgetting that many urban events are not only hard, or impossible, to quantify but also subject to the vagaries of political influences. Harvard sociologist Daniel Bell has spoken of "the fallacy of misplaced concreteness."[10] He refers to the search of the social scientists for "scientific" certainty, a search that can lead them further and further from the reality they seek to describe.

Realistically pursued, urban research can be, and is, useful. Indeed, it is indispensable. But in the short run, it is not likely to precipitate any miracles. In the long run, for it takes time, we can hope that research by able people will increase our understanding of the fundamental urban problems and lead to public programs that will help relieve them. The path may be long, but we should and must not fail to pursue the wisdom required to improve our cities and the lives of those who inhabit them.

Toward Better Urban Research

Improved Research Management

In its management of urban research, HUD and its predecessor (HHFA) have tried a number of approaches. In the brief and abortive effort in the early 1950s, there was a minimum of planning to direct research efforts toward problems of critical policy or program importance. On the whole, HHFA responded to proposals of academic researchers and chose those that appeared most promising. At the other extreme, in the mid-1970s, HUD Assistant Secretary Charles Orlebeke undertook to direct research through a quite detailed plan, derived through consultation with the various operating and staff heads, to establish their perceived needs. An approach somewhere between these extremes of nondirection and detailed direction was favored by Assistant Secretary Harold Finger. The relationship between the researchers and the research managers is important to the success and relevance of the research undertaken. Researchers need guidance. They also need to be intimately familiar with the programs and goals of the departments they serve. Passivity on the part of the research manager leads to random shots in the dark. But overprogramming from on high can turn the researcher into a mechanic, stifling his imagination and inventiveness.

The best role for research management is to keep researchers well informed of the department's aims and problems without stifling their imaginations. A research plan is desirable, and the department's general research goals should be identified, but enough flexibility should be retained to give full play to the researcher's imagination. If aware of the department's general aims and problems, a good researcher can frequently design more original and productive research than the program managers themselves. Thus, a flexible approach to research planning will produce the best results. Moreover, there must be not only full communication between research managers and the researchers but also full trust. A researcher who believes that his efforts are not respected is hardly likely to produce his best work. Under these circumstances the researcher's greatest assets—his imagination and inventiveness—will not be given the fullest opportunity for expression.

Failures Are Inevitable

Those who direct and pay for urban research as well as those who practice it must recognize that all research, even that in the much applauded hard sciences, involves trial and error. Harry Finger has said that HUD Secretary George Romney could not accept the long time it took for the researchers to come up with "practical" answers and why they were sometimes wrong.

Mr. Romney had to make policy without hard data and could not wait for research results. As a result, he and other policymakers sometimes question the value of research that has a long lead time. Most researchers recognize this. They should make every effort to educate their clients—not always a pleasant job and sometimes an impossible one.

Research Requires Sustained Support

Stop-and-go research is not a very productive enterprise. It is, however, a tendency built into the political process. Let us hope, now that urban research has finally been established as a tolerably respectable undertaking, that public support will be sustained as well as enlarged.

Thorough Testing of New Program Ideas

One of the government's greatest weaknesses is its tendency toward what Anthony Downs calls "compulsive innovation." In our political process, new administrations are likely to consider all inherited programs inherently bad and all new ideas inherently good, even though many of the new ideas are conceived quickly under pressure of some urgent deadline or other. In our newly found humility, we have learned that it is hard to know in advance how people and institutions will respond to new federal programs and, thus, how effectively they will work. Because of this, the prudent way for government to design workable new programs is through carefully designed program experimentation and testing. As Schultze, Rivlin, and associates have asserted, "the best way—perhaps the only way—of finding out how individuals and institutions will respond [to new programs] would seem to be to try out the new programs in advance of their installation."[11] The testing of new program ideas is one of the most productive uses of research in government—for example, HUD's experiments in housing allowances as a means of subsidizing housing for the poor. But it was difficult to get congressional approval of these experiments. Much the same thing was proposed by the Model Cities Task Force with quite different political results. In our political system, it is probably too much to hope that every new program idea will be permitted the luxury of an advance testing period. Thus, the most prudent course is probably to test new program ideas when it is politically feasible and when it is not, to proceed with a program while continuously evaluating its performance.

Evaluation of Program Results

HUD, far too often, has launched new programs that then became permanent fixtures without ever evaluating their actual results; without finding out whether they produced the desired results, some unexpected result, or accomplished nothing at all. HUD has made real efforts to evaluate the 1974 Block Grant Program for Community Development through contracts with the National Association of Housing and Redevelopment Officials and through the Brookings Institution. But many other permanent programs have never been so evaluated—for example, residential rehabilitation, a very popular subject today and one on which much money has been and is being spent. Yet we know practically nothing about the long-term effects of rehabilitation on neighborhoods—the only true test of its effectiveness. The Urban Institute has published a useful book on program evaluation. The conclusions were: program evaluation is greatly needed, little is done, and the techniques for program evaluation are inadequate.[12] Program evaluation is a little-done, much-needed objective for HUD research. Harry Finger believes that every federal program must be considered an experiment and its results carefully measured. Thus, they can be modified from experience. If modification proves impossible, the new understandings can be used later.[13]

New Insights Into Hard Problems

Despite years of federal effort in housing and urban matters, there are still some quite basic urban issues on which our understanding is dim or nonexistent. These problems must be better understood if our cities are to be improved. They require serious, extended study by the most brilliant minds we can bring to the task. This should be a high and continuing HUD goal.

13
Policies and People

Obviously, HUD cannot perform effectively without well-trained, dedicated personnel. Particularly crucial in this respect are the fifty or sixty persons who play a decisive role in creating workable and acceptable policies and in administering them efficiently. This "policymaking elite," to use Harold Wolman's phrase, consists of political appointees as well as career professionals.[1] Conversely, mediocre, inept leadership produces poor policies and worse results. Far from being the sprawling, impersonal bureaucracy manned by faceless drones, as the popular myth has it, HUD is people.

In his study of HUD's decision-making process from 1967 through 1969, Wolman wrote, "A persistent finding throughout this study . . . was that specific individuals could and did make significant contributions to the nature of policy through the force of their personality or through the chance occurrence of finding themselves in the right place at the right time."[2] Wallace Sayre, a longtime student of government, has made the same point:

> The higher executives and professionals of the federal service stand with the President and the Congress, at the center of the nation's policy process. Much of the process of decision-making is in their hands. The assembly of information, the discovery of alternatives, the analytical appraisal of these choices, the synthesis of risks and opportunities into innovative yet realistic

recommendations, the process of bargaining and accommodation which transforms proposals into accepted policies, the execution of resulting plans and proposals—in each of these stages effective participation by the higher executives and professions is indispensable . . . without their contributions at a high level of quality the political system cannot meet the increasingly complex demands being made upon it.[3]

In his thoughtful book on the presidency, Richard Neustadt gives a striking illustration of the importance of the right people at the right place at the right time. The Marshall Plan—certainly one of our country's most humanitarian and successful postwar policies—was, according to Neustadt, the work of four men: President Truman, Secretary of State George Marshall, Averell Harriman, and Republican Senator Arthur Vandenberg. Neustadt further notes that "Here, as everywhere, the outcome was conditioned on who they were and what he was and how each viewed events, and on their actual performance in response."[4]

The creation, establishment, and management of government programs requires people who can perform these very different functions:

1. creation of the plan (this role may be performed by HUD people or by its advisers)
2. transforming the idea into a politically accepted reality
3. managing the program
4. assisting and acting for the program manager or secretary
5. orchestrating and guiding the Department's many programs
6. influencing the general climate to make innovation possible

These functions require quite different skills. Some people can perform several of these special functions. It is a rare person who can perform them all. Obviously, therefore, teamwork is important.

In HUD, various people have performed with varying success in various roles. The catalog that follows is by no means complete. But it does illustrate the important influence of people who, by design or chance, happened to be in the right place at the right time. As we shall see, the element of chance is often significant: for every person who had an important influence on the policies and performance of HUD, there is perhaps a "mute inglorious Milton," who might have had an influence had he been in the right place at the right time. This catalog starts with the present and goes backward through the history of HUD and its predecessors. The evaluations of individual performance are as objective as this writer can make them. However, subjective judgments cannot be avoided completely—clearly, what is failure to one is often positive achievement to another.

The Innovators

It is hard to trace the creation of a truly new idea and even harder to credit it to a single individual. Some innovations are the work of several people and constitute a synthesis of their conflicting views. Other innovations seem to spring up spontaneously from different people in different places, as often happens in the natural sciences. Still others mature over years. Nearly all are profoundly affected by the atmosphere, needs, and intellectual climate of the times. We need not belabor the mysterious nature of creation. What concerns us here is who was in the strategic position to present a new idea to those in government who could and did act upon it.

Richard Nathan and Frank Fisher

The 1974 shift from special-purpose categorical programs for inner-city improvement to a general block grant to localities with relatively few strings attached was a major HUD policy change. It resulted from a clash and ultimate reconciliation between two dramatically opposed conceptions. The first conception came largely from Richard Nathan of the Nixon Office of Management and Budget. Its purpose was to further Nixon's "new federalism" by removing as many social programs from Washington as possible and by putting responsibility for their administration in local government with a minimum of federal interference. The second conception came from Frank Fisher, HUD's regional administrator in Chicago, later assigned to HUD headquarters. He devised a procedure under which a locality would submit annually for federal review a plan showing how it intended to use and coordinate HUD's various inner-city improvement programs. Fisher's idea was to improve program coordination, improve planning, and reduce excessive red tape. It was *not* designed to diminish federal control over use of federal funds for the purposes intended. Nathan and Fisher conceived and developed their ideas without knowing about the work of the other. Their plans came to HUD Under Secretary Richard Van Dusen, who, along with Dana Mead of the White House Domestic Council, worked out a compromise: some of the elements of federal review of local plans and explicit identification of the federal objectives (espoused by Fisher) and many elements of Nathan's transfer of decision making to the cities. The result was neither the federal "cop out" that the Nixon administration first conceived nor the higher degree of federal review that Fisher's plan contemplated. In a sense, each won and each lost. Such inconclusive compromises are, of course, common in federal policy development.

HUD Secretary James Lynn, Senator Sparkman, Congressmen Barrett and Ashley, and George Gross

By 1973, those concerned with housing subsidies had split into two camps. HUD Secretary James Lynn and many others favored a housing allowance payment to low-income families to rent or finance housing of their choice. The argument was that this would give poor families more freedom and cost the government less. Senator Sparkman, chairman of the Senate committee with jurisdiction over HUD's programs, Representative Barrett, chairman of the housing subcommittee in the House, and many others believed that this approach would only inflate the cost of housing and that federally subsidized construction of additional units for the poor was essential. Representative Ashley, a senior member of the housing subcommittee, and George Gross, its chief counsel, managed to negotiate a compromise with Secretary Lynn: subsidies for poor families to rent existing housing as well as subsidies for new and rehabilitated housing. This compromise was enacted as Section 8 of the Housing and Community Development Act of 1974.[5]

Secretary George Romney, Lester Condon, et al.

George Romney was convinced that production and management of housing should be separated in HUD, just as marketing and production are separated in industry. He was also convinced that HUD's field offices should be multiplied and given increased discretion, just as industry encourages franchises and dealerships in many locations. Condon, HUD's assistant secretary for administration, was given the responsibility for fleshing out Romney's innovative, but disastrous, organizational ideas. Condon was undoubtedly assisted and influenced by several members of his career staff who had long harbored a justified desire to get control of the once-recalcitrant FHA and to make HUD a single, cohesive entity. The objectives of Romney, Condon, and his associates were admirable—they all desired effective service to the public. But they chose the wrong means to that end.

Another Romney innovation was his drive for a high volume of subsidized housing production. It was a spectacular success in terms of production achieved. But Romney paid a high price for it: FHA's administrative capacity was strained beyond the breaking point, and some program abuses and outright criminality resulted.

The other innovations of the Romney era—Operation Breakthrough and Project Rehab—have been discussed in previous chapters. Both were formulated by his staff, all but two of whom were career professionals.

A Career Professional

John Kennedy's major legislative innovation in the urban field, the sweeping Housing Act of 1961, is illustrative of the support a career professional can provide his political superiors if he happens to be at the right place at the right time and is prepared to take the risks of speaking up. Shortly after John Kennedy appointed Robert Weaver HHFA administrator and while he was still assembling his top staff, the White

House sent word that the president wanted in a few weeks a draft of a housing message dealing with the problems of the cities. This had been a major theme of Kennedy's election campaign.

To respond, Weaver set up a task force. It was composed of a mixture of his new appointees (including Neal Hardy, the federal housing commissioner, and a few others not yet cleared), several persons from outside the federal government, a few HHFA career people, including the author of this book, and a career man brought from the Bureau of the Budget. When I learned that there was no staff agenda, I prepared one on my own initiative, without being authorized to do so. This list of major proposals was welcomed by Weaver and other members of the task force and reflected in Kennedy's housing message issued March 9, 1961.

Neal Hardy and Philip Brownstein

When Weaver took office in 1961, one of the clearest needs was to modify the traditional role of the venerable and much-admired FHA as well as to persuade it that it was indeed an integral part of HHFA, no longer the independent agency it long had been.

The writer is in possession of an unpublished manuscript by a former head of FHA which quotes an opinion of its general counsel questioning the authority of President Eisenhower to interfere in FHA's activities beyond the mere nomination of the administrator, with the consent of the Senate. These men were highly competent in real estate matters, but their perception of the role and obligations of an agency of the executive branch of the federal government had become sadly myopic. FHA's actions, since it became part of the National Housing Agency in 1942 and later of HHFA, had reflected this warped attitude— much to the frustration of numerous NHA and HHFA administrators.

Weaver and many others saw the need to bring FHA into the HHFA family. But as HHFA administrator, Weaver's authority was still limited to general supervision and coordination. The question was, therefore, how to perform this delicate job. Weaver decided that the best tactic was to appoint as head of FHA a man who shared his own views and was, at the same time, a respected expert in mortgage finance. His first appointment to FHA was Neal J. Hardy. When Hardy resigned after two years, Weaver appointed Philip N. Brownstein, a man of similar views and professional competence.

The effects of this shrewd move were immediate and ultimately dramatic. FHA became deeply involved in stimulating the flow of mortgage funds into declining inner-city areas, long boycotted by FHA and mortgage lenders. It immersed itself in the difficult problems of rehabilitating run-down, inner-city areas and even slums. It supported the efforts of the Urban Renewal Administration and even took the lead in cooperative efforts to make urban renewal rehabilitation more effective. FHA also took responsibility for administering subsidized programs to provide housing for families of moderate income and later for the very poor. Five years later, HHFA held a three-week training conference on urban renewal rehabilitation attended by Washington and local urban renewal and FHA staff. The session was both conceived and conducted by FHA.

Hardy started and Brownstein completed a remarkable change in the policies of FHA and another remarkable change in the attitude of most of its far-flung staff of 7,000 people. The appointment of Hardy and subsequently Brownstein was no accident. The role this writer was privileged to play in redirecting FHA was largely accidental. It resulted from earlier career identification with FHA, long association with Hardy, and many years of employment in the HHFA administrator's office, working on policy development and evaluation. This experience afforded me acquaintance with all the FHA high priests and easy identification with FHA. Then, too, I knew and shared Weaver's objectives. Thus, I was selected to help "bring FHA into HHFA," had an opportunity to participate in the process, and observed the transformation. But my role was only to assist. The major credit for accomplishing Weaver's intention to change the FHA must go to Hardy for his innovative skills, to Philip Brownstein for his superb administrative skills, and to Weaver for his judgment in choosing them.

Marie McGuire

In 1961, Weaver appointed Marie McGuire as commissioner of the Public Housing Administration. Aided by great charm and intimate knowledge of the program, she brought about two important innovations in that embattled program. First, she brought a deep understanding that housing the poor has social as well as physical dimensions. Thus, she worked hard and successfully to increase the humaneness of public housing management. Second, she adopted and sold a new method of contracting for the construction of public housing. It was called the "turnkey system." For years, public housing projects had been designed by architects retained by local housing authorities; then these projects were offered to contractors for construction bids, principally to firms involved in heavy construction, including office buildings, factories, and apartments. The turnkey method cut short this frequently tedious and time-consuming procedure. Under turnkey, the local housing authority outlined the general character of the structures it wanted, identifying the number of units of different sizes, the public spaces, and so on. Then it asked builders to submit prices for the delivery of a building meeting these general standards. This turned over to the builder most of the responsibility of selecting a site, designing and building the structure, making inspections, applying for city approvals, and related matters. The turnkey approach had an unexpected, but important, side effect: it attracted to public housing construction those longtime archenemies—the home builders. Macy's married Gimbels. This was a revolution of incalculable political consequence. In 1977 a prominent home builder was president of the national housing conference, the principal lobby for public housing. Twenty years ago, no one in his right mind would have predicted this development. Joseph Burstein, Commissioner McGuire's general counsel, also deserves a large share of credit for the turnkey innovation. It was his fertile legal brain that developed the turnkey idea, established its legality, and furthered its acceptance.

Mrs. McGuire could not reverse public housing's unhappy trend toward large high-rise monoliths—unsuitable for family living and invitations to the vandalism, crime, and the general social disorders that turned many a public housing project into an instant slum. But she did see the problem and started scattered-site public housing—much of it leased from existing owners. In this innovation she received a big legislative assist from the Republican leadership on the House Banking and Currency Committee. Mrs. McGuire also supported much public housing for the elderly, a form she had pioneered when in San Antonio. The laws facilitating public housing projects exclusively for the elderly, passed in the late 1950s, again saved that politically beleaguered program by making it possible for local housing authorities to find sites for projects in the central city. Public housing for the elderly was readily accepted by cities that had become unreceptive to any other type. Old folks were not only accepted; they presented local housing authorities with no difficult management problems.

Robert C. Wood, Walter Reuther, and Others

The Model Cities Program was the boldest and most ambitious innovation that occurred during Weaver's years as HUD secretary (see chapter 5). The idea is generally credited to the Johnson task force chaired by Robert C. Wood. Within that prestigious group, Walter Reuther was the most ardent and persuasive advocate of the plan. But, as often happens, Weaver and his staff were working on a similar idea—the meshing of physical and social improvements to uplift slum neighborhoods through the cooperative actions of several departments. Harold Wolman quotes an unnamed high HHFA official to the effect that such a plan was fully developed and ready to be announced by HHFA; but the White House held it up, according to this official, because the Wood task force was planning to announce the same plan. To be sure, the HHFA plans probably did not contain all of the elements of the Model Cities Program, and Wolman's quotation refers to urban renewal plans of a broad scope developed in New Haven and Detroit.[6] However, HHFA Administrator Robert C. Weaver was indeed thinking of ways to coordinate housing improvement and human services in slum neighborhoods. But the Wood task force was at the right place at the right time. It had the president's ear, and he supported their proposal. Thus, whoever may have thought of it or something like it first, the Wood task force qualifies as the innovator.

As we have seen in chapter 12, Robert Wood also contributed signficantly to the creation of a respectable HUD program of research. This policy innovation was largely the product of his creative ideas and ingenious tactics.

Albert Cole

Albert Cole, a defeated four-term Kansas congressman with a record of consistent opposition to public housing, urban renewal, and many other housing programs, was appointed HHFA administrator by President Eisenhower shortly after he was elected president. As Senator Hubert Humphrey said of the appointment, it "is like putting a fox in charge of a chicken coop."[7] But Humphrey's dire prediction proved wrong. Cole grew with his new responsibilities and became a vigorous supporter and administrator of HHFA's programs in an administration not greatly concerned with social programs. Cole advocated, within the administration, the creation of an urban department. He also contributed significantly to the Housing Act of 1954, certainly the most important HHFA legislative innovation in an otherwise passive period.

On September 12, 1953, Eisenhower announced the appointment of the President's Advisory Committee on Government Housing Policies and Programs. The committee was charged with making a thorough reassessment of HHFA's programs, policies, and organization. Administrator Cole was named chairman. What alarmed those concerned with progressive housing and urban programs was the people appointed to the committee. Of the twenty-two members, seven were bankers, and one was a realtor—neither group was famed for its support of such things as urban renewal, public housing, urban planning, or even liberal terms on FHA-insured mortgages. Furthermore, it appeared that Eisenhower's staff had gone out of its way to select the most conservative and even reactionary men it could find. Many predicted that the Advisory Committee would scuttle HHFA and most of its programs.

It did just the reverse. The Advisory Committee proposed

a broadening and liberalization of most of HHFA's programs, particularly urban renewal and public housing. It also proposed liberalization of FHA's mortgage insurance programs to support rebuilding on land cleared by urban renewal. Its report is a thoughtful, constructive document, covering a broad range of urban issues.[8]

To this near-miraculous result, Albert Cole contributed significantly, mostly through his deft performance as chairman. The virtuoso performance of two other men played an equally crucial role in extracting positive results from a largely negative committee.

James Rouse

James Rouse, a mortgage banker from Maryland, was chairman of the subcommittee on urban renewal. He saw the need for inner-city renewal. He was convinced that the 1949 legislation, which focused entirely on bulldozing slums and building apartments and office buildings on the land so cleared, must be broadened to include slum prevention, neighborhood conservation, and rehabilitation as well as clearance. He also believed cities should be required to do their own part—through code enforcement and planning—before they received federal aid for urban renewal. With conviction, force of personality, and sheer eloquence, Rouse persuaded the Advisory Committee to accept his sound modifications of the Urban Renewal Program. He also personally drafted the portions of the committee's final report expressing his vision of what urban renewal ought to be. James Rouse was and is a remarkable businessman. He emphatically demonstrated his special qualities of mind and personality at a time when the very future of urban renewal was at stake.

Ernest Bohn

Ernest Bohn, longtime director of Cleveland's Public Housing Authority, was named chairman of the subcommittee on housing for low-income families. He, too, was a remarkable man, but in a style quite different from that of Rouse. Rouse overwhelmed a reluctant committee with a direct assault of reasoned persuasion. Bohn, faced with a committee almost unanimously opposed to public housing, won with a dazzling display of wit, guile, and carefully cloaked evangelism. The committee staff were puzzled, then alarmed, when for weeks Bohn held no meetings of his subcommittee. This was neither neglect nor laziness. It reflected his shrewd conclusion that each of his subcommittee members had to be converted one by one in what now might be called encounter sessions. The results of this tactic astounded seasoned observers acquainted with the usual pallid workings of government advisory committees. Bohn gained the committee's support for an expansion of public housing, then in one of its frequent periods of near-terminal political illness. Beyond that, the reborn Bruce Savage, a onetime ardently anti–public housing realtor from Indianapolis, later became commissioner of the Public Housing Administration—and a good one.

David Krooth and Leon Keyserling

In 1937 federally subsidized housing for the poor was not a new idea—there was already much in England and in Western Europe. The innovation that facilitated the birth of public housing in this country was a complex but ingenious financing formula that greatly improved its political acceptability. Under this formula, some of the subsidies were not readily visible. One was the exemption from federal income taxes of interest payments on bonds issued by local housing authorities. Another was the waiver of local property taxes. The visible subsidy—the federal annual contributions contract—produced the least possible immediate impact on the federal budget. David Krooth was then a lawyer with the New Deal's Public Works Administration. Leon Keyserling was then staff assistant to Senator Robert Wagner of New York.

Riefler, Babcock, Colean, and Fisher

As we saw in chapter 7, the basic conception of FHA's system of federal insurance to support and stimulate origination of high-ratio, long-term private home mortgages came from the fertile mind of Winfield Riefler, then an economic adviser in the Treasury Department and probably the first man to hold that now familiar post in the federal government.[9] Riefler's concept was refined by Frederick M. Babcock, who invented its system for rating mortgage risks, and Miles Colean, who established the standards against which FHA judged the soundness of housing construction as well as subdivision planning. Ernest Fisher developed FHA's system for local market analysis. All these inventions were to have an impact on mortgage lending and home building far beyond the transactions FHA directly assisted. These, too, are striking illustrations of how the right men in the right place at the right time can have a great influence on government policy.

Turning the Idea into a Reality

Transforming ideas into policies usually involves drafting of legislation, the mobilization of support in Congress and elsewhere, as well as the bargaining and compromise that are so essential. Of these, the actual drafting, while complex, is the least difficult. In HUD and in HHFA, these delicate and demanding tasks have been done largely by lawyers. HUD and HHFA have been blessed with a long line of exceptionally gifted legislative lawyers—experts in the art of the politically possible. Former Secretary Weaver has expressed the opinion that he had "the best lawyers in town."[10]

Foard and Fefferman

During the 1950s, 1960s, and early 1970s, Ashley Foard and Hilbert Fefferman performed with notable success the complex job of turning policy ideas into legislative reality. Both were highly skilled career professionals. Foard was the gentle, unassuming craftsman. Fefferman, equally skilled as a legislative drafter, was more aggressive. His special forte was that of the political tactician. Together, they made up a team of complementary opposites. Both were completely dedicated to the public service, nonpartisan, with a capacity for long hours and hard work. During most of this long period, their efforts were ably supported by Carl Coan, Sr., the knowledgeable staff director of the Senate subcommittee on housing and by others on the staff of the equivalent House subcommittee. This legislative team played a crucial role in the shaping of nearly twenty major laws on housing and urban affairs. These laws authorized many of HUD's present activities.

B. T. Fitzpatrick

B. T. Fitzpatrick served with distinction as HHFA general counsel and deputy administrator from its creation in 1947 through the early years of the Eisenhower administration. Fitzpatrick was a legislative genius. Working intimately with Joseph McMurray, then staff director of the Senate Banking and Currency Committee, and with many of the era's most influential senators and congressmen, he was a principal force behind the creation of a permanent HHFA, the passage of the landmark Housing Act of 1949, and at least nine other major legislative enactments. He also trained those who were to follow him. The contributions of Fitzpatrick, at a time when housing programs were being extended to cover more and more urban issues and when the first permanent agency was being organized, can hardly be exaggerated.

Managing the Programs

No idea turned into law can serve the public purpose unless it is administered effectively. There have been many good administrators during the long history of HUD, HHFA, and its early predecessors. There have also been some poor ones. A few program administrators stand out because of their unusual capacity to perform in this challenging role.

Philip Brownstein

Philip Brownstein directed the FHA from 1963 to 1969. It was a time when the once-admirable FHA had succumbed to hardening of the arteries, that most common of bureaucratic diseases. It was also a time when circumstances required a major change in FHA's purposes, programs, and attitudes. During this difficult period, Brownstein managed the FHA with surpassing skill. A disciplined man with great vision, he changed FHA's direction while improving its efficiency. Very few men could have achieved as much. It is a tribute to his administrative skill that when Secretary Weaver and Under Secretary Wood left office, they both said that, to their surprise, the FHA had proved both the most efficient and most responsive of HUD's operating elements.

Stanley Baughman

When the Federal National Mortgage Association was transferred to HHFA in 1950, Stanley Baughman was made its president. He quickly reorganized and streamlined its organization. He also directed its operations for over fifteen years with exceptional skill and a jaundiced attitude toward the waste of public funds. Baughman is universally recognized as one of the ablest program managers HHFA has ever had.

Philip Klutznick

During World War II, the Public Housing Administration was turned into a means of providing housing for workers in war industries and military personnel. Philip Klutznick managed this radically transformed organization with brilliance and produced the results needed. His efforts gave vital support to a country at war.

Stewart McDonald and William Flanders

As we have seen, the creation of the FHA in 1934 revolutionized mortgage finance in the United States and spawned a new type of home-building industry. This could not have been done without creativity and good management. The latter was provided by Stewart McDonald, the second of FHA's administrators. He was a hard-headed, sometimes brusque, businessman. He ran the early FHA with a firm hand and produced a highly disciplined, productive organization. In this job he was ably supported by William Flanders, a pleasant and forceful private real estate operator. Flanders handled the delicate job of selecting capable people to direct FHA's far-flung field offices in the face of the inevitable pressures for political patronage. He also helped McDonald turn the fledgling organization into a cohesive, highly motivated unit with great esprit de corps. He was both respected and loved by FHA's personnel. As late as the 1950s, Flanders's picture could be seen in the offices of most of FHA's executives, long after he had departed.

The "Assistants-To"

In his study of the federal service, John Corson distinguishes between program managers and those who provide managerial support. Among the latter are what he calls "assistants-to," professionals who aid their bosses in a wide range of activities.[11] The job of these people is to extend the influence of their superiors by carrying out their objectives and by representing them in numerous ways and in a variety of situations. It is a delicate job, requiring broad knowledge, great tact, and persuasiveness. Many, of course, have served in this role. Some were highly effective; other less so; some did more harm than good. For purposes of illustration, we will discuss two who performed well and one whose success in other roles did not extend to this.

Neal J. Hardy

Under HHFA Administrator Raymond Foley and briefly under Albert Cole, Neal Hardy held the title of assistant administrator for Plans and Programs. This title suggests policy analysis. In fact, under Foley, Hardy's role was much more than that. He was Foley's alter ego: as such, he made policy, handled relations with HHFA's often reluctant operating units, handled relations with the White House and other federal agencies, and dealt with the numerous outside groups seeking to exert influence on HHFA's policies. These last ranged from the practical, well-organized home builders to the often unsophisticated, but earnest, representatives of various public interest and consumer groups. To this multitude of responsibilities, Hardy brought a wide knowledge, imagination, flexibility, persuasiveness, and tact. During the Korean War, for example, HHFA was assigned joint responsibility with the Federal Reserve Board for administering restraints on mortgage credit under what was known as Regulation X. By this time, the brilliant Winfield Riefler was assistant to the chairman of the Federal Reserve Board. Regulation X required delicate and technically complex decisions to be made jointly by the austere Federal Reserve Board and the very different, socially oriented HHFA. Communication was not easy. Winfield Riefler soon let it be known that Neal Hardy was the only man in HHFA with whom he would discuss the joint assignment. Not a few other groups, of vastly differing interests and knowledge, felt the same way. To say that Hardy became indispensable to Foley is no exaggeration.

Jay Janis

Jay Janis, a home builder from Florida, became special assistant to HUD Secretary Robert Weaver. He represented Weaver both inside and outside HUD with a gentle, tactful force. His actions accomplished Weaver's purposes while leaving everyone with whom he dealt feeling flattered rather than pressured. HUD is lucky that current Secretary Patricia Harris has appointed Jay Janis as her under secretary.

Joseph Burstein

As we have seen, Joseph Burstein is a brilliant, imaginative legal adviser. His important contributions to housing are many and widely recognized. When HHFA Administrator Weaver appointed Marie McGuire commissioner of the Public Housing Administration, she searched in vain for an effective deputy commissioner. In this vacuum, Joseph Burstein gradually assumed the role of de facto deputy. But this brilliant man was miscast in the assistant-to role. He lacked the qualities that made Hardy and Janis so effective, and the result was discord within the Public Housing Administration. The able Mrs. McGuire's effectiveness was reduced by an able man in the wrong place at the wrong time.

Agents of Change

The climate of opinion surrounding HUD exerts an important, if indirect, influence on its programs and policies. Ideas are important weapons.

Anthony Downs

Anthony Downs is an economist, head of a private consulting firm, and perhaps the most prolific current writer on urban affairs. (As this book goes to press, Downs has just joined Washington's Brookings Institution.) His books and articles have influenced informed opinion in many ways. Some of his ideas have already had their impact on HUD, others will in the future.

Paul Douglas and Edgar Kaiser

In the 1960s, President Johnson appointed former Senator Paul Douglas and industrialist Edgar Kaiser chairmen of two separate committees to study urban problems and recommend solutions. The report of the Kaiser Committee had almost immediate influence on HUD's legislation. Douglas's report had less immediate impact. But because it was such a masterly analysis of urban issues, its influence is already evident and will continue to be evident.

Anderson and Jacobs

Several influences established the climate that made possible and even inevitable Robert Weaver's change in the character of the urban renewal program, that is, greater emphasis on neighborhood preservation and revival and on humanizing the program and less emphasis on clearance. Two will be mentioned here—Martin Anderson's *The Federal Bulldozer* and Jane Jacobs's *The Life and Death of American Cities*. Anderson's book was simplistic, partisan, and filled with error. Jacobs's book was a naive glorification of life in Greenwich Village. Both bitterly attacked slum clearance. Of Jacobs's book, Lewis Mumford wrote, "This doughty opponent of urban renewal projects . . . bulldozes out of existence every desirable innovation in urban planning during the last century . . . without even a pretense of critical evaluation . . . I will say no more of Mrs. Jacobs's lack of historical knowledge and scholarly scruple except that her disregard of easily ascertainable facts is all too frequent."[12] Despite their shallowness and error, these two books of the mid-1960s greatly influenced public and even professional views on urban renewal. Ironically two flawed books with a single valid note helped bring about the sensible redirection in urban renewal that James Rouse had so responsibly urged a decade before.

Miles Colean

Miles Colean has written two books that significantly influenced the climate of opinion. The first, *American*

Housing, came before the passage of the Housing Act of 1949. The second, *Renewing Our Cities,* was published before the 1954 legislation and is generally credited with giving urban renewal the name by which it is known.

Charles Abrams

Charles Abrams, a prolific author, teacher, and gadfly, has exerted immense influence on urban policies through the years. He has done this through his books and through his influence, as teacher, on a generation of urban specialists.

The Administrators and Orchestrators

The job of the HUD secretaries, and before them of the HHFA administrators, was to guide and orchestrate the programs of the various operating elements and to establish broad policy objectives. The complex requirements of the job have been discussed in chapter 3. The performance of each secretary has also been discussed. Before them, the men who performed comparable roles were John Blandford, Wilson Wyatt, Raymond Foley, Albert M. Cole, and Norman P. Mason.

John Blandford, who headed the National Housing Agency, was a trained public administrator with great vision of the future role that his temporary, wartime agency might some day perform. He also assembled men of great ability who were later to play influential roles in HUD's creation.

Wilson Wyatt was on the scene only a year. He was energetic and eloquent. But his short tenure left little lasting imprint, in part because his energies were addressed to the acute but temporary needs of returning veterans.

Raymond Foley grew with the job and presided over HHFA when it was being enlarged from a purely housing agency to one concerned with urban affairs generally. He was a wise man and an effective user of able people, such as Hardy and Fitzpatrick. His influence on HHFA's early development was great. He also possessed considerable ability to deal with the Congress. In a very real sense, Foley was the man who assembled the program elements that later were to become an urban department.

Albert M. Cole was HHFA administrator during most of

the Eisenhower presidency. In addition to his role in generating the important Housing Act of 1954, Cole proved an unexpectedly effective administrator. He vigorously supported urban renewal, battled with the then cautious FHA in a sometimes vain effort to gain its support for the construction of apartment houses on land cleared by urban renewal, and supported creation of an urban department in the face of the president's lack of interest. Cole's relations with his career staff were warm, and he trusted and used them. The quality of his appointments to top positions in HHFA was mixed. Some were able; some not.

Norman P. Mason succeeded Cole as HHFA administrator during the twilight of the Eisenhower administration. A former lumber dealer from New England and former FHA commissioner, his skills and experience, like those of George Romney later, gave him only limited understanding of the sweeping challenges of his position. Since Mason's tenure was short, one can only guess whether he would have grown with the job, as Foley and Cole did.

The web of policy formation and execution in HUD, as elsewhere in government, is an intricate one. But the process is neither automatic nor anonymous. The force of a single personality can modify it—for better or worse. The force of a few personalities can decisively shape HUD's policies and their administration.

14

The Underlying Impediments to Urban Improvement

It must be clear by now that the many efforts of HUD and its predecessor agencies to alleviate our urban problems have achieved only partial success. Some of HUD's programs have improved the urban condition, some have failed. Many have had an ambiguous impact. Public housing served many (but not enough) poor families well—but it ran into many problems as its clients changed and as high-rise construction became necessary. FHA made a notable impact on mortgage finance and home building, but its influence has declined in recent years. Urban renewal, Model Cities, and other programs directed toward the improvement of slum conditions cannot be called spectacular successes. HUD's efforts to improve urban planning and eliminate racial discrimination have faced elusive and often intractable barriers.

In the preceding chapters we have examined the immediate causes of the successes and failures of HUD's programs. We have also noted the absence of coherent public policy in some fields (housing subsidies, for example). We have seen how the burden of contradictory purposes has handicapped the urban renewal program. HUD's partial command over federal actions influencing the problems with which it was attempting to deal has likewise been discussed. Again and again, we have observed that conditions in the general economy (unemployment, inflation, the cost and availability of credit) have a far greater effect on some of the most crucial urban problems than greater effect on some of the most crucial urban problems than anything HUD can do. The antiquated state of local government in our urban areas has also been seen to be a major impediment to rational planning and fiscal equity.

Lurking beneath all these difficulties that HUD faces are even deeper impediments, which have been touched upon but not elaborated. This chapter is devoted to these deeper issues. They lie at the root of HUD's frequent frustrations and of the frustrations of many other federal agencies trying to deal with the intricate problems of our society today.

The Limits of Government

The traditional structure of federal agencies is centralized and hierarchical. This structure has served us well for decades, but it works best when the problem to be solved or the service to be delivered is simple and straightforward. Up until the early 1960s, the jobs expected of the federal government were generally within the capacity of the traditional form of federal bureaucracy. Namely, these government functions consisted of writing checks for Social Security beneficiaries and similar forms of income support. They also involved the construction of roads, dams, post offices, and similar physical improvements. A third kind of pre-1960 federal responsibility that the standard bureaucracy was fairly well equipped to handle was general housekeeping—such as maintaining public parks, printing the currency, and collecting customs duties.

To discharge these relatively clear public functions, the only things required were an appropriation of funds, the establishment of a federal agency, and the hiring of competent bureaucrats to plan and carry out the jobs.[1]

But in the 1960s, the responsibilities given to our traditional bureaucracies became more complex and subtle. Thousands of individual decisions were required, each dealing with a unique complex of variables and interactions. Obviously, this was different from writing checks or building dams: the many individual decisions required could hardly be encompassed in the standard government regulation or operating manual. Hence there are many examples of the growing complexity of federal responsibilities: the rehabilitation of slum neighborhoods; the many-sided Model Cities Program; public housing, especially in its later years, when social problems became more important than simple physical improvement of housing; and, in closely related fields, the delivery of health care and pollution control. Under the burden of these very complicated assignments, the federal apparatus began to falter. It was overwhelmed by assignments for which the centralized, hierarchical bureaucracy was not well designed. Moreover, the traditional federal agency found it difficult, if not impossible, to measure the results of its efforts. A dam is a dam, and it either holds back the water or it does not. But improvements in the conditions and aspirations of poor families are not so easily measured.

An HEW director of policy analysis studied that department's capacity to deliver its health and welfare services to eligible clients. He found that an individual needing a single service had one chance in four of receiving it. He also found that the average client needed not one but seven types of services. Multiplying these fractions, he concluded that the chances of an eligible client getting all the human services he needed was close to zero. HEW was not alone. The agencies responsible for controlling air and water pollution experienced a similar difficulty in carrying out their assignments.

This development creates a dilemma. As Eugene R. Skolnikoff has put it, "the great benefit of the market for self-regulation must be increasingly sacrificed because it is not adequate to serve social goals. But the capability of political institutions to carry out the planning and regulation thereby required is also in question."[2]

As the public lost confidence in the government's capacity to provide the services or exercise the controls expected of it, some thought that better coordination was the solution. Others concluded that decentralization of decision making was the solution. (The Community Development Block Grant Program is an example of the second proposed solution.)

Charles L. Schultze, to whom I am indebted for his analysis of this question, thinks neither coordination nor decentralization is the answer. He believes federal programs aimed at changing the behavior of individuals and institutions require quite different methods, that today's complex problems require multiple decisions, each involving special circumstances and therefore an individual judgment. These, he argues, cannot be solved by the customary bureaucratic regulations nor handled by the customary bureaucrat, no matter how able. As he puts it, "The omniscient bureaucrat has not been born."[3] The approach Schultze favors involves federal incentives and penalties designed to produce decisions on the private market that accord with the public purpose by making them more profitable. As an example, he suggests that private firms would find a way not to pollute our rivers if government-designed penalties and rewards made it more profitable to take the necessary actions. In a moment of rhetorical exuberance, Schultze went so far as to say, "We need an Adam Smith for the social sector."[4]

Many thoughtful students of government disagree. They think Schultze's proposal suffers from oversimplification. Others think his approach is likely to work in only a limited number of circumstances and hardly ever in the urban field.[5]

Schultze does not deny that designing the right kind of incentives will be "extremely difficult."[6] President Carter's proposed energy program contains many incentives and penalties. It also shows how difficult it is to design just the right incentives and penalties to influence the behavior of individuals and institutions in the desired way.

There Is Much We Do Not Understand

We simply do not understand many aspects of human and institutional behavior nor how to design public programs we need. This is true of crime, of antisocial behavior in the slums, of education, poverty, urban planning, and many other aspects of the urban environment. As they have come to recognize this hard fact, many of the exuberant social engineers of the 1960s have become both humble and discouraged. Charles Haar, one of the architects of the Model Cities Program, has recently written of the "bankruptcy of the liberal mind."[7] The Urban Institute has recently said, "in 1976 there is less consensus on the ultimate causes of many serious urban problems, and even less consensus on the measures that would ameliorate them, than there was in 1966. . . . Confidence in our ability to frame solutions has declined even as understanding of the problems has grown."[8]

Nathan Glazer has practically given up on the government's capacity to alleviate the still widespread discrimination against and segregation of blacks and other minorities.[9] Others are of the same mind. Some now advocate experimentation to improve our understanding of the problems and of how to deal with them more effectively.

But excessive pessimism is as bad as excessive optimism. As Schultze has observed, "Giving up the search for solutions to urgent social problems would be both irresponsible and dangerous."[10] The new humility among many urban scholars is probably a healthy development, but it does not justify inaction.

Our Permissive Society

Few would dispute that ours has become a highly permissive society. This is reflected in many contemporary institutions and art forms that we have made and now tend to make us. We are surrounded and seduced by television, magazines, advertising, paperback books, and music that glorify self-interest, materialism, and a hedonistic preoccupation with instant gratification. The message is cleverly packaged, using language, art, and visual impact as a means of psychological manipulation. Many serious students believe these messages attack us both at the conscious and subconscious levels. The highly respected scholar, Joseph Schumpeter, has described the attack of modern advertising "upon the subconscious which takes the form of attempts to evoke and crystallize pleasant associations of an entirely extra-rational, very frequently of a sexual nature."[11] Evidently, America's creed of "life, liberty, and the pursuit of happiness" has gone wild. Liberty becomes license, and happiness becomes a false, self-defeating caricature of the real thing.

The insidious use of modern merchandising techniques has invaded politics. Candidates for public office are now promoted as if they were lipstick, face cream, or the newest fashion in clothes. As someone noted, it is unlikely that Abraham Lincoln could be elected president today. Too often we vote for contrived images rather than for men.

The fragile balance between individual liberty and the necessary restraint of liberty has eroded. The important point is that a society so pervaded by the doctrine of permissiveness is less likely to produce responsible citizens, not to mention stable neighborhoods. Our democracy requires above all the participation of citizens who are not only informed but responsible and willing to sacrifice individual self-interest for the common interest—when that is required.

The Other Side

It is America's good fortune that its people are, by and large, far better than the hedonistic images that surround and pound upon them. Heroism is not dead in America. Neither are charity and moral responsibility. Most of us have neighbors who display virtues of a very high order. Our universities are full of students motivated to some kind of public or private service. Even in our urban slums, most people act with remarkable faith and courage in the face of the squalor in which they are trapped. Frank Hurcules—a long-time resident of New York's Harlem—is thoroughly familiar with its seamier side—the run-down buildings, the crime, the terror, the despair. Yet he insists that Harlem also possesses courage, zest, and a good deal of humor. He thinks it is "a triumphant, not a defeated community." Harlem, he says, "celebrates the invincibility of the human spirit."[12]

The Leaders and the Led

At this stage in its history, our country needs more than anything else to reform its political and private institutions.[13] If institutions do not shape human behavior, they certainly influence it. We need institutions, therefore, that will appeal to and reinforce the best in human nature to replace those that play upon the worst of human instincts.

The reform of our institutions is the task of national leadership. In political life, a cleansing leadership is especially important. It is also very difficult—for three reasons. First, the events of the past decade have led people to become cynical of government and its leaders. For this, there is considerable justification. Clearly, a faith in government must be restored. Second, the major issues facing our society are technically complex and require a sustained response. It is only human to respond more quickly to crises that are clearly perceived as well as immediately desperate. Winston Churchill's famous speeches during World War II dealt with a clear and immediate danger that could be communicated in simple and eloquent phrases; "We will fight [for our lives] on the beaches" is something that all Englishmen could understand. President Carter's speeches on energy conservation represent a far more difficult kind of leadership. The nature of the danger is difficult to comprehend and long-range, and the proposed remedies are intricate. Churchill's crisis was far easier to communicate than Carter's. The energy crisis may be "the moral equivalent of war," but it is far harder for the average American to grasp as something immediate and urgent. Third, there is a complicated reciprocal relationship between the leader and those he tries to lead. People cannot be led and mobilized to do things for a purpose with which they do not instinctively agree. Winston Churchill's personal physician has stated in his memoirs that Churchill had no true empathy with the British people. He spoke not for them but for himself. He just happened to say what the people of that beleaguered isle wanted to hear and were already willing to make sacrifices for.[14]

In Conclusion

Today, the question that puzzles serious thinkers is whether the deterioration in America's politics and in its capacity for collective consensus on grave national problems (energy, pollution, the cities, all of which are closely interrelated) is a long-term trend or a passing cycle. There are many good reasons for hope. Daniel Bell has observed, "Within limits, men can remake themselves and society, but the knowledge of power must coexist with the knowledge of its limits. This is, after all, the most enduring truth about the human condition."[15]

Sir Dennis Brogan, the English historian and lifelong observer of the American scene, has put the same hopeful view in quite different words. Noting the contrast between democratic government and nondemocratic government, he said nondemocratic government "is like a splendid ship, with all its sails set; it moves majestically on, then hits a rock and sinks forever." On the other hand, "democracy is like a raft. It never sinks, but damn it, your feet are always in the water."[16]

Appendix

Major Legislative Enactments and Executive Orders*

1. Federal Home Loan Bank Act, 1932 (Federal Home Loan Bank Board)
2. Home Owners' Loan Act of 1933
3. National Housing Act, 1934 (Federal Housing Administration)
4. United States Housing Act of 1937 (Public Housing)
5. Lanham Act—War Housing, 1940
6. Establishment of the National Housing Agency, 1942
7. Veterans' Emergency Housing Act of 1946
8. Establishment of Housing and Home Finance Agency (by Executive Order), 1947
9. Housing Act of 1948 (Research)
10. Housing Act of 1949 (Slum Clearance and Urban Redevelopment)
11. Housing Act of 1954 (Research; Urban Planning, extension of slum clearance to include rehabilitation; first use of term *urban renewal*; additional public housing)
12. Housing Act of 1959 (Housing for Elderly)
13. Housing Act of 1961 (FHA below-market-rate housing, planning for urban mass transportation, open space land)

---

*A general description of the contents of these and other legislative and executive actions can be found in U.S., Congress, House, Committee on Banking, Currency and Housing, *Evolution of Role of the Federal Government in Housing and Community Development* (Washington, D.C.: U.S. Government Printing Office, 1975).

14. Housing Act of 1964 (Direct 3 percent loans for rehabilitation)
15. Housing and Urban Development Act of 1965 (Rent supplements; advanced acquisition of land)
16. Department of Housing and Urban Development Act, 1965
17. Demonstration Cities and Metropolitan Development Act of 1966 (Model Cities Program)
18. Civil Rights Act of 1968
19. Housing and Urban Development Act of 1968 (National Housing Goals, Sections 235 and 236, subsidized loans for ownership and rental of housing)
20. Moratorium on Housing Subsidy and Community Funds, Executive Decision, 1973
21. Housing and Community Development Act of 1974 (block grants for community development, Section 8 Program for subsidizing rents on new and existing housing)
22. The Housing and Community Development Act of 1977 (modification of block grant apportionment formula, special multiyear Urban Development Action Grants for neighborhood revitalization in severely distressed cities and counties)

Notes

Chapter 1

1. J. L. Sert, *Can Our Cities Survive?* (Cambridge, Mass.: Harvard University Press, 1942).

2. *Goals for Americans,* The Report of the President's Commission on National Goals (New York: Prentice Hall, 1960).

3. Anthony Downs, *Opening up the Suburbs* (New Haven: Yale University Press, 1973).

4. George Sternlieb and Robert W. Burchett, *Residential Abandonment* (New Brunswick, N.J.: Rutgers University Press, 1973).

5. Ibid.

6. Harvey S. Perloff, ed., *Agenda for the New Urban Era* (Chicago: American Society of Planning Officials, 1975).

7. Ibid.

8. Barbara Ward, *The Home of Man* (New York: W. W. Norton and Co., 1976).

9. *Marketing and Mobility,* Report of the Panel of the Interagency Task Force on Motor Vehicle Goals Beyond 1980, Department of Transportation (Washington, D.C., 1976).

10. Perloff, *Agenda for the New Urban Era.*

11. *Building the American City,* Report of the National Commission on Urban Problems (Washington, D.C.: U.S. Government Printing Office, 1968).

12. Ward, *The Home of Man.*

13. Arnold A. Rogow, *The Dying of the Light* (New York: G. P. Putnam's Sons, 1975).

14. Edward A. Banfield, *The Unheavenly City Revisited* (Boston: Little, Brown and Co., 1971).

Chapter 2

1. U.S., Congress, House, Committee on Banking, Currency and Housing, *Basic Laws and Authorities on Housing and Community Development,* 94th Cong., 1st sess. (Washington, D.C.: U.S. Government Printing Office, 1975).

2. Quoted in Mark I. Gelfand, *A Nation of Cities* (New York: Oxford University Press, 1975).

3. Ibid.

4. Ibid.

5. Ibid.

6. Ibid.

7. Ibid.

8. Among the people who played a role in generating support for an urban department between 1950 and 1965 were: Paul Ylvisaker, then with the Ford Foundation; Robert C. Wood, then a professor at MIT; Edward Logue, redevelopment director in New Haven; Joseph P. McMurray, then staff director of the Senate Committee on Banking and Currency; B. T. Fitzpatrick, a lawyer and former deputy administrator of HHFA; Nelson Rockefeller, then governor of New York and adviser to President Eisenhower; Senator Joseph Clark of Pennsylvania and James Sundquist, his executive assistant; Congressman Albert Rains; Mayors Richard Lee of New Haven, Richardson Dilworth of Philadelphia, and Richard Daley of Chicago; Chester Bowles, former governor of Connecticut and ambassador to India; and Albert M. Cole, administrator of the Housing and Home Finance Agency in the Eisenhower administration.

9. Memo from Arthur A. Kimball to the President's Advisory Committee on Government Organization, November 9, 1956.

10. William L. C. Wheaton, "A New Cabinet Post," *The Federal Government and the Cities,* Washington, D.C., 1961.

11. The events leading to the establishment of HUD are fully covered in Frederick N. Cleaveland, *Congress and Urban Problems* (Washington, D.C.: The Brookings Institution, 1969), and in Gelfand, *A Nation of Cities.*

12. David S. McLellan, *Dean Acheson: The State Department Years* (New York: Dodd, Mead, 1976).

Chapter 3

1. M. Carter McFarland, "Unlearned Lessons in the History of

Federal Housing Aid," *City Magazine* (Washington, D.C.), Winter 1972.

2. Based on an interview with Robert C. Weaver, September 1976.

3. Marvin H. Bernstein, *The Job of the Federal Executives* (Washington, D.C.: The Brookings Institution, 1958).

4. Wallace S. Sayre, "The Public Service," in *Goals for Americans* New York: Prentice Hall, 1960).

5. John J. Corson and R. Shale Paul, *Men Near the Top* (Baltimore: The Johns Hopkins Press, 1966).

6. Quoted in *The Washington Post*, April 3, 1977.

7. Some federal agencies do go out of business when their job is completed, for example the Home Owners Loan Corporation, which closed its doors in June 1953, after bailing out a large percentage of American homeowners whose mortgages were foreclosed during the Great Depression.

8. James Nathan Miller, "The 'Unholy Trinities' That Undermine America," *Reader's Digest*, March 1977.

9. Political scientist Harold Wolman, who studied HUD's policymaking process during the years 1965-1967, found that organized interest groups had relatively little influence on HUD's major policy decisions. Harold Wolman, *Politics of Federal Housing* (New York: Dodd, Mead, 1971).

10. McFarland, "Unlearned Lessons."

11. Ibid.

12. Marriner Eccles, *Beckoning Horizons* (New York: Alfred A. Knopf, 1966).

13. Richard E. Neustadt, *Presidential Power* (New York: John Wiley and Sons, 1962).

14. Ibid.

15. For an accurate description of Romney's reorganizations and their effects, see Horace B. Bazan, *The Fragmentation of FHA* (Washington, D.C.: Mortgage Bankers Association of America, 1974).

16. Albert M. Cole, HHFA administrator during the Eisenhower administration, told the author that if he had been faced with the same organizational choices, he would have "leaned" toward Weaver's decision.

17. *Washington Post*, March 20, 1976.

Chapter 4

1. U.S., Congress, House, Committee on Banking, Currency and Housing, *Evolution of Role of the Federal Government in Housing and Community Development, a Chronology of Legislation and*

Executive Actions (Washington, D.C.: U.S. Government Printing Office, 1975).

2. From a conversation in November 1976 with Paul Ylvisaker, dean, Graduate School of Education, Harvard University.

3. American Institute of Architects, *A Plan for Urban Growth: Report of the National Policy Task Force* (Washington, D.C., 1972).

4. Dorn C. McGrath, Jr., "Population Growth and Change: Implications for Planning," *Aspects of Population Growth* (Washington, D.C., 1969).

5. See American Institute of Planners, *National Planning Policy* (Washington, D.C., 1974).

6. Ward, *The Home of Man.*

7. Elliot Richardson, *The Creative Balance* (New York: Holt, Rinehart and Winston, 1976).

8. William Gorham and Nathan Glazer, *The Urban Predicament* (Washington, D.C.: The Urban Institute, 1976).

9. From a conversation in November 1976 with Dean Harvey Perloff, School of Agriculture and Urban Planning, University of California at Los Angeles.

10. National Commission on Urban Problems, *Building the American City.*

11. Daniel Bell, *The Cultural Contradictions of Capitalism* (New York: Basic Books, Inc., 1976).

12. Conversation with Harvey Perloff.

13. Melvin B. Mogulof, *Governing Metropolitan Areas* (Washington, D.C.: The Urban Institute, 1971).

14. Perloff, *Agenda for the New Urban Era.*

15. Mogulof, *Governing Metropolitan Areas.*

16. Gorham and Glazer, *The Urban Predicament.*

17. W. W. Rostow, "The American National Style," *Daedalus* 87, no. 2 (Spring 1958): 110-144.

18. Lewis Mumford, *The Urban Prospect* (New York: Harcourt, Brace and World, Inc., 1968).

19. Philip Arctander, "Dangerous Dogmas of Urban Planning and Research," *City Magazine* (Washington, D.C.), Winter 1972.

20. Marion Clawson, "Environment and Land Use," in Perloff, *Agenda for the New Urban Era.*

21. Ibid.

22. American Institute of Architects, *A Plan for Urban Growth.*

23. Donald Canty, *Architectural Forum*, August-September 1964. Many responsible students of the problem believe land banking to be unwise; others believe it would be politically impossible to accomplish. The National Commission on Urban Problems could

not agree on this issue. Its report contains a minority view expressing strong support for the idea. We will never know which experts are right until it is tried.

24. Testimony of Robert Embry before the Committee on Banking, Currency and Housing, Washington, D.C., September 1976.

25. From a conversation, in September 1976, with former HUD secretary, Robert C. Weaver.

Chapter 5

1. Housing and Community Development Act of 1974, P. L. 93-383, August 22, 1974.

2. Ibid.

3. From a discussion with Dean Harvey Perloff, at UCLA, in November 1976.

4. From a discussion with Louis Winnick, of the Ford Foundation, August 1976.

5. From a speech delivered by Charles L. Schultze at the First National Conference on Congregate Housing for Older People, Washington, D.C., November 1975. The content of this conference has been published by U.S., Department of Health, Education and Welfare, *Congregate Housing for Older People* (Washington, D.C.: U.S. Government Printing Office, 1977).

6. Charles L. Schultze (with Edward Fried, Alice Rivlin, and Nancy Teeters), *Setting National Priorities—the 1973 Budget* (Washington, D.C.: The Brookings Institution, 1972).

7. From a discussion with Mr. Brownstein in August 1976.

8. From a conversation with Paul Ylvisaker, dean, Graduate School of Education, Harvard University, September 1976.

9. Charles M. Haar, *Between the Idea and the Reality* (Boston: Little, Brown and Co., 1975).

10. Quoted in the testimony of Robert C. Wood before the House Committee on Banking, Currency and Housing, U.S. Congress, Washington, D.C., October 1976.

11. David B. Walker, Advisory Commission on Intergovernmental Relations, from speech delivered at the December 1976 meeting of the Washington Chapter of Lambda Alpha, the International Land Economics Fraternity.

12. U.S., Department of Housing and Urban Development, *Community Development Block Grant Program* (Washington, D.C.: U.S. Government Printing Office, December 1975).

13. *NAHRO Community Development Monitoring Report* (Washington, D.C., April 1976).

14. *Housing and Development Reporter* (Bureau of National Affairs, Washington, D.C.), April 5, 1976.

15. From a conversation with Neal J. Hardy, former commissioner of FHA, November 1976.

16. Based on a discussion with Robert C. Weaver in September 1976.

17. Catherine Bauer, "Redevelopment: A Misfit in the Fifties," in *Future of Cities and Urban Redevelopment*, ed. Coleman Woodbury (Chicago, 1952).

18. Housing Act of 1949, P. L. 81-171.

19. Robert A. Caro, *The Power Broker* (New York: Vantage Books, 1975).

20. Martin Anderson, *The Federal Bulldozer* (Cambridge, Mass.: MIT Press, 1964).

21. William L. Slayton, commissioner, Urban Renewal Administration, testimony before the House Committee on Banking and Currency, U.S. House of Representatives, 1963.

22. Perloff, *Agenda for a New Urban Era.*

23. See M. Carter McFarland, *Residential Rehabilitation in the Harlem Park Area, Baltimore, Maryland* (Washington, D.C.: Housing and Home Finance Agency, June 1963); and M. Carter McFarland and Walter K. Vivrett, *Residential Rehabilitation* (Minneapolis: University of Minnesota Press, 1966).

24. See "Goals and Accomplishments of Residential Rehabilitation," from HUD Secretary Robert C. Weaver's testimony before the Senate Committee on Banking and Currency, July 17, 1967 (mimeo by HUD).

25. See M. Carter McFarland, *The Rehabilitation and Revival of Decayed or Decaying Residential Neighborhoods*, a study prepared for the Research Service of the Library of Congress, February 3, 1977. Published in hearings before a subcommittee, pt. 8—Substandard Housing, Committee on Appropriations, House of Representatives (Washington, D.C.: U.S. Government Printing Office, 1977).

26. Ibid.

27. Haar, *Between the Idea and the Reality.*

28. Ibid.

29. Ibid.

30. Dan Rather, *The Palace Guard* (New York: Warner paperback ed., 1975).

31. Ibid.

32. For a full account of the Model Cities Program, see Haar, *Between the Idea and the Reality*; and Bernard J. Freeden and Marshall Kaplan, *The Politics of Neglect* (Cambridge, Mass.: MIT Press, 1975).

33. Conversation with Robert C. Weaver, September 1976.

34. Based on conversation with Ralph Taylor in August 1976.

35. Based on information supplied by former HUD Legislative Counsel Hilbert Fefferman, June 1977.

36. Based on a discussion with Jay Janis in November 1976.

37. Conversation with Robert C. Weaver, September 1976.

38. This apt phrase is borrowed from Haar, *Between the Idea and the Reality*.

39. Martha Dertrick, *New Towns In-Town* (Washington, D.C.: The Urban Institute, 1972).

40. Harvey Perloff (with Tom Berg, Robert Fountain, David Vetter, and John Weld), *Modernizing the Central City* (Cambridge, Mass.: Ballinger Publishing Co., 1975).

41. Schultze el al., *Setting National Priorities—the 1973 Budget.*

42. From a speech delivered to a meeting of the National Housing Conference, Washington, D.C., April 19, 1977.

Chapter 6

1. Housing Act of 1949, preamble, Public Law 81-171, July 15, 1949.

2. Ernest M. Fisher, *Urban Real Estate Markets: Characteristics and Financing* (New York: National Bureau of Economic Research, 1951).

3. Anthony Downs, "The Successes and Failures of Housing Policy," *The Public Interest*, Winter 1974.

4. National Commission on Urban Problems, *Building the American City.*

5. Miles L. Colean, *The Impact of Government on Real Estate Financing in the United States* (New York: National Bureau of Economic Research, 1950).

6. Ibid.

7. Message from the President of the United States, *First Annual Report on National Goals* (Washington, D.C.: U.S. Government Printing Office, January 28, 1969).

8. Charles L. Schultze (with Edward Fried, Alice Rivlin, and Nancy Teeters), *Setting National Priorities—the 1972 Budget.* (Washington, D.C.: The Brookings Institution, 1971).

9. Henry Aaron, *Shelter and Subsidies* (Washington, D.C.: The Brookings Institution, 1972).

10. From a conversation with Robert C. Weaver, September 1976.

11. National Commission on Urban Problems, *Building the American City*.

12. Joint Center for Urban Studies of MIT and Harvard University, *The Nation's Housing: 1975-1985* (Cambridge, 1977).

13. The President's Domestic Council, *1976 Report on National Growth and Development* (Washington, D.C.: U.S. Government Printing Office, 1976).

14. HUD Secretary Patricia Harris, speech before the National Housing Conference, Washington, D.C., March 1977.

Chapter 7

1. The National Housing Act, P. L. 73-479, June 27, 1934.

2. Eccles, *Beckoning Horizons*.

3. Ibid.

4. Miles Colean, *A Backward Glance: An Oral History* (Washington, D.C.: Mortgage Bankers Association of America, 1975).

5. Based on a conversation with Miles Colean in late 1976.

6. Quoted in M. Carter McFarland, "The New in FHA," *The Mortgage Banker*, February 1962.

7. Based on a conversation with Professor Saulnier in mid-1976.

8. Ibid.

9. McFarland, "The New in FHA."

10. Conversation with Miles Colean in late 1976.

11. National Commission on Urban Problems, *Building the American City*.

Chapter 8

1. Downs, "The Successes and Failures of Housing Policy."

2. Ward, *The Home of Man*.

3. From notes made on this chapter by Philip N. Brownstein.

4. Charles J. Orlebeke, "A Framework for Housing Policy," in Perloff, *Agenda for the Urban Era*.

5. HUD Statistical Report on Section 8, May 31, 1976 (mimeo).

6. Milton Semer and Julian Zimmerman, "A Review of Federal Subsidized Housing Programs," Washington, D.C., 1974. (Unpublished report prepared under contract with HUD.)

7. Rogow, *The Dying of the Light.*

8. A conversation with Mrs. McGuire, 1976.

9. Housing and Urban Development Act of 1968, P. L. 90-448, August 1, 1968.

10. It is interesting to note that some of FHA's founders, notably Frederick M. Babcock and Miles Colean, grasped the logic of Weaver's vision far better than the second and third generation of FHA technicians, who tended to elevate to immutable, Biblical verities the original FHA policies.

11. Remarks of P. N. Brownstein, FHA assistant secretary-commissioner at Director's Conference, *FHA's Job Today*, October 23, 1967.

12. It is the belief of Philip Brownstein, among others, that FHA could perform both its traditional and its social functions without confusion by applying its normal underwriting standards to subsidized applications, taking into account the lower rents made available by subsidies.

13. Downs, "The Successes and Failures of Housing Policy."

14. U.S., Congress, House, Committee on Banking and Currency, *Investigation and Hearing of Abuses in Federal Low- and Moderate-Income Housing Programs* (Washington, D.C.: U.S. Government Printing Office, 1970).

15. Ibid.

16. Aaron, *Shelter and Subsidies.*

17. Schultze et al., *Setting National Priorities—The 1972 Budget.*

18. Downs, "The Successes and Failures of Housing Policy."

19. See *Hearings* on the Housing Act of 1937, *Report of the Subcommittee on Housing,* of the *Senate Committee on Post War Planning* (1945); and *Report of the President's Advisory Committee on Government Housing Policies and Programs* (1953).

20. Orlebeke, "A Framework For Housing Policy."

21. U.S. Department of Housing and Urban Development, *Housing in the Seventies* (Washington, D.C.: U.S. Government Printing Office, 1974).

22. Speech of HUD Secretary Harris before the National Housing Conference, Washington, D.C., March 1977.

23. U.S., Congress, Library of Congress, Congressional Research Service, *Critique of "Housing in the Seventies"* (Washington, D.C.: U.S. Government Printing Office, 1974).

24. Ibid.

25. Ibid.

26. McFarland, "Unlearned Lessons."

27. Orlebeke, "A Framework for Housing Policy."
28. Ibid.
29. Semer and Zimmerman, "A Review of Federal Subsidized Housing Programs."
30. McFarland, "Unlearned Lessons."
31. Gorham and Glazer, *The Urban Predicament.*
32. Sherman J. Maisell, "Stabilization and Income Distribution Policies and Housing Production," *Resources for Housing* (San Francisco: Federal Home Loan Bank Board of San Francisco, 1976).
33. See speeches by Patricia Harris and Stuart Eizenstat before the National Housing Conference (the former in March 1977, the latter in April 1977).

Chapter 9

1. Henry Schechter, *The Residential Mortgage Financing Problem*, prepared for U.S., Congress, House, Committee on Banking and Currency, Subcommittee on Housing (Washington, D.C.: U.S. Government Printing Office, 1971).
2. Ibid.
3. Maisell, "Stabilization and Income Distribution Policies and Housing Production."
4. *Report of the Commission on Mortgage Interest Rates to the President of the United States and to the Congress* (Washington, D.C.: U.S. Government Printing Office, 1969).
5. Schechter, *The Residential Mortgage Financing Problem.*
6. Ibid.
7. *The Economic Report of the President* (Washington, D.C.: U.S. Government Printing Office, 1957).
8. *The Economic Report of the President* (Washington, D.C.: U.S. Government Printing Office, 1967).
9. Speech by Oakley Hunter, president of the Federal National Mortgage Association, before the Conference of the National Association of Housing and Redevelopment Officials, San Francisco, 1975.
10. For thorough studies of credit cycles and their causes see *The Residential Mortgage Financing Problem; Report of the Commission on Mortgage Interest Rates;* Oliver Jones and Leo Grebler, *The Secondary Mortgage Market* (Los Angeles: University of California Press, 1961); and *Resources for Housing.*
11. Maisell, "Stabilization and Income Distribution Policies and Housing Production."

12. J. M. Clark, *Strategic Factors in Business Cycles* (New York: National Bureau of Economic Research, 1934).

13. Maisell, "Stabilization and Income Distribution Policies and Housing Production."

14. *The Residential Mortgage Financing Problem.*

15. National Commission on Urban Problems, *Building the American City.* Professor Leo Grebler of UCLA disagrees with this view. See Leo Grebler, "The Role of the Public Sector in Residential Finance," in *Resources for Housing.*

16. National Commission on Urban Problems, *Building the American City.*

17. Ibid.

18. Charles L. Schultze, *Setting National Priorities—The 1971 Budget* (Washington, D.C.: The Brookings Institution, 1970).

19. *Report of the Commission on Mortgage Interest Rates.*

20. From notes made on a draft of this chapter by Dr. Henry Schechter, who was kind enough to review it.

Chapter 10

1. *The President's Message on the Cities,* March 2, 1965.

2. These cost figures are taken from the National Association of Home Builders.

3. Anthony Downs, "The Coming Rental Housing Shortage," unpublished paper, Chicago, 1977.

4. Oakley Hunter, "A Housing Policy for Today," speech delivered at the 36th National Convention of the National Association of Housing and Redevelopment Officials, Los Angeles, October 1975.

5. Based on a conversation with Anthony Downs.

6. From an unpublished paper prepared by Anthony Downs.

7. Conversation with Anthony Downs.

8. Joseph P. Fried, *Housing Crisis—USA* (Baltimore: Penguin Books, 1972).

9. U.S., National Bureau of Standards, "Consumer Reaction to Living in Operation Breakthrough," a study prepared for HUD in June 1976. Mimeographed.

10. Real Estate Research Corporation, "Evaluation of Operation Breakthrough," report prepared for HUD, Chicago, 1976. Mimeographed.

11. National Bureau of Standards, "Consumer Reaction."

12. Real Estate Research Corporation, "Evaluation."

13. Based on Mr. Finger's notes on an earlier draft of this chapter.

14. Based on a conversation with Harold Denton, February 1977.

15. Based on a conversation with Professor William Wheaton, Berkeley, California, November 1976.

16. Downs, "The Successes and Failures of Federal Housing Policy."

17. McFarland, "Unlearned Lessons."

18. The cost figures used in the preceding paragraphs were provided by the Economics Department of the National Association of Home Builders.

19. National Commission on Urban Problems, *Building the American City*.

20. Ibid.

21. Dick Nitzer, a study prepared for the National Commission on Urban Problems, Washington, D.C., 1968.

22. The report of the National Commission on Urban Problems contains an excellent analysis of housing costs as well as numerous recommendations for public actions.

Chapter 11

1. The Civil Rights Act of 1968, Public Law 90-284, April 11, 1968.

2. Alexis de Tocqueville, *Democracy in America* (1862; reprint ed., New York: Vantage Books, 1945).

3. Gunnar Myrdal, *The American Dilemma* (New York: Harper and Row, 1944).

4. *Report of the National Advisory Commission on Civil Disorders* (Washington, D.C.: U.S. Government Printing Office, 1968).

5. Federal Register, Rule 24 (Docket No. R-71-119), *Project Selection Criteria*, Washington, D.C., 1972.

6. Federal Register, Title 24 (Docket No. R-72-108), *Advertising Guidelines for Fair Housing*, Washington, D.C., 1972.

7. David Falk and Herbert M. Franklin, *Equal Housing Opportunity* (Washington, D.C.: The Potomac Institute, 1976).

8. Myrdal, *The American Dilemma*.

9. Ibid.

10. See The United States Commission on Civil Rights, *Twenty Years After Brown* (Washington, D.C., 1975). The same point was made by HUD's assistant secretary for equal opportunity in a speech

before the National Housing Conference in Washington, D.C. in late 1976.

11. U.S. Commission on Civil Rights, *The Federal Civil Rights Enforcement Effort—1974* (Washington, D.C., 1974).

12. U.S. Commission on Civil Rights, *Twenty Years After Brown.*

13. Gorham and Glazer, *The Urban Predicament.*

14. Perloff, *Agenda for the New Urban Era.*

15. Gorham and Glazer, *The Urban Predicament.*

16. Ibid.

17. *The Washington Post,* June 29, 1975.

18. Reported in *Time Magazine,* November 1976.

19. Nathan Glazer, *Affirmative Discrimination* (New York: Basic Books, Inc., 1975).

20. Banfield, *The Unheavenly City Revisited.*

21. An observation made by Robert C. Weaver.

22. Downs, *Opening Up the Suburbs.*

23. Richard Kluger, *Simple Justice* (New York: Alfred A. Knopf, 1976).

24. Bell, *The Cultural Contradictions of Capitalism.*

25. Falk and Franklin, *Equal Housing Opportunity.*

26. Ibid.

27. Ibid.

28. Ibid.

29. From Dr. Weaver's notes made on an early draft of this chapter.

Chapter 12

1. The Housing Act of 1948. Public Law 80-901, August 10, 1948.

2. The Housing Act of 1949. Public Law 81-171, July 15, 1949.

3. U.S., Department of Housing and Urban Development, *Science and the City* (Washington, D.C.: U.S. Government Printing Office, 1967).

4. Ibid.

5. The opinion of former HUD assistant secretary for research, Harry Finger.

6. Richardson, *The Creative Balance.*

7. Doris Haar, research executive at HEW.

8. Gorham and Glazer, *The Urban Predicament.*

9. Based on a conversation with Charles L. Schultze, January 1977.

10. Bell, *The Cultural Contradictions of Capitalism.*

11. Charles L. Schultze (with Edward W. Fried, Alice M. Rivlin,

and Nancy Teeters), *Setting National Priorities, The 1975 Budget* (Washington, D.C.: The Brookings Institution, 1974).

12. Joseph S. Wholey, et al., *Federal Evaluation Policy* (Washington, D.C.: The Urban Institute, 1970).

13. From a conversation with Harold Finger.

Chapter 13

1. Wolman, *Politics of Federal Housing.*
2. Ibid.
3. Wallace S. Sayre, "The Public Service."
4. Neustadt, *Presidential Power.*
5. For the details of these two illustrations of policy innovation, I am indebted to Hilbert Fefferman, former HUD associate general counsel for legislation.
6. Wolman, *Politics of Federal Housing.*
7. Gelfand, *A Nation of Cities.*
8. *Report of the President's Advisory Committee on Government Housing Policies and Programs* (Washington, D.C.: U.S. Government Printing Office, 1953).
9. Eccles, *Beckoning Horizons.*
10. Based on an interview with Robert C. Weaver in New York, September 1976.
11. Corson and Paul, *Men Near the Top.*
12. Mumford, *The Urban Prospect.*

Chapter 14

1. Schultze, *Setting National Priorities—the 1973 Budget.* Also, Charles L. Schultze, "Can the Economy Support New Social Initiatives?" *Congregate Housing for Older People,* U.S., Department of Health, Education and Welfare (Washington, D.C.: Government Printing Office, 1977).
2. Eugene B. Skolnikoff, "Is Policy Possible?" *The Wilson Quarterly,* Autumn 1976.
3. Schultze et al., *Setting National Priorities—the 1973 Budget.*
4. Ibid.
5. Among those who question Schultze's idea are Robert C. Weaver and James Sundquist of the Brookings Institution.
6. Schultze, *Setting National Priorites—the 1973 Budget.*
7. Haar, *Between the Dream and the Reality.*

8. Gorham and Glazer, *The Urban Predicament.*

9. Glazer, *Affirmative Discrimination.*

10. Schultze, *Setting National Priorities—the 1973 Budget.*

11. Joseph A. Schumpeter, *Capitalism, Socialism and Democracy* (New York: Harper and Row, 1950).

12. Frank Hurcules, "To Live in Harlem," *National Geographic,* February 1977.

13. Robert Wood, testimony before the House Committee on Banking, Currency and Housing, October 1976.

14. Lord Moran, *Churchill, the Struggle for Survival* (Pleasantville, N.Y.: Reader's Digest Condensed Books, 1966).

15. Bell, *The Cultural Contradictions of Capitalism.*

16. Quoted in *Time,* May 2, 1977.

Index

Aaron, Henry, 103, 144
Abrams, Charles, 130, 239
Advertising, 245
Advisory Committee on Intergovernmental Relations, 61, 73
Affirmative action, 197, 201. *See also* Racial discrimination; Racial segregation
Affirmative Marketing Regulations, 190. *See also* Racial discrimination; Racial segregation
Aluminum Company of America (ALCOA), 173
American Housing, 238-239
American Institute of Architects, 53-54, 131
American Motors, 172
Anderson, Martin, 77, 238
Appraisers, 191
Appropriations Subcommittee (House of Representatives), 206, 207
Architects, 159, 178
Arden, Illinois, 182
Ashley, Thomas, 224
Australia, 182
Automobiles, 7-9. *See also* Transportation; Traffic congestion; Pollution

Babcock, Frederick, 116, 117, 191, 232
Baltimore, Maryland, 66-67
Banfield, Edward C., 12, 43
Banking and Currency Committee (U.S. House of Representatives), 141
    Subcommittee on Housing, 224
Banking and Currency Committee (U.S. Senate), 224, 234
    Subcommittee on Housing, 233
Banks, commercial. *See* Commercial banks
Barrett, William, 224
Bauer, Catherine, 2, 76, 116, 130
Baughman, Stanley, 235
Bebout, John, 209
Bell, Daniel, 216, 247
Below Market Interest Rate Program (BMIR). *See* FHA subsidy programs
Bernstein, Marvin, 29
Beyer, Glenn, 209
Blacks, 4-5, 131. *See also* Racial discrimination; Racial segregation
Blandford, John, 239

Block grants for community development, 223
description of, 70-71; evaluation of, 91-92; experience with, 74-76; 1977 revisions of, 93-94; research on, 219; strengths and weaknesses, 71-74
Bohn, Ernest, 130, 231-232
Boston, Massachusetts, 80
Brookings Institution, 29, 104, 144, 209, 214, 219, 237
Brownstein, Philip N., 73, 139-140, 147, 226, 227, 234, 235
Budget circular A-95, 61
Budget, federal, 58, 137, 143, 148
Building codes. *See* Codes
Building materials, 159
Building permits, 179
Bureaucracy, maladies of, 30-31, 32-33
Bureau of Public Roads, 57
Bureau of the Budget, 226. *See also* Office of Management and Budget
Burstein, Joseph, 228, 237

Califano, Joseph, 31
Canada, 182
Can Our Cities Survive?, 1, 2
Career public servants, 29, 30, 31, 44-45, 50
Carter, Jimmy, 31, 47, 49, 91-92, 131, 146, 165, 215, 244, 247
Carter administration, 91, 126
Cedar-Riverside Project, 90
Central city, 7, 10
Chattanooga, Tennessee, 75
Churchill, Henry, 1
Churchill, Winston, 247
Civil Rights Commission, 188, 192, 193, 197
Civil rights legislation, 187
Civil Rights Act of 1964, 188, 192; Civil Rights Act of 1968, 188, 190, 192, 199; Executive

Order 110703, 187, 188; HUD administration of, 193
Civil rights movement, 197. *See also* Racial discrimination; Racial segregation
Civil War, 189
Clark, J. M., 159
Clawson, Marion, 66
Closing costs, 179, 180, 183-184
Coan, Carl, Sr., 233
Codes
building, 180-181, 184-186; housing, 52-54, 78-84
Cole, Albert, 47, 230-231, 236, 239-240
Colean, Miles, 100, 115, 116, 117, 232-233, 238-239
Coleman, James, 196
College housing. *See* Housing
College of Charleston, South Carolina, 212
Columbia, Maryland, 55, 175. *See also* New communities
Commercial banks, 109, 111, 156. *See also* Mortgage lenders
Community Facilities Administration (CFA), 20
Condon, Lester, 225
Construction costs. *See* Housing
Consumer protection, 119, 120
Cornell University, 209, 211
Corson, John, 20, 236
Council of Economic Advisers, 3 158, 162, 165
Councils of Governments (COGs), 61, 62
Credit controls, selective, 164. *See also* Housing finance
Crime, 199, 213, 244

Denton, Harold, 175
Department of Agriculture, 205, 206, 208
Department of Commerce, 49
Department of Defense, 211
Department of Health, Educa-

tion and Welfare, 49, 213, 214
Department of Housing and Urban Development (HUD) creation of, 15-20; missions of, 23, 24; performance of HUD's secretaries, 39-50; problems faced by a secretary, 26-36; skills required of a secretary, 36-39
Department of Justice, 188, 192
Department of Labor, 49, 186
Depression, Great, 117-118
Desegregation (in housing). *See* Racial segregation
Detroit, 7, 42, 55, 229
Dickens, Charles, 2
Direct loans (for housing), 164. *See also* Public housing; FHA subsidy programs; Section 8 Program
Discount points (on mortgages), 158. *See also* Housing
Division of Slum Clearance and Urban Redevelopment. *See* Urban Renewal Administration
Domestic Council (White House), 49, 91, 152, 165, 224
Don Quixote, 133
Douglas, Paul, 238
Down payments (on mortgages), 157. *See also* Housing finance
Downs, Anthony, 3, 102, 126, 141, 144-145, 147, 169, 177, 198, 200, 209, 218, 237-238

Eccles, Marriner, 115
Economic Report of the President, 157-158
Economy, national. *See* National economy
Ehrenkrantz, Ezra, 209
Einstein, Albert, 199
Eisenhower, Dwight D., 47, 116, 133, 226
Eisenhower administration, 230, 234, 240
Eizenstat, Stuart, 91, 165

Emancipation Proclamation, 189
Embry, Robert, 66, 67
Emergency Home Financing Act of 1970, 111-112
Eminent domain, 76, 182-183
Energy crisis, 247; waste of, 5, 8-9. *See also* Automobiles; Traffic congestion; Pollution
England, 182, 232
Environmental protection, 113, 179
Equal opportunity HUD assistant secretary for, 188, 193; HUD efforts to achieve, 189, 190, 195. *See also* Civil rights legislation; Racial discrimination; Racial segregation

Fahey, John, 34, 115-116
Fairhope, Alabama, 182
Family income. *See* Incomes (family)
Federal Bulldozer, 77, 238
Federal Deposit Insurance Corporation, 107
Federal government. *See* Government, federal
Federal Home Loan Bank Board (FHLBB), 34, 107, 109-110, 111, 112, 115, 123, 161-162, 188
Federal Home Loan Mortgage Corporation (FHLMC), 109, 112, 161
Federal Housing Administration (FHA) As an element of HUD, 19-20; decline and reasons for, 110-114; early accomplishments, 114-120; future need for, 121-123
Federal National Mortgage Association (FNMA) authority to purchase conventional mortgages, 109, 111-112; countercyclical effective-

ness, 161; original functions, 107-108; purchase of FHA below-market interest rate mortgages, 135-136; tandem plan, 160
Federal Reserve Board, 155-157, 162, 164-165, 236
Federal Savings and Loan Insurance Corporation, 109-110
Fefferman, Hilbert, 87, 233-234
FHA subsidy programs, 125
  Below Market Interest Rate (BMIR), 135-137; rent supplements, 130, 137-138, 141, 142, 144, 147; Section 202, 127, 129; Section 235, 127, 129, 138-139; Section 236, 127, 129, 138, 147, 150
Filtering, theory of, 102-103, 126, 158
Finger, Harry, 174-175, 212-217, 219
Fiscal crisis of local government, 7
Fiscal policy, 163-164
Fisher, Ernest, 99, 116, 206, 233
Fisher, Frank, 223-224
Fitzpatrick, B. T., 234, 239
Flanders, William, 116-117, 235
Florida, 62
Foard, Ashley, 233-234
Foley, Raymond, 236-237, 239, 240
Ford, Gerald, 46, 196
Ford, Henry, 171
Ford administration, 200
Ford Foundation, 209
Ford Motor Company, 209
Frieden, Bernard J., 73

Gabel, Hortense, 209
Gardner, John, 87
General Electric Company, 171, 209
General Motors Corporation, 171
Ghettos, 2, 3, 198

Glazer, Nathan, 57, 197, 245
Gorman, William, 57
Government, federal, 242-244
Government, local, 6, 7, 60-61, 65, 67, 203-204
Government, state
  role in urban affairs, 66
Government National Mortgage Association (GNMA), 108, 123-124, 128, 160
Grebler, Leo, 103, 162
Greenwich Village, 238
Gross, George, 225
Growth, urban, 5, 6
Guaranteed market contracts, 176. *See also* Technology

Haar, Charles, 73, 84, 244
Haldeman, H. R., 42
Hardy, Neal J., 226-227, 236-237, 239
Harlem, 246
Harriman, Averell, 222
Harris, Patricia, 25, 47-50, 75, 106, 146, 152, 200, 237
Health care, 243
Highway program, 56-57
Highways, urban, 7. *See also* Transportation
Hills, Carla, 25, 46-47, 72-73, 128, 147
Hobson, Julius, 201
Holleb, Doris B., 6, 195
Home builders, 118-119, 133-34, 136, 171
Home ownership for the poor, 138-139, 150-151
Home Owners Loan Corporation, 117
Home purchasers, 156-157, 158-159, 169
Home renters, 169
Homesteading. *See* Rehabilitation
Hoover, Herbert, 123
Housing

costs, 161-186; demand, 26, 103-104; for colleges, 20; for the elderly, 20; for war workers, 235; goals, 102-105; industry, 118-119; market, 98-101; open, 201; substandard, 105, 148. *See also* Public housing; FHA subsidy programs; Section 8 Program; Housing finance

Housing Act of 1949, 76, 102, 203, 206-207, 234, 239

Housing Act of 1954, 230

Housing Act of 1961, 225-226

Housing allowances, 144, 145, 148-149, 224
  experiments in, 213, 218. *See also* Public housing; FHA subsidy programs; Section 8 Program

Housing and Community Development Act of 1964, 203

Housing and Community Development Act of 1977, 48-49, 92-93, 129

Housing and Home Finance Agency (HHFA)
  as HUD's predecessor, 16, 97; elevation to cabinet status, 15-16, 19-20; research program of, 206-208

Housing Assistance Plan. *See* Block grants for community development

Housing costs. *See* Housing

Housing cycles. *See* Housing finance

Housing expediter, 176. *See also* Wyatt, Wilson

Housing finance
  as a HUD mission, 15; federal aids to, 98 (*see also* FHA; VA; FNMA; GNMA; FHLBB); importance of, 98-99; sources of (*see* Mortgage lenders); subsidized (*see* Public housing;

FHA subsidy programs; Section 8 Program)

Housing for Low and Moderate Income Families, the case for, 125, 126, 127. *See also* Public housing; FHA subsidy programs; Section 8 Program

Housing subsidies. *See* Public housing; FHA subsidy programs; Section 8 Program

Howard, Ebenezer, 1

How the Other Half Lives, 1

HUD. *See* Department of Housing and Urban Development

Humphrey, Hubert, 230

Hunter, Oakley, 158

Hurcules, Frank, 246

Incomes (family), 168-169

Income tax
  Federal, 182-183; state, 182-183

Income taxes. *See* Taxes

India, slums in, 2

Inflation, 154, 159, 161, 180, 241-242

Informal organization, 27-28

Inner city, loans in, 139-140

Institute for Defense Analysis, 209

Institute on Urban Development (proposed), 167

Insurance companies, 118, 156. *See also* Mortgage lenders

Interest rates, 161
  President's Commission on, 163

Intergovernmental Cooperation Act of 1968, 61

Internal Revenue Code, deductions for home ownership, 150, 151

International Business Machines (IBM), 209

Jacobs, Jane, 238-239

Janis, Jay, 87, 239

Jobs for blacks, 200-201

Johnson, Lyndon B., 15, 39, 41, 42, 89-90, 146, 211, 238

Keyserling, Leon, 232
Kluger, Richard, 199
Klutznick, Philip, 235
Korean War, 236
Krooth, David, 130

Labor Unions, 185
Land
banking of, 65, 66, 182-183; cost of, 182; research into, 204; speculation in, 57, 58; tax on, 182, 184; use of, 175, 213-214
Latin America
land taxation in, 182; slums in, 2-3
Leadership
national, 246-247; presidential, 246, 247; skills required of HUD secretary, 36-39
L'Enfant, 63, 64
Levittown, New Jersey, 6
Life and Death of American Cities, 238
Lincoln, Abraham, 189, 245
Lindsey, John, 170
Little, Arthur D., Company, 81, 214
Little Rock, Arkansas, 75
Local government. *See* Government, local
Local housing authority, 127, 130, 133. *See also* Public housing
Logue, Edward, 80
Low income families, 2, 10, 12. *See also* Public housing; FHA subsidy programs; Section 8 Program; Poverty; Poor families
Lustron Corporation, 176
Lynn, James, 25, 45-47, 145, 147, 224-225

Maisell, Sherman, 151, 155
Marshall, George, 222

Marshall Plan, 222
Mason, Norman, 240
Massachusetts Institute of Technology (MIT), 208-209
Mass production (of housing), 171. *See also* Operation Breakthrough
McDonald, Stewart, 121
McGuire, Marie, 134, 228, 229, 237
Mead, Dana, 224
Message on the Cities (of President Lyndon B. Johnson), 167
Metropolitan government. *See* Government, local
Minneapolis–St. Paul, Minnesota, 62
Minority groups, 26. *See also* Racial discrimination; Racial segregation; Civil rights
Mitchell, John, 130
MIT-Harvard Joint Center for Urban Studies, 105, 211
Model Cities Program
as addition to HUD's authority, 41; as a policy innovation, 229-230; conception and passage, 84-85; lessons learned from, 86-89; short life, 85-86; subsumed into Block Grant Program, 70
Mondale, Walter, 140
Moratorium (on HUD's programs), 127-128, 145-147
Mortgage bankers, 159. *See also* Mortgage lenders
Mortgage Bankers Association of America, 124
Mortgage credit. *See* Housing finance
Mortgage finance. *See* Housing finance
Mortgage Guarantee Insurance Corporation (MGIC), 111
Mortgage insurance
by FHA, 19-20, 108-109, 114-

116, 119, 122, 121-123; by VA, 108-109, 112; private, 111, 122-123. *See also* Housing finance; FHA; VA
Mortgage lenders. *See* Commercial banks; Insurance companies; Mutual savings banks; Savings and loan associations; Pension funds; FNMA; GNMA; FHLMC
Moses, Robert, 76-77
Mumford, Louis, 1, 2, 64, 238
Mutual savings banks, 156. *See also* Mortgage lenders
Myrdal, Gunnar, 189, 191

Nashville, Tennessee, 75
Nathan, Richard, 223-224
National Academy of Science, 208
National Aeronautics and Space Administration (NASA), 209, 210, 212
National Association of Home Builders, 145. *See also* Home builders
National Association of Housing and Redevelopment Officials (NAHRO), 74, 219. *See also* Public housing; Research, urban
National Bureau of Standards, 173, 174
National Commission on Urban Problems, 60, 104, 161-162
National Development Bank, 164
National economy
    effect on urban problems, 2, 3, 159, 164; stabilization of, 163-164, 241
National Homes Corporation, 173
National Housing Agency (NHA)
    as a HUD predecessor, 97; creation of, 34; quality of staff, 28
National Housing Conference, 146

National Institute of Building Sciences, 204
Neustadt, Richard, 38-39, 222
New communities, 90
    in Britain, 55. *See also* New Communities Program; Columbia, Maryland; Reston, Virginia
New Communities Program, 41, 53, 55. *See also* New communities
New Deal, 116, 123
New Federalism, 71-72, 223
New Haven, Connecticut, 80, 229
New towns. *See* New communities
New Towns-in-Town, 89-90
New York City, 60, 75, 77, 131
New Zealand, 182
Nitzer, Dick, 184
Nixon, Richard M. 42, 45-46, 71, 145
Nixon administration, 125, 128, 146, 211, 224

Oak Ridge National Laboratory, 209
Office of Management and Budget, 61, 162, 165. *See also* Bureau of the Budget
Office of Science and Technology (White House), 208
Older neighborhoods
    loans in, 139. *See also* Slums
Open space, 52
Operation Breakthrough, 167, 171-175, 176-177, 180, 181, 213, 225. *See also* Technology
Oregon, 62
Orlebeke, Charles, 145, 147, 217
Owen, Wilfred, 209

Paine, Thomas, 209
Pension funds, 118. *See also* Mortgage lenders

Percy, Charles, 139
Perloff, Harvey S., 11, 58, 61, 72, 89, 90, 209
Philadelphia, Pennsylvania, 60
Pittsburgh, Pennsylvania, 175
Plan for Urban Growth, A, 53
Planned Unit Development (PUD), 175, 185. *See also* Land
Planners, 10, 26, 58
Planning (urban)
    by other government departments, 53; highway program and, 56-57; HUD's success in generating, 53-56; HUD's tools for, 52-53; metropolitan, 61-62; obstacles to, 58-60; purpose of, 52
Political appointees, 38, 48
Pollution, 8-9, 12, 243
Poor families, 213
Poverty, 9, 244
President's Advisory Committee on Government Policies and Programs, 230-231
President's Commission on Civil Disorders, 11, 180. *See also* Riots, urban
President's Commission on Mortgage Interest Rates, 163
Presidential leadership. *See* Leadership
Private mortgage insurance, 121-122. *See also* Mortgage insurance
Program evaluation, 219
Project Rehab, 81, 83. *See also* Rehabilitation
Project selection criteria, 60-61, 66-67, 190, 195. *See also* Racial discrimination; Racial segregation; Civil rights
Property taxes, 65-66, 179, 184
Proxmire, William, 48
Pruit-Igoe Project, 131-132, 134
Public facilities, loans for, 70
Public housing 125
    as element of HUD, 20; early

years of, 130-131; evaluation of, 134-135; for elderly, 132; setbacks, 131
Public servants. *See* Career public servants
Public Works Administration, 232

Racial apartheid. *See* Racial segregation
Racial covenants, FHA's use of, 191. *See also* Racial Discrimination; Racial segregation
Racial discrimination (in housing), 5, 189, 190
    and affirmative marketing regulations, 190; FHA's early encouragement of, 191; limitations on HUD's power to prevent, 192-194; progress in reducing, 194-195, 241; public housing's early record in, 191
Racial segregation (in housing), 4-5
    HUD's mission to prevent, 188; legal powers (*see* Civil rights legislation); project selection criteria, 190; research in, 204
Racial quotas (in jobs and education), 197
Racial relations advisers, 191-192
Ratcliff, Richard U., 207
Reader's Digest, 77
Real Estate Research Corporation, 174
Realtors, 26, 193
Recession, 161
Reconstruction Finance Corporation, 108
Redlining (in mortgage lending), 194
Regulation X, 236-237. *See also* Federal Reserve Board; Mortgage finance
Rehabilitation, 79-83, 214, 217-218, 227, 231. *See also* Project Rehab

Reifler, Winfield, 115, 120, 232-233, 236
Renewing Our Cities, 239
Rent Supplement Program (FHA). *See* FHA subsidy programs
Republic Steel Corporation, 173
Research, urban
  by HHFA, 206-208; funds for, 203, 205-206; quality of, 206, 214, 216-217. *See also* Urban Institute
Resources for the Future, 209
Reston, Virginia, 55. *See also* New communities
Reuther, Walter, 229-230
Richardson, Elliot, 57, 213
Riis, Jacob, 1
Riots, urban, 4, 11
Rivlin, Alice, 218
Rogow, Arnold A., 12, 131-132
Romney, George, 25, 42-45, 48, 81, 128, 132, 141, 143, 145-147, 167, 171-172, 173, 177, 190, 212, 217-218, 225
Roosevelt, Franklin D., 34, 115
Roosevelt, Theodore, 1
Rosenblith, Walter, 209, 215
Rouse, James, 175, 231, 238
Rouse-Watts Company, 173
Rutgers University, 3, 209

San Antonio, Texas, 229
Santayana, George, 34
Saulnier, Raymond, 116
Savage, Bruce, 232
Savings and loan associations
  as an industry, 109, 110; growth of, 110-111; performance in credit cycles, 156, 161. *See also* Mortgage lenders
Sayer, Wallace, 30, 221
Schechter, Henry, 157, 160, 163
School busing, 189, 196. *See also* Civil rights
Schultze, Charles L., 3, 73, 91, 144, 163, 215, 218, 243-244

Schumpeter, Joseph, 245
Science and the City, 210, 215
Secretary of HUD
  office of, 20-21; problems faced by, 16-24
Section 8 Program, 127-129, 236
Section 202 Program. *See* FHA subsidy programs
Section 235 Program. *See* FHA subsidy programs
Section 236 Program. *See* FHA subsidy programs
Separate but Equal Doctrine, 189. *See also* Supreme Court
Sert, J. L., 1
Shaw, George Bernard, 89
Silverman, Abner, 138
Slum Clearance Program, 70. *See also* Urban Renewal Program
Slums, 1-5, 9, 12, 134, 196, 213
Smith, Adam, 244
Social costs, 159
  of housing cycles, 159
Social Security, 147, 242
Solar energy in housing, research in, 204, 213
South Bronx, 4
Southern Regional Council, 74-75
Sparkman, John, 146, 224-225
Special revenue sharing. *See* Block grants for community development
Spokane, Washington, 142
Sprawl, urban, 5-6, 56, 183
Stabilization (of economy), 164. *See also* National economy
Standard Metropolitan Statistical Areas (SMSA), 60
State housing finance agencies, 127-128
Steiner, Richard L., 90
Sternlieb, George, 3, 4
Stockholm, Sweden, 183
Straus, Nathan, 121, 133
Subdivision regulations, 184-185. *See also* Planning

Substandard housing. *See*
  Housing
Suburbs, 5, 6, 121
Supreme Court, 189, 194, 197

Taft, Robert, 47, 130, 145
Tandem Plan, 160-161. *See also*
  GNMA
Taxes
  federal income, 102; local, 58-
  59; property, 102, 181; tax
  exemptions, 102
Taylor, Ralph, 87
Technology (for housing produc-
  tion), 170-177
Television, 245
Thomas, Albert, 207-208
Tocqueville, Alexis de, 188
Traffic congestion, 2. *See also*
  Transportation; Automobile
Transportation
  Department of, 56-57; mass
  transit, 52 (*see also* Auto-
  mobile; Congestion; Pollu-
  tion); planning of, 52; urban,
  9
Treasury, Department of, 49,
  162, 165, 232
Truman, Harry, 38, 44, 175, 222

Unearned increment (from land),
  183
Unemployment, 180
United States Housing Author-
  ity, 130-133. *See also* Public
  housing
University of California at
  Berkeley, 237
University of California at Los
  Angeles (UCLA), 237
University of Pennsylvania, 237
Urban Development Action
  Grants, 93-94
Urban Institute, 90, 144-145, 150,
  195, 202, 212-213, 215, 219
Urban planning. *See* Planning

Urban Predicament, The, 215
Urban problems
  lack of interest in, 11; serious-
  ness of, 11-12
Urban Regional Policy Task
  Force, 49
Urban Renewal Administration,
  20, 80. *See also* Urban Renewal
  Program
Urban Renewal Program, 41, 52,
  54, 76-79, 94, 227, 229, 231, 239,
  241
Urban research. *See* Research,
  urban
Urban sprawl, 5-6
User charges for public services,
  184

Vandalism, 134
Vandenberg, Arthur, 222
Van Dusen, Richard, 43, 224
Veterans Administration (VA)
  loan guarantee program, 107,
  108-109, 110, 111, 123; mortgages, 158; racial policies,
  187-188
Veterans Emergency Housing Act
  of 1946, 176
Vietnam war, 196

Wagner, Robert, 130, 232
Walker, David, 73-74
Ward, Barbara, 8, 12, 57, 126, 152
Washington, D.C., 55, 64, 89-90,
  142, 152, 201, 211
Washington Post, 45
Water and sewer facilities
  effect on urban planning
  (*see* Community Facilities
  Administration); grants for,
  70
Weaver, Robert C., 25, 29, 39-42,
  42, 44, 67, 75, 78, 79, 87-88, 103,
  132, 134, 139, 189, 191, 192, 200-
  201, 215, 225-226, 227, 229, 233,
  234, 237

Webb, James, 210
Wehrli, Robert, 174
Welfare payments, 147-148
Welfare services, 243
Western Europe, 232
White House, 225-226, 229
Winnick, Louis, 72
Wolman, Harold, 221, 229
Wood, Robert C., 41-42, 70, 85, 88, 203, 208-209, 215, 229-230
Woods Hole Conference, 215
Woods Hole Summer Study Center, 208, 215

Workable program, 53. *See* Planning; Codes
World War II, 133, 153
Wyatt, Wilson, 176-177, 239. *See also* Housing expediter

Ylvisaker, Paul, 52, 73
Youth revolt, 196

Zoning, 57, 58, 59, 65, 184-185, 193, 195
changes in, 179; exclusionary, 63; flexibility in, 172, 175